CHURCH MURDERER

❑

Convinced that the body will be found at any moment—particularly when he is told that witnesses saw him with Blanche that afternoon—he prepares for arrest. In fact, nothing happens; days go by and he is still free. But he knows that this cannot go on forever. Sooner or later, the bellringer will notice a smell of decay and will investigate. Now, living in a kind of nightmare, he feels that if he is going to be hanged, he might just as well repeat the pleasure of possessing one of those infinitely desirable young churchgoers who seem to embody the allure of the whole female species.

And so Blanche's best friend is persuaded to enter the library . . .

**—from THE KILLERS AMONG US
Book II
Sex, Madness, and Mass Murder**

THE KILLERS AMONG US

BOOK II

SEX, MADNESS & MASS MURDER

COLIN WILSON
author of *Written in Blood*
& DAMON WILSON

WARNER BOOKS

A Time Warner Company

Originally published in Great Britain by Robinson Publishing Ltd. under the title, *A Plague of Murder*.

WARNER BOOKS EDITION

Cover design by Mike Stromberg
Cover photos courtesy of The Bettmann Archive

Warner Books, Inc.
1271 Avenue of the Americas
New York, NY 10020

Visit our Web site at
http://warnerbooks.com

A Time Warner Company

Printed in the United States of America

First Warner Books Printing: March, 1997

10 9 8 7 6 5 4

CONTENTS

1

INTRODUCTION

WHEN FBI AGENT ROBERT RESSLER COINED THE TERM *serial killer* in the early 1980s, he introduced an extremely useful distinction into criminology. Before that, anyone guilty of multiple homicide was called a mass murderer. Since Ressler, anyone who kills repeatedly out of *calculation* is a mass murderer, while anyone who kills out of some kind of psychological *compulsion* is a serial killer. I have a book called *Mass Murder* by L. C. Douthwaite, published in 1928, in which three of the ten cases—Earle Nelson, Fritz Haarmann and Neill Cream—are what we would now call serial killers. Others, like "Brides in the Bath" Smith and French Bluebeard Landru, are just as clearly mass murderers, since they killed solely for profit—although because Landru chose this method of making a living because he was an obsessive seducer, we have to admit that there was an element of the serial killer in his makeup.

What is so strange about the second half of the twentieth century is that there are now so many "compulsive" killers. In my *Encyclopedia of Murder*, published in 1961, there were only about a dozen serial killers, including Jack the Ripper. Now it would be possible to devote a whole encyclopedia to serial killers.

What has gone wrong? Why are they multiplying at such a rate?

The obvious reason is that our society has more freedom than any other in history. The few serial killers of the remote past, like Gilles de Rais, who murdered children, Countess Bathory, who murdered servant girls, and Vlad the Impaler, who murdered anyone he could lay his hands on, were members of the aristocracy, and therefore had a great deal of freedom—freedom to be bored and spoiled and self-indulgent. Their servants and tenants were too hungry and overworked to commit murder for pleasure. Now the advance in civilization has raised the standard of living to a level that would have been inconceivable even in the 1940s. And this higher degree of leisure and comfort and *choice* means that a large percentage of our society enjoys a degree of freedom that was once only enjoyed by the rich.

The most powerful of human needs are security, food and drink, and sex. In the past, the poor often committed robbery because they were half starved. But murder for sex was almost unheard of because when you are hungry and tired, sex takes second place. It is therefore inevitable that, as society becomes more affluent, sex crime will increase.

A recent example is the British sex killer Fred West (discussed in Volume 1 of this book). It is true that he suffered a head injury in his teens that seems to have amplified his sex drive until he wanted to possess every attractive woman that he saw. Yet in this he was not really so different from most healthy young males. In a novel called *Eternal Fire*, Calder Willingham invented a character called Harry Diadem, who is an obsessive seducer. He told me that, during a party in his home, a male guest had a little too much to drink and declared expansively: "*I* am Harry Diadem. *You* are Harry Diadem. We're all" (with a drunken gesture at the other males in the room) "Harry Diadem." And we have to acknowledge that he at least had a point.

Now West's wife Rose was a nymphomaniac with lesbian tendencies. And she undoubtedly had no kind of brain abnormality. But when they turned their home into a lodging house, and Fred took advantage of as many female guests as possible, Rose joined in the orgy with enthusiasm, and not only seduced the male lodgers, but also forced her attentions on unwilling females, who were usually tied down on a bed. Rose West makes it clear that it would be a mistake to think of sex maniacs solely as predatory males; *she* was Harry Diadem too.

The West case raises one of the most ominous and worrying questions about the increase in sex crime. Fred West began simply as a rapist. One of their victims, who had been their *au pair* girl, was offered a lift, taken back to the house, then sexually assaulted by both of them. After that, she was allowed to go home. She reported them to the police, but they escaped with a fine. After that, they began killing their rape victims. But it is now clear that, long before he was caught, Fred West was having sex with the victims only after they were dead; before that, he inflicted pain and indignities on them, often suspending them from a beam in the basement.

This is one of the most baffling things about sex crime—that it so easily escalates into torture. Most normal males will find this incomprehensible, even those who find it easy enough to understand a multiple rapist. The Gainesville serial killer Danny Rolling points out in his autobiography that when dozens of male university students were asked if they would rape a beautiful girl if they could get away with it, the majority answered yes. But I doubt whether any of them would enjoy inflicting pain on the victim.

It seems that as sex killers murder victim after victim, the degree of sadism increases. Ted Bundy described how, when he first followed a girl with the intention of knocking her unconscious, and she went into a house before he could carry out his purpose, he felt shattered and conscience stricken, and swore that he would never surrender to such madness again. Yet in the case of his final victim, an underage girl, he refused to tell the interrogating officer what he did to her because it was too horrible. Why did Bundy become increasingly sadistic?

Now it might seem reasonable to ask: why bother to ask such a question? Why bother to write about murder at all—unless out of some morbid compulsion or the cynical desire to make money?

The answer is that it touches upon one of the most profound problems of human nature, a problem that *must* be understood if we are to understand ourselves.

I have always been aware that human beings are utterly confused in their attitude towards their "objects of desire." If I am hungry, then the need to eat is an urgent physical desire. If it remains unsatisfied, I shall die. And we tend to think of all our desires in this way: "satisfying a need."

But sex-starvation has never killed anyone. So what kind of "need" does sex satisfy?

Doctor Johnson remarked: "The knowledge that he is to be hanged in a fortnight concentrates a man's mind wonderfully." I would argue that most of our "needs" boil down to a need to *concentrate the mind*. When we get tired of routine, we allow the mind to become slack, and this slackness is called boredom. And when the mind is slack and bored, it is impossible to appreciate anything. Even your favorite amusements seem oddly dull.

Therefore we seek out things that will *focus and concentrate* the mind. A bored woman may go out and buy herself a new dress. Or she *may* even think of taking a lover. Sex is one of the favorite human methods of concentrating the mind. The reason the "sex maniac" enjoys sex is that it concentrates his mind wonderfully.

But there is one basic difference between the sex killer and some oversexed but otherwise normal male. The sex killer is willing to harm another human being to satisfy his desire. This is the all-important Rubicon that lies between good and evil.

One of the most typical recent cases took place in Canada. In August 1995, Paul Bernardo, a multiple rapist and killer, was sentenced to life imprisonment for kidnaping, raping, and murdering two teenage girls. The baffling feature about the case is that he was aided and abetted by his wife Karla Homolka, who received twelve years.

Bernardo was a rapist before he met Karla in 1987. He had been attacking and raping women—usually anally—in the Scarborough district of Toronto for years. Within an hour of meeting Karla in a hotel restaurant, Bernardo was in bed with her—he was 23, she 17. Bernardo had a strong sadistic streak; he needed to dominate women. She had a strong masochistic streak and liked to be dominated. At their first party together they sneaked into a bedroom and he found that she had a pair of handcuffs; she allowed him to handcuff her to the bedpost before he tore off her clothes.

He told her he was a rapist, and she found it thrilling. And when she asked him what he wanted for Christmas, he replied: "Your sister Tammy," and she agreed to help him to rape her 15-year-old sister. They drugged her drink, then anesthetized her with halothane, after which Bernardo raped and sodomized her. Unfortunately, Tammy vomited in her sleep and choked to death. Yet even this was not enough to convince Karla Homolka that she was wrong to help this man rape her sister. She kept the panties her sister was wearing, and later gave them to Bernardo to use in masturbation.

Now deep into *folie à deux*, she continued to help him during the kidnap, rape, and murder of two schoolgirls. It was only when his beatings became too violent that she finally left him and told her aunt her secret.

Here we can see how easily this "Rubicon" is crossed. Bernardo is a "satyr," who is in a permanent state of sexual excitement; it seems to him that women are being deliberately provocative by simply having female sexual characteristics. Karla dreams about a handsome, dominant male who will achieve greatness with her at his side. Yet there is no reason why they should not satisfy one another in a mutual fantasy and achieve a stable relationship. Unfortunately, he has already crossed the Rubicon in turning his fantasies into rape. She finds this exciting and agrees to help him rape her sister . . . .

And now we suddenly become aware that this is a far bigger problem than mere *folie à deux*. It is latent in the whole human species, particularly the male. The Victorians did their best to propagate the fiction that men fall in love with sweet, demure women, conquered by their goodness, and are only too anxious to marry them and support a family. The truth is that most male sexual desire is as impersonal as the desire of a hungry man for food. Fortunately, most men and women find partnership agreeable and end by settling down and raising children. But there are always the "rogue males" who see this as a form of surrender. Casanova simply wanted to possess as many women as possible and avoid any permanent attachment. And oddly enough, we do not regard this as unforgivable. In fact, we find Mozart's Don Giovanni an amusing scamp and are not really convinced that he has done anything that merits being dragged off to hell.

There is nevertheless a sense in which Don Giovanni has crossed the same Rubicon as the serial killer. He wants women purely for sexual pleasure and is not willing to allow the relationship to become personal.

The same is true of Goethe's Faust. He is lonely and frustrated, and the Devil offers him fulfillment. Faust sees the innocent Gretchen in the street and says: "All right, I want *her*." The Devil obliges and helps Faust seduce her. Gretchen gets pregnant, kills the baby, and is sentenced to death. This is not entirely Faust's fault—he tries to help her, but she feels she has sinned and refuses.

The modern reader feels this is absurd. She has not "sinned," merely behaved like a woman in love. Yet Goethe has put his finger on the moral dilemma. Faust has sold his soul in exchange for Gretchen; he has crossed the Rubicon. The rest follows inevitably.

Paul Bernardo, like Ted Bundy, began as a peeping Tom. At this stage he probably felt he was doing no one any harm. He was still on this side of the Rubicon. But desire and opportunity soon turned him into a rapist. At this point, Goethe would have said, he had sold out to the Devil. He had taken the fatal step of deciding he had the right to harm other people.

It seems a hard conclusion, but it is difficult to see how to avoid it. Nature urges males to cross the Rubicon by making women desirable. The serial killer takes nature at its word by committing rape. The "normal" male sees a pretty girl at a dance and wonders how he can steer her towards his bedroom. Surely, the difference is in degree, not in kind?

I must admit that there are times when I am tempted to abandon the strictly scientific view of the criminologist and think that killers like Bundy are Fausts who have surrendered to the Devil. But in order to be logical. I have to recognize that nature and the Devil have entered into a partnership of convenience.

As we shall see, sex murder—in the sense of murder committed purely for sexual satisfaction—is a fairly recent phenomenon. There have, of course, been notable exceptions—we have already mentioned Gilles de Rais and Countess Elizabeth Bathory—but throughout the eighteenth and most of the nineteenth century, sex crime, in our modern sense of the word (i.e. murder purely for sexual satisfaction) was unknown. The first sex killer to achieve universal notoriety was the unknown killer who called himself Jack the Ripper.

Between August 31, 1888, and November 9, 1888, five murders took place within an area of half a mile in the East End of London. The killer's method was to cut the throat of the women—probably from behind—then to cut open the stomach and pull out the intestines. On several occasions he took away certain organs.

The first of the Ripper murders to attract the attention of the general public was that of a prostitute named Mary Ann Nicholls (known as Polly), who was found just before dawn on Friday, August 31, lying on the pavement in Bucks Row, Whitechapel, with her throat cut. It was not until she had been removed to a nearby mortuary that it was discovered that the abdomen had been slashed open from the ribs to the pelvis. Polly Nicholls, 42, had been sleeping in a fourpence-a-night doss house, but had been turned away the evening before because she had no money. She had gone off looking for a male who would give her a few pence in exchange for sex in an alleyway. In fact, her killer had displayed exceptional coolness in cutting her throat within a few feet of an open bedroom window; the people in the room had heard nothing.

It was in the vicinity of such an alleyway, used for casual sex, that the body of 47-year-old Annie Chapman was found sprawled on her back in the early hours of September 8. She lay in the yard of a lodging house at 29 Hanbury Street, a few coins lying ritualistically around her. Two front teeth were missing; so were her ovaries and kidneys. Again, the killer had murdered her quickly and silently close to a house-ful of people.

The murders caused widespread anger and panic. There were noisy meetings in the street, and editorials demanded action from the police. And on September 28, the Central News Agency received a letter signed "Jack the Ripper," and threatening more murders. When it was published two days later, the gruesome soubriquet captured the public imagination. As if reacting to the clamor, "the Ripper" committed a double murder that same night. He was interrupted immediately after he had cut the throat of a woman named Elizabeth Stride in the backyard of a workmen's club in Berner Street; a carter drove into the yard and saw a man bending over the body. By the time he had raised the alarm, the man had fled. He walked half a mile to Mitre Square, on the edge of the City and picked up a prostitute named Catherine Eddowes, who had just been released from jail for drunkenness. There he cut her throat and disemboweled her, removing the left kidney and some of the entrails. After this the killer cut off part of her apron, then went and washed his hands in a public sink in an alleyway; the apron fragment was found a quarter of a mile away to the north, and blood-stains on it suggested that it had been used to wipe the blood off the knife. Someone had written on a wall above it, "The Juwes [or Jews] are The men That Will not be Blamed for nothing." Sir Charles Warren, the Commissioner of Police, ordered the words to be erased in case they caused antise-mitic violence.

Another "Jack the Ripper" letter, which must have been posted soon after the double murder, reached the Central News Agency the next day, apologizing for not sending the ears of the victim, but explaining that he had been inter-rupted. And on October 16, George Lusk, the president of the Whitechapel Viligance Committee, also received a letter ("from hell, Mr. Lusk") enclosing half a human kidney, taken from someone suffering from Bright's Disease (as Catherine Eddowes was), and stating that the writer (who signed himself "Catch me when you can") had fried and eaten the other half.

October 1888 passed without incident, but on the morning of November 9, 1888, the body of 24-year-old Mary Kelly was found in her rented room in Millers Court, mutilated beyond recognition. The killer had obviously spent a long time in dissecting the body and removing most of the organs and entrails, slicing off the breasts, and cutting the skin off the face so it looked like a skull. A pile of burnt rags in the grate suggested he had done this by firelight. This time no body parts had been taken away.

This, as far as we know, was the last of the Ripper murders.

The uproar caused by Mary Kelly's murder led to the resignation of Sir Charles Warren and to renewed efforts by the police and a committee of public vigilantes to trap the murderer. But although three more cut-throat murders of prostitutes were attributed to Jack the Ripper during the next three years, the public had, in fact, heard the last of the sadistic disemboweler of Whitechapel.

Over the years there have been at least two dozen books claiming to have established the identity of Jack the Ripper once and for all. I have found none of these convincing. In my own view the most likely suspect so far is a man who is himself known as a murder victim.

In 1993, *The Diary of Jack the Ripper* by Shirley Harrison revealed that a handwritten notebook signed "Jack the Ripper" had turned up in Liverpool. Apparently the original finder was an out-of-work scrap dealer called Mike Barrett, who claimed that he had been given the Diary by a friend named Tony Devereux, with the comment: "Do something with it."

In a book on poisoning, Barrett came upon the Maybrick case and learned that the Maybricks had lived in Battlecrease House, which was mentioned in the Diary as the home of the man who signed himself "Jack the Ripper." The author of the Diary—to judge from internal evidence—was James Maybrick, a Liverpool cotton merchant who died in 1889, apparently poisoned by his wife Florence. The defense was based on the fact that Maybrick habitually swallowed arsenic, strychnine, cocaine, and other drugs as stimulants. Nevertheless, Florence was convicted and sentenced to death; at the last minute, her sentence was commuted to fifteen years' imprisonment.

In 1880, eight years before the murders, the 41-year-old Maybrick had fallen in love with 18-year-old Florence on a transatlantic crossing; they married and moved into Battlecrease House, in Aigburth, Liverpool. Their relationship soured when Florence discovered that he had a mistress—whom he still saw regularly—and several children. She banished him from her bed. Worse still, she began to have affairs with other men; she even stayed in a London hotel with a lover named Alfred Brierley. The writer of the Diary seems to be a man who lives in a frenzy of jealousy; he often refers to his wife as "the whore."

Maybrick was frequently in London on business and stayed in the Whitechapel area. He had known Whitechapel well since his early days as an apprentice in London and had married a woman named Sarah Robertson there (so the marriage to Florence was apparently bigamous). He seemed a highly plausible candidate for the Whitechapel killer.

The publisher of *The Diary of Jack the Ripper* made the serious mistake of offering it to the *Sunday Times* for serialization. It was a disastrous miscalculation. The *Sunday Times* had been deeply embarrassed over the affair of the forged Hitler diaries, which historian Trevor Roper had endorsed as genuine; now it took the opportunity to denounce the Ripper Diary as a fraud, on the grounds that the handwriting was unlike that of Maybrick's will, which was written in "copperplate." Unfortunately, no other example of Maybrick's handwriting seems to exist—although he must certainly have used a less formal hand for personal letters.

Six months later, the Diary's finder, Mike Barrett, announced that he had forged the Diary using a modern ink called Diomine. He withdrew the claim within hours, explaining that he was drunk at the time (he was an alcoholic), and had made it in order to hurt his wife Anne, who had recently left him. And although Barrett's handwriting is not remotely like that of the Diary, and the ink in which it was written has been proved not to be Diomine, the claim has stuck, so that most people now have a vague notion that the Diary has been proved a fraud.

The contrary is true. In July 1994, Barrett's wife Anne admitted to Paul Feldman—producer of a video on the Diary, who had spent a fortune researching its provenance—that the Diary had been in the possession of her family for years, originally belonging to her grandfather, then her father. It had been given to her by her father, Billy Graham, but she had taken no interest in it. She was not even sure whether Jack the Ripper was a real or fictional character. Because her husband was trying hard to become a writer, she had decided to give him the Diary, to see if he could turn it into a literary project that might prevent him from drinking so heavily. Since they were on such bad terms, she decided to give him the Diary through his friend and drinking companion Tony Devereux, and to simply hand it to him with the comment: "Do something with it." Devereux followed her instructions, handing over the brown paper parcel without even opening it.

Anne Barrett's father was dying of cancer; nevertheless, he agreed to see Paul Feldman. Feldman had been tracking down James Maybrick's many descendants—mostly the illegitimate line—and was convinced that Billy Graham was a Maybrick. He was stunned when Graham admitted—on tape—that in fact he was the grandson of Florence Maybrick, who had called herself Graham when she came out of prison. Feldman also recalled that when Florence revisited England from America—long after her release from prison—she had commented that she wanted to see her children, when in fact she had only one surviving child by Maybrick.

Feldman's researches have established convincingly that Florence had already had an illegitimate child in Liverpool before she met Maybrick, and that the child had been "farmed out" to a family named Graham. The evidence for this is circumstantial, yet very persuasive. Towards the end of the Diary, the writer remarks, "I have told Bunny all"—Bunny was Maybrick's pet name for Florence. It seems, therefore, highly probable that the Diary was originally in Florence's possession, that after her death it was passed on by her solicitor to her illegitimate son, William Graham, and by him to his son Billy—who confirms that he gave it to his daughter Anne.

When the Diary was examined by the American expert on forged documents Kenneth Rendell, Rendell announced that it *was* a forgery—dating from 1921, plus or minus twelve years. This is obviously absurd; the Diary is either a *modern* forgery, dating from after 1986, or it is almost certainly genuine. The ink expert Alec Voller—who works for Diomine—also looked at the Diary and stated unhesitatingly that the fact that the ink had "bronzed" indicated that it was at least ninety years old.

In my own view, James Maybrick is far and away the likeliest Ripper candidate so far.

1

PORNOGRAPHY AND THE RISE OF SEX CRIME

ALL THIS IS IMPORTANT TO THE UNDERSTANDING OF THE CRIMINAL mentality, particularly the serial killer. At the time I am writing these words, a religious cult in Waco, Texas, is under siege by the FBI. A psychologist who has been studying cult members comments that such people are not necessarily unintelligent and easily influenced—that such cults often target highly intelligent people, but concentrate on them when they are in a state of emotional vulnerability, perhaps after the break-up of a love affair, the loss of a job, the failure to pass an exam. Then the potential convert is in a state of low self-esteem, and looks around for something that will give him a sense of exercising his power to choose, his ability to *act*—because action brings relief.

In the Postscript to my history of forensic detection *Written in Blood*, I cite the parallel example of Arthur Koestler, who, after he had lost all his money in a poker game, got drunk at a party, spent the night with a girl he disliked, and discovered that his car radiator had frozen and burst, experienced an intense urge to "do something desperate" that resulted in the decision to join the Communist Party. In a man with a tendency to physical violence it could just as easily have led to murder.

The case of serial killer Ted Bundy reveals the same pattern. In his early twenties Bundy fell in love with a girl from a wealthy family and they became engaged. He decided to study Chinese because he reasoned that America would enter diplomatic relations with China and need interpreters. But he found the work too hard and dropped out of the course. The girl broke the engagement, which had the effect of totally undermining his self-esteem. Yet it was not this event that caused him to become a serial killer, even though he subsequently developed into a Peeping Tom. He became a law student and worked for the Office of Justice Planning, then became an election worker for a candidate for state governor. His self-confidence increased. Five years after being thrown over, he met his former fiancée, persuaded her to marry him, and spent a weekend with her. Then he dumped her as she had dumped him. And it was this act of calculated revenge that turned him from a Peeping Tom into a sex murderer. It gave him the courage—and the contempt for women—to turn his fantasies into reality.

The same psychological mechanism explains the rise in the crime rate during times of economic recession. It is not simply that people steal for money. It is because the psychological trauma of being without a job leads to the feeling of "anger with fate," and the desire to express it by *abandoning former inhibitions* and "hitting out." Graham Greene's favorite quote from Gauguin was: "Life being what it is, one dreams of revenge." After one of the Moors murders, Ian Brady—who proclaimed himself an atheist—shook his fist at the sky and shouted: "Take that, you bastard!" The serial killer Carl Panzram even believed that by killing innocent people—usually children—he was gaining a kind of "compensatory" revenge on people who had made him suffer.

This element of violent irrationality has always been a basic element in human nature. Shakespeare catches it in *Julius Caesar* when a man being attacked by a mob protests that he is Cinna the poet, not Cinna the conspirator, and his attackers shout: "Tear him for his bad verses." But until the nineteenth century, it was rare for this kind of resentment to find expression in sex crime. Crime was largely the result of social deprivation, so the criminal was interested in money and property, not in sex. In overcrowded slums, brothers and sisters often slept in the same bed, and were introduced to incest from an early age. In *The Complete Jack the Ripper*, Donald Rumbelow quotes a friend of Lord Salisbury who was indignantly separating two children having sex on a slum pavement when the boy cried: "Why do you take hold of me? There are a dozen of them at it down there." Drunken women would offer their bodies for a few pence, and mothers sell their daughters' virginity for five shillings. Sex was so freely available that there would have been no point in killing for it, or even risking the gallows for rape.

Casanova, who died in 1798, embodies the straightforward physical approach to sex. He is fascinated by the magic of women, and by his own ability to persuade them to yield. His first love affair was with two teenage sisters, who allowed him to spend the night in their room so that he could meet a girl with whom he was in love. When the girl failed to show up, they allowed the young abbé—Casanova was in holy orders—to sleep between them. He instantly broke his promise not to lay a finger on them, and seduced first one, then the other. But he tells this story—like that of his innumerable later conquests—in a language of delicate euphemism: "Her natural instincts soon working in concert with my own, I reach the goal; and my efforts, crowned with the most complete success, leave me not the shadow of doubt that I have gathered those first fruits to which our prejudice makes us attach so great an importance." He is enough of an eighteenth-century rationalist to recognize that there is a certain absurdity in attaching so much importance to taking a girl's virginity. And after he has described a dozen or so similar affairs, we begin to recognize that Casanova's conquests are not the result of an overpowering sexual impulse, but of a desire to think well of himself, to aggrandize his ego. He attaches far more importance to other kinds of conquest—for example, impressing contemporary intellectuals like Voltaire and Rousseau, or holding a dinner table enthralled with his conversation.

In the second half of the eighteenth century, a curious change began to come about. It was at this time that pornography suddenly came into existence: that is, sexual description whose basis was the *forbiddenness* of the sexual act. Earlier works like Aretino's *Dialogues* (1536) and the anonymous *School of Venus* (1655) may seem to contradict that assertion; but they can also be seen as works in the great humanist tradition, arguing against puritanical morality. In *The School of Venus*, Fanchon tells her friend Suzanne: "Since Robinet fucked me, and I know what is what, I find all my mother's warnings to be but bugbears and good for nothing but frightening children. For my part, I believe we were created for fucking, and when we begin to fuck we begin to live." Donald Thomas comments: "Compared with the neurotic and sadistic pornography which has made up so much of the erotic literature of the last two centuries, *The School of Venus* seems almost radiant with innocence."

The same argument applies to the anticlerical erotica of the eighteenth century, with titles like *Venus in the Cloister* and *The Monastery Gate, or the Story of Dom Bugger*; it was all about priests seducing their penitents or monks impregnating nuns. (In fact, *Venus in the Cloister* was based on a famous scandal in which a Jesuit named Fr. Girard seduced one of his penitents.) This type of health indecency can trace its ancestry to Boccaccio and Rabelais—the latter writes: "Even the shadow of a monastery is fruitful."

The change to genuine eroticism is marked by John Cleland's *Memoirs of a Lady of Pleasure*—usually known as *Fanny Hill* (1747)—which describes how a young servant girl is introduced into a brothel, then into a life of endless sexual adventure. But *Fanny Hill* was preceded by a far more important novel: Samuel Richardson's *Pamela* (1740), the story of a servant girl who resists all her master's attempts at seduction until he capitulates and marries her. Richardson, a printer-turned-author, firmly believed that he was writing a highly moral tale about a virtuous girl. But the public who lingered over scenes in which her master flings her on a bed and throws her skirts over her head were more interested in how soon she would lose her virginity.

Pamela was the first novel in our modern sense of the word: a kind of soap opera about ordinary people rather than strange, distant lands populated by dusky princes and lovelorn shepherds. Within five years, Europe had become a "nation of readers," and every small town had its lending library. It was then that Cleland introduced a new twist with *Fanny Hill*, in which there was no attempt to pretend that the author's intention was to preach virtue and abstinence.

And yet even *Fanny Hill* is, in a sense, non-pornographic. The sex is Rabelaisian and down-to-earth; when Fanny peers through a crack in the closet-door at the brothel madame about to have sex with her lover, she sees "her fat brawny thighs hung down; and the whole greasy landscape . . . fairly open to my view: a wide open-mouthed gap, overshaded with a grizzly bush seemed held out like a beggar's wallet . . . " The description could hardly be less erotic.

I have suggested elsewhere that the invention of the novel must be regarded as one of the important steps in mankind's

development. The theater had provided the public with entertainment since the days of the ancient Greeks, but the novel
was an invitation to sit alone and use the imagination to conjure up other people's lives. And even though Cleland was
sentenced to the pillory, and then persuaded to write no more
pornography by the grant of a government pension (which
suggests that ministers recognized the danger of free sexual
fantasy), others quickly took his place and created a pornography industry.

By far the most important of these figures was the Marquis de Sade, born in the same year that *Pamela* was published. Thrown into jail for atheism, then for kidnaping and
whipping a beggar woman, Sade was antiauthoritarian to the
point of paranoia. His early fantasies about incest and about
the seduction and rape of children can only be understood in
the light of his hatred of the Christian church. He was obsessed by "the forbidden"—it is typical that he seduced and
ran away with his wife's younger sister, a canoness (or apprentice nun). Finally, sentenced to prison for a third time for
various misdemeanors—including sodomizing prostitutes
and almost killing two of them with an aphrodisiac—he
poured his sexual frustrations into the works for which he is
famous (or infamous), novels like *Philosophy in the Boudoir*
and *Justine*. The first is about the debauching of a virgin by
an incestuous brother and sister, the second about the endless
misfortunes of a pure and virtuous girl. Both might be regarded as blasphemous parodies of Richardson's *Pamela*.
His unfinished *120 Days of Sodom* is an attempt at a novel
that catalogues every possible sexual perversion.

Freed briefly by the French Revolution, Sade was soon
back in prison for writing novels of unparalleled violence
and indecency; *Juliette* ends with a scene in which a mother
allows her little daughter to be violated and burnt alive while

she herself is simultaneously penetrated, vaginally and anally, by two of her lover's henchmen.

In fact, the novels of Sade are even less pornographic than *Fanny Hill*. There is no lingering sensuality, no gloating over sexual fantasy; Sade is more concerned with shouting blasphemies at the top of his voice. He is a man who hates the system so much that his one concern is to defy it. When he describes sexual orgies, it is not to titillate the lecherous, but to upset the guardians of morality.

To understand Sade—and the great majority of serial killers—we only have to recognize that he was an extremely imperious man who loved having his own way. As a born aristocrat, he expected to give orders and have them promptly obeyed. So to be at the mercy of gaolers threw him into a state of sheer outrage. His privileges were always being suspended for losing his temper. In the chronology of his life we read: "October 10, 1787: Sade berates the prison governor and his aide who come to announce to him suspension of his exercise period." Thirteen days later it was restored, but in June of the following year we read: "Sade's exercise period again having been suspended 'for impertinence', and he having been informed in writing, the prisoner nonetheless attempts to descend at his regular hour to the yard, and . . . it was only when the officer pointed his gun at him that he retreated, swearing loudly." Sade was simply incapable of getting used to the idea that he was not an eastern sultan. He never learned to adjust. Frustration of his wishes threw him into a frenzy of rage. And because it was impossible to express that rage by flogging the prison governor and his minions, Sade channeled it into his books. We might say that what fate was trying to teach him was self-discipline; but his imperious temperament made it impossible. And, being highly intelligent, he rationalized his refusal to attempt self-discipline in the only possible way: that is, into a philosophical system in which *everybody* is permitted unlimited violence towards everybody else . . . We shall observe the same syndrome in many of the serial killers of the late twentieth century.

Sade died in the Charenton asylum in December 1814. But his influence was already pervasive. Lord Byron had recently invented a new kind of hero, the world-weary sinner who is also the defiant rebel, and had lived up to his sinister reputation by seducing and impregnating his half-sister, then sodomizing his wife. By the time of Byron's death in exile in 1824, Sade's works already enjoyed a wide underground circulation in England (a country that always seems to have been peculiarly obsessed by sexual morality and immorality), and a new pornography industry was flourishing. And the essence of this new pornography was an obsession with *forbiddenness*. It is full of scenes in which schoolteachers seduce their pupils and butlers seduce the little daughter of the household. In *The Power of Hypnotism*, a youth who has learned hypnosis in Germany uses it to seduce his sister, after which the two of them use it to have sex with their mother and father. Later in the book, the vicar and his two little nieces are hypnotized into joining in an orgy. Nothing could be more unlike the boisterous couplings in Boccaccio or Rabelais, or even in *Fanny Hill*. And Casanova would simply have scratched his head, and wondered why any normal person should want to have sex with his own family members when the world is full of desirable girls. This is sex raised to an unhealthy intensity by the use of a kind of morbid imagination.

Let us try to understand just what has happened.

Sex depends fundamentally upon a certain sexual energy which accumulates in the genitals, like water accumulating in a cistern. Without this energy, neither male nor female can experience sexual excitement. This energy is released by friction—preferably with the genitals of someone of the opposite sex. But when the cistern is full to the top, almost any friction can cause it to brim over—for example, accidentally pressing against a tabletop.

But no matter how full the cistern, it would be difficult to achieve full release without some sense of purpose or direction, which serves as a channel. In animals, this channeling is caused by the smell of the female in season. Human sex has ceased to be seasonal, and the channeling is achieved by a certain sense of "forbiddenness." The pleasure of sexuality lies in the male's feeling that the body of an attractive female is "forbidden territory" until she can be persuaded to give her consent. And no matter how gentle and considerate the male, this desire to enter "forbidden territory" must be recognized as a form of aggression.

In primitive societies, the forbiddenness is complicated by a social taboo. The male has to approach the parents of the girl he wants to marry and obtain their consent—perhaps even pay them for her. And now, in a sense, she is no longer "forbidden." Yet here human imagination comes to the rescue. He continues to want her, even when she is his wife, because it is easy to remember when she was "forbidden."

We must recognize another important point that is true of *all* desire. It can be intensified by wanting something badly. You enjoy your dinner more when you are hungry. But you also enjoy it more when you have been looking forward to it. Romantic love is essentially a kind of imaginative build-up, a "looking forward" to possessing the object of desire. This is a simple but all-important observation: that we can enjoy something twice as much simply by "taking thought" about it, building up a certain anticipation. Conversely, it is easy to cease to enjoy something by being too casual about it, by taking it for granted.

So "romantic love"—as expressed by the troubadours, and by Dante and Petrarch and Shakespeare—was an interesting step forward in human history. Human beings were learning to intensify animal sexuality with the use of imagination. But this must be immediately qualified by saying that it was true only for a small number of people. For the "average man," sex remained as simple and crude as the coupling of two dogs.

With the rise of the novel, more and more inveterate daydreamers learned to use the imagination and to "cultivate their sensibilities"—that is, to "conjure up" other realities, other times and places.

Inevitably—human nature being what it is—an increasing number of these began to use imagination for sexual purposes—that is, for masturbation. There is a very narrow dividing line between a teenage girl imagining being carried off by Byron's Corsair, and allowing herself to daydream of being ravished by him. And if we look closely at Heathcliff in *Wuthering Heights*, it is easy to see that Emily Brontë daydreamed of a male who was even more brutal and earthy than Byron's swashbuckling heroes. It may seem unnecessarily crude to ask: Did Emily Brontë masturbate as she thought about Heathcliff? But the question is more important than it looks. It makes us aware that imagination was pushing human beings towards the dividing line between the "permitted" and the "forbidden." And—since forbiddenness is another name for criminality—towards the criminal.

In Victorian pornography, this criminal element has become all-important. Now it is a question of seeking out the forbidden for its own sake. Sexual excitement ceases to be associated with naked lovers in bed; instead, the quintessential situation is someone peering through a keyhole or a crack in the lavatory door at something he is "not supposed to be looking at." The penis is regarded as a kind of burglar whose task is to get into forbidden places.

What is happening is that this power of the imagination— to increase a pleasure by anticipating it—is being used to create a new kind of sex, what we might call "superheated sex."

Normal "animal" sex can only reach a certain intensity, no matter how much a man wants a woman and vice versa. When they are in bed, close physical contact soon turns into the "flow experience," in which there is a mutual release of energy. No matter how much they try to control the flow, it soon leads to sexual fulfilment. What the Marquis de Sade discovered was that the initial desire can be made far more intense, far more feverish, by taking advantage of the fact that male sexuality is based on aggression. Moreover, imagination can be used to drag out the whole process to far more than its normal length. "Animal" intercourse might last from a minute to a quarter of an hour or so. But "superheated sex" can be kept on the boil for twice or three times that period.

Now in fact, Sade's idea of sex was always far more aggressive than that of the normal male. Even as a young man, he wanted to beat prostitutes and be beaten. He once tried to explain his idea of sex by saying that any kind of blow— even chopping wood with an axe—gives a feeling of satisfaction. Most males are likely to consider this a little peculiar—to feel that Sade is extending sex beyond the idea of the normal sexual impulse. But anyone who reads Sade's works in chronological order can understand how this came about. Sade's first major work is the novel *Justine*, completed in the Bastille in 1787, when he was 47. He had been in prison for eight years. The basic argument of *Justine* is that crime leads to prosperity, while virtue leads to misfortune. Justine is a sweet, timid, modest girl of remarkable beauty; her elder sister Juliette, equally beautiful, is depraved from an early age. Their parents die while they are still in a convent, leaving them destitute, and they are thrown out into the world. The wicked Juliette prospers, while Justine is humiliated, beaten and raped with appalling regularity. Sade obviously felt that he had been badly treated by the world—which on the whole was true—and the novel was intended partly as a Swiftian satire on human selfishness. Sade takes an entirely cynical view of kings, judges and priests; he claims that all indulge their vices to the full, while urging restraint on the rest of society. But, according to Sade, God does not exist, there is no "moral law," and man was sent into the world solely to enjoy himself. So he is trying to awaken his fellow men to "the truth" about society, and to overthrow those in authority. Unfortunately, his logic is totally distorted by his hatred of authority and religion, so that he simply refuses to imagine what would happen if everybody set out to satisfy their desires to the full.

In fact, Sade was already writing a novel in which he asks the question: what would happen if a group of human beings was rich and powerful enough to satisfy their desires to the full? The *120 Days of Sodom* is a vast catalogue of the "forbidden," in which four libertines, who include a bishop and a Lord Chief Justice, spend four months indulging every form of perversion, from the rape of children and virgins to ritual murder. Towards the end, even Sade gets tired of the horrors, and the final scenes are only sketched in outline. He left this work behind in the Bastille when he was released, and it was only found by accident many years later.

So Sade, who has been violently restrained—and rather badly treated—by authority now used his imagination to devise situations that amounted to a continuous scream of defiance. In fact, as an individual, Sade was far from "sadistic." He was a genuinely affectionate father, and when he had a chance to sentence his hated mother-in-law to death—as a member of a revolutionary tribunal—he allowed her to go free. But he was crazed with hatred of authority, and his work may be seen as a kind of continuous sex crime of the imagination. A serial killer like Carl Panzram is a kind of Sade who put his daydreams into practice.

Oddly enough, Sade's work is seldom pornographic, in the sense of being sexually stimulating. He never gloats over the lascivious preliminaries and the physical details of sex; when one of his characters commits incest, he merely "ravishes" his daughter, then teaches her "all the mysteries of love." Sade is more interested in expressing his sense of grievance by pouring out indecencies; basically, he is like a schoolboy sticking out his tongue at the headmaster.

What is obvious to the modern reader of Sade is that he is a man who is trying to create a *sexual illusion,* a kind of daydream. If he shows signs of waking up, he redoubles the "wickedness" to try and stimulate his imagination. When Sade actually seduced his sister-in-law, the apprentice nun, he must have found out that, after the initial thrill, it soon ceased to feel wicked. But Sade's characters never get tired of "the forbidden." After Juliette has seduced her clergyman father, she then looks on as he is murdered by her lover. But, as we can see from the *120 Days,* Sade's imagination was unable to sustain the sexual daydream; he kept on inflating the sexual illusion until it burst like a bubble.

Victorian pornography never went this far. It was only concerned with creating an atmosphere of feverish sensuality, with great emphasis on the preliminaries. One well-known piece of Victorian pornography, the anonymous *Raped on the Railway* (1894), clearly reveals the difference between sex in the eighteenth and in the nineteenth centuries. It begins with a prelude on Euston station (to increase our anticipation of what is to come), then a chapter in which a painter named Brandon tries to persuade a veiled lady with whom he is sharing the compartment to "let me contemplate those heavenly features I so burn to portray." When he tries to lift her veil, she produces a revolver; but before she can fire it, the train brakes suddenly and flings her into his arms.

There follows a long digression in which the author tells the reader about the painter's earlier life and love affairs; finally he returns us to the carriage, in which the lady—introduced as Mrs. Sinclair—is now lying in a "swoon." The painter unbuttons her dress "exposing to view two small but beautifully round breasts just showing their little pink nipples above the corset which confined them." After kissing these, he "carefully turned back her skirt, and the fine linen petticoats underneath it exposing to view a pair of well-shaped legs encased in black silk stockings, and encircled by very natty-looking garters with red bows." "Pulling apart her thighs as gently as though he were touching a sleeping child," he opens the slit of her drawers. "The charms he sought were, however, hidden from his eyes by a chemise of the finest cambric. Carefully lifting this he saw before his entranced eyes, now gleaming with lust, a forest of golden brown curly hair which extended, in a triangular shape from the line where the thighs join the body, all over the belly. At the apex of this triangle, there peered through a thicker and curlier tuft of hair the pouting red lips of a pretty and very tempting-looking abode of love."

All this is quite unlike Cleland or Sade. The writer is trying to create in the reader, moment by moment, the actual sensations of a man in the grip of sexual excitement. It is also clear that the writer finds her underwear very nearly as exciting as her body. This is a refinement of sexual desire that Casanova would have found incomprehensible.

As he is about to enter, the lady wakes up. The painter wrestles with her until she is exhausted, then succeeds in penetrating her. She struggles violently until he thrusts into her and "poured into her vagina the warm flood which she would have been so glad to receive and mingle with her own love fountain, if the tool which was shooting the warm jets into her had come as a friend and not as an enemy."

After the rape is over, he begs her forgiveness, offering to let her shoot him; she finally agrees to say nothing about the rape if he will promise not to speak to her for the rest of the journey.

But a guard at the next station deduces from her "tottering walk" and the disarray of her clothes what has happened, and when a man in the next compartment makes a joke about needing a woman, tells him that the lady next door looks as if she has had a "rare good poking." As Mrs. Sinclair emerges from the toilet, one of the men, described as "a giant," recognizes her as his sister-in-law. With three companions he gets into her carriage. While they doze, the rapist and his victim are both overpowered and tied up. Then the lady is laid face-downward on the seat, and the men begin "very carefully and slowly to draw back the panting woman's dress." "They then served a stout traveling flannel petticoat in the same way, and also a rose-colored silk petticoat that she wore next to her drawers." At this point, the writer pauses to observe that "the latter article of feminine toilette calls for special remark. There is a great psychological significance in the quality of women's drawers." And the next part of the undressing is delayed for a page while he discourses on underwear. Finally, the drawers are removed, and for the next six pages or so, the lady's bottom, "the most wonderful riches that it has ever been the lot of man to gaze upon," is birched until it glows bright red.

Even when she arrives home, Mrs. Sinclair's ordeal is not finished. Her brother-in-law—a member of the Society for National Purity—calls on her and makes a determined attempt to rape her; she finally disables him by bending his penis, which causes him such agony that a doctor has to administer morphine.

It is impossible not to recognize the resemblance between *Raped on the Railway* and Sade. The fact that the brother-in-law is a member of the Society of National Purity suggests that all such people are hypocrites—in fact, that they are rapists at heart—while the description of the woman's struggles as her brother-in-law tries to rape her ("her underclothing was in a frightful state, the pink silk petticoat . . . being torn in several places, and her clean white drawers nearly wrenched from the strings that attached them to her waist") is reminiscent of *Justine's* tribulations.

Yet the difference between *Justine* and *Raped on the Railway* is also enormous. *Justine* is simply "violated," and the details are left to the imagination. Mrs. Sinclair's breasts, her buttocks, her genitals, her petticoat, her underskirt and her drawers are all described with obsessive precision. Compared to Cleland or Sade, the author of *Raped on the Railway* is in a kind of fever; we can almost hear his heavy breathing as he describes her underwear. All this is the result of a century and a half of novel-reading.

The main difference between the two books lies in the happy ending of *Raped on the Railway*. In the last chapter, the lady's husband is conveniently killed off in the Boer war; Brandon calls on her, and they end in one another's arms. Yet as the book closes in an atmosphere of reconciliation and morality, we become aware of the paradox involved in the author's attitude to sex. Brandon and Mrs. Sinclair will now become husband and wife. But will Brandon's eyes continue to "gleam with lust" every time his wife takes off her clothes? Obviously not; they will become an ordinary married couple, for whom sex is a pleasure that lasts ten minutes or so, and then is followed by sleep. All this dwelling on rounded breasts, white thighs (and the "abode of love" between them), pink silk petticoats and fine linen drawers, is a kind of embroidery, a deliberately intensified *illusion*, that has nothing to do with the simple fact of sexual intercourse as described by Cleland. It has been *added* by the Victorian imagination, and is the outcome of a century of romanticism, of regarding women as untouchable goddesses or compassionate angels.

In fact, this feverish romanticism had already begun to manifest in another form. In 1886, a book called *Psychopathia Sexualis* caused such a scandal that the British Medico-Psychological Association debated whether to cancel the author's membership. The author was a German "alienist" (as psychiatrists were then called), Richard von Krafft-Ebing. And the book begins with an utterly typical case describing how a middle-aged man showed "increasing perversion of his moral sense," so that he constantly accosted women in the street and asked them to marry him or allow coitus. Placed in an asylum, "the sexual excitement increased to a veritable satyriasis, which increased until he died." "He masturbated continuously, even before others, took delight only in obscene ideas, and thought the men around him were women, and pestered them with obscene proposals." And this portrait of a man totally obsessed with sex is followed by a gallery of sadists, masochists (Krafft-Ebing invented both words), voyeurs, fetishists, transvestites, vampires and necrophiles.

Among the cases of necrophily is one that throws a great deal of light on the development of "the sexual illusion."

Sergeant Bertrand, a man of delicate physical constitution and of peculiar character; from childhood silent and inclined to solitude.

The details of the health of his family are not satisfactorily known; but the occurrence of mental diseases in his ancestry is ascertained. It is said that while he was a child he was affected with destructive impulses, which he himself could not explain. He would break whatever was at hand. In early childhood, without teaching, he learned to masturbate. At nine he began to feel inclinations towards persons of the opposite sex. At thirteen the impulse to sexual intercourse became powerfully awakened in him. He now masturbated excessively. When he did this, his fancy always created a room filled with women. He would imagine that he carried out the sexual act with them and then killed them. Immediately thereafter he would think of them as corpses, and of how he defiled them. Occasionally in such situations the thought of carrying out a similar act with male corpses would come up, but it was always attended with a feeling of disgust.

In time he felt the impulse to carry out such acts with actual corpses. For want of human bodies, he obtained those of animals. He would cut open the abdomen, tear out the entrails, and masturbate during the act. He declares that in this way he experienced inexpressible pleasure. In 1846 these bodies no longer satisfied him. He now killed dogs, and proceeded with them as before. Towards the end of 1846 he first felt the desire to make use of human bodies.

At first he had a horror of it. In 1847, being by accident in a graveyard, he ran across the grave of a newly buried corpse. Then this impulse, with headache and palpitation of the heart, became so powerful that, although there were people near by, and he was in danger of detection, he dug up the body. In the absence of a convenient instrument for cutting it up, he satisfied himself by hacking it with a shovel.

In 1847 and 1848, during two weeks, as reported, the impulse, accompanied by violent headache, to commit brutalities on corpses actuated him. Amidst the greatest dangers and difficulties he satisfied this impulse some fifteen times. He dug up the bodies with his hands, in nowise sensible in his excitement to the injuries he thus inflicted on himself. When he had obtained the body, he cut it up with a sword or pocket-knife, tore out the entrails, and then masturbated. The sex of the bodies is said to have been a matter of indifference to him, though it was ascertained that this modern vampire had dug up more female than male corpses.

During these acts he declares himself to have been in an indescribable state of sexual excitement. After having cut them up, he reinterred the bodies.

In July, 1848, he accidentally came across the body of a girl of sixteen. Then, for the first time, he experienced a desire to carry out coitus on a cadaver.

"I covered it with kisses and pressed it wildly to my heart. All that one could enjoy with a living woman is nothing in comparison with the pleasure I experienced. After I had enjoyed it for about a quarter of an hour, I cut the body up, as usual, and tore out the entrails. Then I buried the cadaver again." Only after this, as B. declares, had he felt the impulse to use the bodies sexually before cutting them up, and thereafter he had done it in three instances. The actual motive for exhuming the bodies, however, was then, as before, to cut them up; and the enjoyment in so doing was greater than in using the bodies sexually. The latter act had always been nothing more than an episode of the principal one, and had never quieted his desires; for which reason he had later on always mutilated the body.

The medico-legal examiners gave an opinion of "monomania." Court-martial sentence to one year's imprisonment.

An account of the case quoted by the sexologist Magnus Hirschfeld includes some important details:

> He denied that he had ever bitten the corpses, as one of the experts asserts.
>
> An interesting feature of the case is that, in addition to and in spite of his necrophile activities, B. entertained relations with girls wherever he was stationed, and completely "satisfied" them. Several girls wanted to marry him. When the impulse manifested itself, which happened at intervals of about a fortnight, the attack being heralded by a headache, he pursued his necrosadistic pleasures. And nothing could deter him. Even shots fired at him by sentries, traps laid for him, the most inclement weather, such obstacles as a pond which he had to swim in the middle of winter, the need to lie motionless in wet clothes in icy cold weather—none of these things deterred him. Finally, he was so severely wounded by a trap shot while climbing over the cemetery wall that he could not escape arrest, thereby providing an explanation of the many desecrations of the cemetery that had become known. Under the influence of the surgeon Marchal de Calvi, under whose treatment he was, B. freely admitted everything stating that he was not sure that he would not do such things again. He also declared that the important thing for him was the act of destruction, not the sexual act.

His attitude to women is rather interesting. He said:—

"I have always loved women to distraction. I have never allowed anyone to offend a woman in my presence. Everywhere I had young and charming mistresses, whom I have been able to satisfy completely and who were devoted to me. This is proved by the fact that some of them, although they came from well-to-do, distinguised families, wanted to follow me. I have never touched a married woman; I always disliked obscene talk. If such talk was started in my presence, I endeavored to turn the conversation to a different subject. I had a strictly religious education and have always loved and defended religion, though I am not a fanatic.

"I have always loved destruction. In my childhood my parents would not give me any toys because I smashed everything. In later years I could not keep anything, even a penknife, longer than a fortnight; by then it was smashed up. It sometimes happens that I buy myself a pipe in the morning, and smash it up in the evening or next morning. In the army I once returned to barracks drunk and smashed everything that I could lay hands on."

This case is interesting because it allows us such a clear insight into the reason for the rise of sex crime. There had, of course, been sadistic disembowellers before the nineteenth century, like Vlad the Impaler (the original "Dracula") and the French Marshal Gilles de Rais (who killed children). But these had been members of an upper class who had the leisure to become bored, and to devote themselves to strange pleasures and fantasies. Bertrand was the son of a peasant. The origin of his sadism lay in "hypersexuality"—sexual desire of almost painful intensity. Fantasies of raping a roomful of women were followed by fantasies of killing them all—a daydream of ultimate power and aggression. (We note that Bertrand is a "man of delicate physical constitution," and inclined to daydream, so these power fantasies are compensatory.) Since he has no contact with human corpses at this period, he is forced to make do with animal corpses; and since these are unsatisfactory for sexual purposes, his aggression finds expression in disembowelling. From then on, he is "imprinted" with an association of sex and disembowelling. At 24, Bertrand began to kill and disembowel dogs while he masturbated. So when he came across an open grave with a corpse (a female) the desire to enact his fantasies was overwhelming; he described in his confession the "insane frenzy" with which he began to beat the corpse with a spade.

The progression, then, is simple: intense sexual desire that finds outlet in daydreams, then in fantasies of rape followed by murder, then in disembowelling animal corpses, then sadistic acts on living dogs, then necrophily on female corpses. (In spite of Krafft-Ebing's assertion, Bertrand said that he felt only disgust when he disinterred a male corpse.) And the medium which causes this progression from fantasy to necrophily is *aggression*. Yet Bertrand continues to feel a powerful inhibition about attacking living women. And so, as far as we can judge, did most of the males suffering from "hypersexuality."

In the second half of the nineteenth century, this inhibition finally broke down. Krafft-Ebing also describes one of the first recorded sex crimes in our modern sense of the word:

Alton, a clerk in England, goes out of town for a walk. He lures a child into a thicket, and returns after a time to his office, where he makes this entry in his notebook: "Killed today a young girl; it was fine and hot." The child was missed, searched for, and found cut into pieces. Many parts, among them the genitals, could not be found. A. did not show the slightest trace of emotion, and gave no explanation of the motive of circumstances of the horrible deed. He was a psychopathic individual, and occasionally subject to fits of depression and *taedium vitae*. His father had had an attack of acute mania. A near relative suffered from mania with homicidal impulses. A. was executed.

Krafft-Ebing has it slightly wrong; the clerk was called Frederick Baker, and the town was Alton, Hampshire. It happened in July 1867, and the victim was an 8-year-old girl named Fanny Adams, whom Baker accosted and lured away from her playmates with a promise of sweets, then murdered in a hop garden.

Here, as in the case of Sergeant Bertrand, we can see that the sheer intensity of sexual fantasy leads to dreams of violence and murder. When he finally puts these dreams into action, it is not enough to commit rape: he also has to mutilate the victim and scatter the parts of her body over such a wide area that the phrase "sweet Fanny Adams" has become a slang term meaning "nothing."

Five years later, in 1872, one of the first Jack the Ripper–type killers, Vincent Verzeni, was arrested. The case is again described by Krafft-Ebing:

Vincenz Verzeni, born in 1849; since January 11, 1872, in prison; is accused (1) of an attempt to strangle his nurse Marianne, four years ago, while she lay sick in bed; (2) of a similar attempt on a married woman, Arsuffi, aged twenty-seven; (3) of an attempt to strangle a married woman, Gala, by grasping her throat while kneeling on her abdomen; (4) on suspicion of the following murders:—

In December a fourteen-year-old girl, Johanna Motta, set out for a neighboring village between seven and eight o'clock in the morning. As she did not return, her master set out to find her, and discovered her body near the village, lying by a path in the fields. The corpse was frightfully mutilated with numerous wounds. The intestines and genitals had been torn from the open body, and were found near by. The nakedness of the body and erosions on the thighs made it seem probable that there had been an attempt at rape; the mouth, filled with earth, pointed to suffocation. In the neighborhood of the body, under a pile of straw, were found a portion of flesh torn from the right calf, and pieces of clothing. The perpetrator of the deed remained undiscovered.

On August 28, 1871, a married woman, Frigeni, aged twenty-eight, set out into the fields early in the morning. As she did not return by eight o'clock, her husband started out to fetch her. He found her a corpse, lying naked in the field, with the mark of a thong around her neck, with which she had been strangled, and with numerous wounds. The abdomen had been slit open, and the intestines were hanging out.

On August 29, at noon, as Maria Previtali, aged nineteen, went through a field, she was followed by her cousin, Verzeni. He dragged her into a field of grain, threw her on the ground, and began to choke her. As he let go of her for a moment to ascertain whether any one was near, the girl got up and, by her supplicating entreaty, induced Verzeni to let her go, after he had pressed her hands together for some time.

Verzeni was brought before a court. He is twenty-two years old. His cranium is of more than average size, but asymmetrical. The right frontal bone is narrower and lower than the left, the right frontal prominence being less developed, and the right ear smaller than the left (by 1 centimeter in length and 3 centimeters in breadth); both ears are defective in the inferior half of the helix; the right temporal artery is somewhat atheromatous. Bull-necked; enormous development of the *zygomœ* and inferior *maxilla*; penis greatly developed, *frœnum* wanting; slight divergent alternating strabismus (insufficiency of the internal rectus muscle, and myopia). *Lombroso* concludes, from these signs of degeneration, that there is a congenital arrest of development of the right frontal lobe. As seemed probable, Verzeni has a bad ancestry—two uncles are cretins; a third, microcephalic, beardless, one testicle wanting, the other atrophic. The father shows traces of pellagrous degeneration, and had an attack of *hypochondria pellagrosa*. A cousin suffered from cerebral hyperæmia; another is a confirmed thief.

Verzeni's family is bigoted and low-minded. He himself has ordinary intelligence; knows how to defend himself well; seeks to prove an *alibi* and cast suspicion on others. There is nothing in his past that points to mental disease, but his character is peculiar. He is silent and inclined to be solitary. In prison he is cynical. He masturbates, and makes every effort to gain sight of women.

Verzeni finally confessed his deeds and their motive. The commission of them gave him an indescribably pleasant (lustful) feeling, which was accompanied by erection and ejaculation. As soon as he has grasped his victim by the neck, sexual sensations were experienced. It was entirely the same to him, with reference to these sensations, whether the women were old, young, ugly, or beautiful. Usually, simply choking them had satisfied him, and he then had allowed his victims to live; in the two cases mentioned, the sexual satisfaction was delayed, and he had continued to choke them until they died. The gratification experienced in this garrotting was greater than in masturbation. The abrasions of the skin on Motta's thighs were produced by his teeth, whilst sucking her blood in most intense lustful pleasure. He had torn out a piece of flesh from her calf and taken it with him to roast at home; but on the way he hid it under the straw-stack, for fear his mother would suspect him. He also carried pieces of the clothing and intestines some distance, because it gave him great pleasure to smell and touch them. The strength which he possessed in these moments of intense lustful pleasure was enormous. He had never been a fool; while committing his deeds he saw nothing around him (apparently as a result of intense sexual excitement, annihilation of perception—instinctive action).

After such acts he was always very happy, enjoying a feeling of great satisfaction. He had never had pangs of conscience. It had never occurred to him to touch the genitals of the martyred women or to violate his victims. It had satisfied him to throttle them and suck their blood. These statements of this modern vampire seem to rest on truth. Normal sexual impulses seem to have remained foreign to him. Two sweethearts that he had, he was satisfied to look at; it was very strange to him that he had no inclination to strangle them or press their hands; but he had not had the same pleasure with them as with his victims. There was no trace of moral sense, remorse and the like.

Verzeni said himself that it would be a good thing if he were to be kept in prison, because with freedom he could not resist his impulses. Verzeni was sentenced to imprisonment for life (Lombroso, "Verzeni e Agnoletti," Rome, 1873). The confessions which Verzeni made after his sentence are interesting:—

"I had an unspeakable delight in strangling women, experiencing during the act erections and real sexual pleasure. It was even a pleasure only to smell female clothing. The feeling of pleasure while strangling them was much greater than that which I experienced while masturbating. I took great delight in drinking Motta's blood. It also gave me the greatest pleasure to pull the hair-pins out of the hair of my victims.

"I took the clothing and intestines because of the pleasure it gave me to smell and touch them. At last my mother came to suspect me, because she noticed spots of semen on my shirt after each murder or attempt at one. I am not crazy, but in the moment of strangling my victims I saw nothing else. After the commission of the deeds I was satisfied and felt well. It never occurred to me to touch or look at the genitals or such things. It satisfied me to seize the women by the neck and suck their blood. To this very day I am ignorant of how a woman is formed. During the strangling and after it, I pressed myself on the entire body without thinking of one part more than another."

Verzeni arrived at his perverse acts quite independently, after having noticed, when he was twelve years old, that he experienced a peculiar feeling of pleasure while wringing the necks of chickens. After this he often killed great numbers of them and then said that a weasel had been in the hen-coop.

It is interesting to note that Verzeni found intestines and the female clothing equally exciting. And this suddenly enables us to understand the emphasis on underwear in *Raped on the Railway*. Mrs. Sinclair is at first remote, untouchable, even her face hidden behind a veil. So the artist Brandon sees her as a sexual object, not as a fellow human being—moreover, as a sexual object whose "forbiddenness" merits aggression. The silk underskirt and the drawers are symbols of her forbiddenness. And the difference between the erotic fantasy of *Fanny Hill* and the pornographic fantasy of *Raped on the Railway* is essentially a difference of aggression. Cleland is interested only in the straightforward pleasures of the "two backed beast," of the mutual satisfaction men and women can obtain from of their genitals. *Fanny Hill* is a straightforward transference of the pleasures of the bed into fiction, a kind of substitute for an hour in bed with a member of the opposite sex. *Raped on the Railway* is intended as more than a substitute; it is intended to give a higher degree of pleasure by taking its (male) reader on an excursion into the forbidden, in which aggression is expressed first in rape, then in spanking.

The irony of the situation is that it is the development of the human imagination that has led to all this "superheated sex" with its flavor of criminality. Imagination means that human beings are no longer contented with the narrowness and boredom of their everyday lives; they dream of far horizons and a richer and more satisfying kind of experience. But this enriched imagination is also placed at the service of their sexual fantasy and their will-to-power. The result is a product like *Raped on the Railway*, which takes at least three hours to read, and is therefore far more extended than a normal sexual experience.

Imagination, of course, is not the whole explanation. The social changes brought about by the Industrial Revolution, which packed hundreds of thousands of human beings into a thoroughly artificial environment in the cities, also played their part. Even more important was the frustration induced by Victorian prudery, in which children were brought up to regard any reference to intimate parts of the body as shameful. Even the word "legs" was unmentionable, and table legs were often covered up with a long tablecloth, or even a kind of stocking, in case they brought a blush to the cheeks of young ladies.

Because we are the heirs of Victorian prudery, we find all this fairly natural, even if rather absurd. But to grasp the real point, imagine what would happen if our society regarded food as shameful and unmentionable, so that only married couples ate together, while single people ate alone, and did their best to give the impression that they had no need of nourishment. A food pornography would develop in which men in a fever of desire would peer through cracks in doors at women eating their dinner, and in which a description of a cherry tart surmounted by a twisted blob of whipped cream would arouse all the illicit thrills of a girl removing her clothes. The sense of wickedness would soon be transferred to food packaging, and fetishists would furtively search through dustbins for empty boxes with erotic pictures of cheesecake and beefburgers. A few dedicated perverts would accumulate drawers full of empty jam jars, opened cans of baked beans, and greaseproof paper in which sausages had been wrapped, while food pedophiles would be attracted only to unripe fruit and baby carrots.

It sounds laughable only because our attitude to food is strictly realistic, like the primitive attitude to sex. We agree that food is one of the great pleasures of life, we sympathize with gourmets who seek out the best restaurants, but we waste no time in daydreaming about ten-course meals. Because food is openly available, and there are no taboos about eating in public, we have not subjected it to the hothouse treatment of the imagination. Yet, biologically speaking, there is a close parallel between our need for food and our need for sex. Both are essential for survival, both can give great pleasure, both can be associated with a will to power (only the rich can afford the finest food). If we make an effort to grasp the underlying reality of sex as we grasp the underlying reality of food, we see that it is based on the man's and woman's mutual need to find a partner, and that the essence of such a relation is that it is based on a sense of *difference*: that obvious yet all-important recognition that men are different from women. The male's sexual pleasure springs from a sense of overcoming this difference. And in a world in which sexual desire was still as "normal" as our need for food, sexual satisfaction would lead to a simple, monogamous relation, with little or no interest in other partners, and certainly no interest in the kind of *abstract* sexuality—the sexual illusion—that is satisfied by erotic daydreams.

To grasp this is to grasp what has happened to sex since the late eighteenth century. Imagination has turned it into a kind of gigantic shadow of itself, like the Specter of the Brocken, and the straightforward bawdiness of Aretino and *The School of Venus* has been transformed into something far more steamy, criminal and neurotic.

In the first half of the nineteenth century, sex crime became increasingly common, particularly in urban areas—Henry Mayhew even produced a map in the mid-1840s showing where "carnal" attacks were most common—and the prevalence of sadistic crime slowly increased, although to judge by the cases mentioned by Krafft-Ebing and Hirschfeld it seldom resulted in murder. (The rape of children was not uncommon, because children were more "forbidden" than adult women.) Even as early as 1790, women in London were terrified by a man who became known as "the Monster," who slashed at their clothes with a sharp knife, which sometimes caused painful cuts. One girl, Anne Porter, was slashed in the buttocks, and on undressing, found a wound nine inches long and four inches deep. Six months later, she recognized her attacker in the street, and her male companion followed the man home and made a kind of citizen's arrest. The "monster" proved to be a slightly built man named Renwick Williams, a maker of artificial flowers; although he insisted on his innocence he was sentenced to six years in prison.

Forty years later, in 1829, a man known as "the Ripper of Bozen" stabbed girls in the lower abdomen, and when caught, admitted that "he was suffering from a sexual urge amounting to a frenzy," and that he was obsessed by the urge for days on end until he gave way to it, experiencing orgasm as he slashed the girls.

The following case from Krafft-Ebing is again typical:

C. L., aged forty-two, engineer married, father of two children; from a neuropathic family; father irascible, a drinker; mother hysterical, subject to eclamptic attacks. The patient remembers that in childhood he took particular pleasure in witnessing the slaughtering of domestic animals, especially swine. He thus experienced lustful pleasure and ejaculation. Later he visited slaughterhouses, in order to delight in the sight of flowing blood and the death throes of animals. When he could find opportunity, he killed the animals himself, which always afforded him a vicarious feeling of sexual pleasure.

At the time of full maturity he first attained a knowledge of his abnormality. The patient was not exactly opposed in inclination to women, but close contact with them seemed to him repugnant. On the advice of a physician, at twenty-five he married a woman who pleased him, in the hope of freeing himself of his abnormal condition. Although he was very partial to his wife, it was only seldom, and after great trouble and exertion of his imagination, that he could perform coitus with her; nevertheless, he begat two children. In 1866 he was in the war in Bohemia. His letters written at that time to his wife, were composed in an exalted, enthusiastic tone. He was missed after the battle of Königgrätz.

Krafft-Ebing tries to explain such cases by remarking that "cruelty is natural to primitive man." But here he seems to be missing the point. What has happened in this case—as in that of Sergeant Bertrand, Vincent Verzeni and Jack the Ripper—is that "superheated sex," which is based on "forbiddenness," has become associated with cruelty. The notion that blood and disembowelment can be sexually stimulating will strike most people as incomprehensible; yet all the evidence seems to show that when a person of high sexual drive is subjected continually to the sight and smell of blood, the result is often the development of a sadistic obsession.

One of the most typical of these early cases is described by State Attorney Wulffen and quoted by Hirschfeld:

Eusebius Pieydagnelle was tried in 1871 for four murders. In the speech he addressed to the jury . . . he begged them to sentence him to death. He said he would have killed himself but for the fact that he believed in a Beyond, and did not want to add a further sin to his score.

Pieydagnelle told the jury that he came from highly respectable parents and had had an excellent education. Unfortunately, opposite their house in Vinuville there was a butcher's shop kept by a M. Cristobal. "The smell of fresh blood, and appetizing meat, the bloody lumps—all this fascinated me and I began to envy the butcher's assistant, because he could work at the block, with rolled-up sleeves and bloody hands." Then, in spite of his parents' opposition, he persuaded them to apprentice him to Cristobal. Here he drank blood in secret and wounded the cattle. He derived the greatest excitement when he was permitted to kill an animal himself. "But the sweetest sensation is when you feel the animal trembling under your knife. The animal's departing life creeps along the blade right up to your hand. The mighty blow that felled the bullocks sounded like sweet music in my ears." Unfortunately for him, his father took him away from the butcher, and apprenticed him to a notary. But it was too late. He was seized with a terrible depression, a deep melancholia, and since he could no longer kill animals, he began to kill people. Six times he committed murder under the compulsion of the same urge. He tried to isolate himself from the world and lived in a cave in a wood. But it was all in vain; his impulse was stronger than he. His last victim was his first employer, M. Cristobal. The murderer then gave himself up. His first victim was a girl of 15, and he describes his sensation when he killed her as follows: "As I looked at the lovely creature my first thought was that I should like to kiss her. I bent down . . . But I paused—a stolen kiss is no use. But I could not bring myself to wake her up. I looked at her lovely neck—and at that moment the gleam of the kitchen knife that lay beside the girl struck my eyes. Something drew me irresistibly towards the knife."

Two years after the publication of *Psychopathia Sexualis*, the Jack the Ripper murders created a sensation that reverberated around the world. For the first time, the general public became aware that something strange and frightening was happening. In an introduction to Donald Rumbelow's *Complete Jack the Ripper*, I tried to explain just why the murders pro-

duced such an impact. The Victorians were basically sentimental; they cried at the death of Little Nell and rejoiced at
the conversion of Scrooge in *A Christmas Carol*. They
gasped with horror in the theater as William Corder shot
Maria Marten in the Red Barn, or the Colleen Bawn was
murdered by her spoiled playboy husband. (Both plays were
based on real cases.) Victorian society might be divided by
class barriers, but where sentiment was concerned, it was one
big happy family. The Ripper murders, with their nightmar-
ish mutilations, simply went beyond normal comprehension.
It was as if the killer wanted to *shock* the whole community,
to fling the murders in its face like a hysterical insult. The
crimes seemed to exude the smell of pure evil.

Now, as we have seen, the Ripper murders were a long
way from being the first sex crimes; such crimes had been
going on intermittently throughout the nineteenth century.
But earlier crimes—like those of Vincent Verzeni—were
hardly known outside the countries in which they occurred.
Reuter had opened a news office in London in 1851; but it
was not until Edison invented the "quadruplex" telegraph in
1874—in which four messages could be sent along the same
wire—that the age of the mass communication suddenly
began. Jack the Ripper, with his gruesome pseudonym, was
the first mass murderer to receive worldwide publicity.

In fact, the Ripper murders merely created a general
awareness of something that had been "in the air" since
Sade. They seemed to crystallize the spirit of the *120 Days of
Sodom*. And in the year following the murders, Tolstoy was
to give expression to a troubled awareness of this change in a
short novel called *The Kreutzer Sonata*, about a man named
Pozdnichev, who had stabbed his wife in a fit of insane jealousy. Pozdnichev argues passionately that civilization has
been poisoned by sexual desire. Simple peasants, he declares, eat and drink a great deal, but they use up the energy

in hard physical labor. The leisured classes canalize their excess energies into sex and romance. He tells how, as a teenager, he indulged in masturbation, and finally began making use of prostitutes. This, he argues, is unnatural, a sign of our frenzied and morbid sexuality.

He goes on to describe how his wife and a musician began to take an obvious romantic interest in one another as they played Beethoven's Kreutzer Sonata, and how he became increasingly possessed by jealousy until he caught the two of them alone together, and stabbed his wife. When he begged her forgiveness as she lay on her deathbed, she merely looked at him with "cold animal hatred," and told him that forgiveness was all rubbish. In fact, Tolstoy is arguing that the intimate relations between man and woman are "all rubbish," based on illusion. When a lady who is listening suggests that real love is based on spiritual affinity and identity of ideals, Pozdnichev asks sarcastically: "Do they go to bed together because of identity of ideals?"

The Kreutzer Sonata caused passionate controversy, and even today, few commentators can write about it without taking sides—usually to argue that Pozdnichev is an insane egoist. The truth is that Tolstoy was the one man of genius of his time who saw clearly what had happened to the human sexual urge in the past century: that it had been amplified by the imagination until it had achieved an unhealthy strength. His argument might be paraphrased: "normal" sexual desire is as straightforward and natural as a fruit punch but human beings have deliberately added raw alcohol to make it more interesting. The result is an erotic cocktail that creates a kind of insanity. Tolstoy must have regarded the Ripper murders as a typical example of this insanity. And in blaming Beethoven, he is not entirely wide of the mark. Beethoven signals the beginning of a new kind of romantic music, a music based on a consciousness of the ego. Tolstoy has simply failed to identify the source of this development as Samuel Richardson and the novelists who followed. How could he recognize it when he himself was perpetuating the "egoism" in his own novels? Yet the basic theme of his own *Anna Karenina* is the sexual illusion, and how it leads to tragedy.

There is another respect in which Tolstoy is guilty of muddled thinking. In appealing to the Russian peasant as the "normal" human being, who keeps sex in its proper place, Tolstoy is implying that highly civilized sexuality—the sexual preoccupation displayed by the leisured classes—is somehow abnormal—that it has crossed the line that divides normality from abnormality or perversion. But this fails to recognize that it is totally impossible to draw a clear dividing line between normality and perversion. Perversion depends on a sense of "forbiddenness," a desire to violate taboos, and *all* sex depends on this sense of forbiddenness. The contact of two bodies has to bring a shock of "difference," and without this shock, sex would become either mechanical or simply impossible. In animals, the smell of the female in heat triggers "forbiddenness." In human beings, this function has been handed over to our minds. *All* sex is based on "forbiddenness."

All this raises an interesting question. Tolstoy blames the problem on the leisured class, and there is a sense in which he is obviously correct: earlier "monsters" like Caligula, Gilles de Rais, Ivan the Terrible, Vlad the Impaler, Countess Bathory,[1] all belonged to the upper classes. So why were the majority of sex killers working-class? Why is it still true that nearly all serial killers are working-class? Conversely, if it was the working classes who were packed like sardines into

[1]For a fuller account of these see "A Gallery of Monsters" in my *Second Mammoth Book of True Crime* (Robinson, London, 1990).

unhealthy basements during the Industrial Revolution, creating a sexual free-for-all, then why were the leisured classes also infected with the virus?

In *The Misfits* I have suggested that the answer could lie in Rupert Sheldrake's "hypothesis of formative causation." Sheldrake points out that heredity cannot be explained entirely in chemical terms: DNA and so on. Something else is needed, and embryologists have concluded that the "something else" is a factor called "morphogenetic fields." The wing of a bird or the tentacle of an octopus is shaped by a kind of electrical "mold"—just like the molds into which we pour jellies—which is why many creatures can re-grow a limb that has been cut off. These "molds" seem to be magnetic fields, which shape the living molecules just as a magnet can "shape" iron filings into a pattern. Sheldrake suggests that these "fields" can be used to explain some rather odd observations made by biologists.

For example, in 1920 the psychologist William McDougal performed an experiment at Harvard to see if baby rats could inherit abilities developed by their parents (the "inheritance of acquired characteristics" that Darwinists regard as such a fearful heresy). He put white rats into a tank of water from which they could escape up one of two gangplanks. One gangplank had an electric current running through it, and the first generation of rats soon learned to choose the other one. Then McDougal tried the same experiment on their children, and then on *their* children, and so on. And he found that each generation learned more quickly than its parents—he had proved that the inheritance of acquired characteristics *does* occur.

Now when a scientist performs an experiment on a group of animals, he always keeps an exactly similar group who are *not* subjected to experiments; these are called the "control group"—the purpose being to have a ready standard of comparison. When a colleague of McDougal's—W. E. Agar of Melbourne—repeated his experiment, he also decided to test the control group at the end of several generations. To his baffled astonishment, these *also* showed the same ability to learn more quickly. And that was impossible, for they had merely been sitting passively in cages. It looked as if the control rats had learned by some kind of telepathy.

Not telepathy, says Sheldrake, but by "morphic resonance." The control group of rats "picked up" the morphogenetic field of the trained rats in the same way that an iron bar can pick up the electrical field of a coil of wire and turn into a magnet. Simple induction.

Incredibly, this seems to work not only with living creatures but with crystals. New chemicals, when synthesized for the first time, are often extremely difficult to crystallize. But as soon as one of them has been crystallized in any laboratory in the world, it becomes easier to crystallize in all the others. At first, it was suspected that scientists traveling from one laboratory to another might be carrying fragments of crystals in their clothes or beards—or even that tiny quantities are carried in the atmosphere. Both explanations seem highly unlikely. The likeliest, Sheldrake suggests, is a process of "induction" through morphogenetic fields.

A series of experiments has been performed to test the Sheldrake hypothesis and has produced positive results. At Yale, Professor Gary Schwartz found that people who do not know Hebrew were able to distinguish between real words in Hebrew and false words—because Jews all over the world already know the genuine words. Alan Pickering of Hatfield Polytechnic obtained the same result using Persian script. In another experiment, English-speaking people were asked to memorize two rhymes in a foreign language—one a well-known nursery rhyme, one a newly composed rhyme. The result—as the hypothesis of formative causation predicts—is that they learned the nursery rhyme more easily than the newly composed rhyme.

If Sheldrake is correct, then it becomes altogether easier to understand what has been happening since the time of Richardson. The obvious objection to the "imagination" theory suggested in this book is that the majority of the inhabitants of Europe were illiterate, even in the nineteenth century, so that even the spread of circulating libraries could hardly explain the enormous influence of romanticism and of the "sexual revolution." Could a mere change in literary fashion explain why, by the time Krafft-Ebing came to write *Psychopathia Sexualis*, the capital cities of Europe seemed to have an astonishingly high level of sexual perversion? Is it not more likely, for example, that the explanation lies in the increasing stresses of industrial society? (One answer to that objection is that cases of sex crime in the nineteenth century occurred in rural areas as frequently as in cities.) The hypothesis of morphic resonance suggests an altogether more satisfying explanation. If Sheldrake is correct, we would expect the "imaginative revolution" to spread to every class of society, so that it would affect illiterate working men like Bichel and Pieydagnelle and Verzeni as much as aristocrats like Sade and Byron and Swinburne.

Fortunately—as we shall see in the next changer—sex crime made a fairly slow start. But by the middle of the 1920s, it was apparent that a new type of human predator was at large, and that in some strange and frightening way, the human race had emerged into a new stage of lost innocence.

2

MASS MURDER IN THE NINETEENTH CENTURY

AS WE HAVE SEEN, THE TERM "SERIAL KILLER" WAS FIRST USED in the late 1970s by FBI agent Robert Ressler, who was a member of the "psychological profiling" team at the FBI headquarters in Quantico, Virginia. It was meant to describe someone who kills repeatedly and obsessively, usually with a sexual motive. Before that, such criminals were called "mass murderers." The disadvantage of this term was that it covered two types of killer: those who killed a number of people at roughly the same time, and those whose murders were spread over a lengthy period of time. Most "mad gunmen" who run amok and shoot people at random belong to the first category. So does the unknown killer who murdered the whole Evangelista family in Detroit on July 2, 1930, chopping off the heads of all six. It would seem more sensible to describe this type of "simultaneous" killer as a mass murderer, and reserve the term "serial killer" for criminals like Jack the Ripper or the Boston Strangler.

Unfortunately, we need a third category for murderers who kill many victims over a long period, but whose motive is financial—like the French "Bluebeard" Landru, or the

"Brides in the Bath" murderer Joseph Smith. They are certainly serial killers in the sense that their crimes occur "serially" and not "simultaneously," yet they lack the obsessive quality that is apparent in the crimes of Jack the Ripper. Perhaps the term "multiple murderer" might serve to describe them. But then a further objection arises: in many such cases, there *is* undoubtedly a sexual element present. Landru was as sexually vain as Casanova, and one of his victims was a poor servant girl who became his mistress and from whom he certainly obtained no financial gain. But if this book is not to become impossibly long, such borderline cases must be ignored.

One of the strangest cases of the early nineteenth century is undoubtedly that of the poisoner Anna Zwanziger, and if the sexologist Magnus Hirschfeld is correct when (quoting a State Attorney named Wulffen) he argues that "the poisoner is actuated by inherent sexual–sadistic motives," then she may be regarded as one of the earliest examples of a serial killer.

The daughter of a Nuremberg innkeeper, Anna Maria Schonleben married a solicitor named Zwanziger who was also an alcoholic, and left her in penury. The constant reading of Goethe's gloomy novel *The Sorrows of Young Werther* led her to attempt suicide on two occasions, and she drifted from place to place, working as a domestic. In Weimar she fled with a diamond ring belonging to her employers, and a public advertisement of the theft came to the attention of her son-in-law, who ordered her out of his house. She found a job as a housekeeper with a judge named Glaser, in Rosendorf, Bavaria. It seemed to have struck her that Glaser would make an excellent husband, but there was one impediment: Glaser's wife, from whom he was separated. Anna set about reconciling the two, and was soon able to welcome Frau Glaser back into her home with flowers strewn on the floor. Within a few weeks, Frau Glaser had died in agony. But Judge Glaser showed no sign of wanting to transfer his affection to his housekeeper, who was thin, sallow and 50 years old. Perhaps he was alerted by the stomach ailments suffered by guests after they had eaten meals prepared by Anna; at all events, she decided to move to the house of another judge at Sanspareil, a younger man named Grohmann, who was unmarried but suffered from gout. Regrettably, he had a fiancée, and Anna became increasingly jealous. When the marriage banns were published, Judge Grohmann died suddenly; his doctor attributed the death to natural causes.

Once more Anna found herself a job as a housekeeper to a member of the legal profession, a magistrate named Gebhard. He was also married, and his wife was pregnant; but her health was poor. When she died, accusing the housekeeper of poisoning her, no one took the accusations seriously. But Gebhard, like the others, showed no sign of wanting to marry Anna. Moreover, as his servants expressed intense dislike of the skinny widow, and told stories of violent colics suffered by those who incurred her displeasure, he finally decided to dismiss her. Half an hour or so after she had left in a carriage for Bayreuth, most people in the household became ill—including the baby, to whom Anna had given a biscuit soaked in milk. It was recalled that Anna had refilled the salt box before she had left, and its contents were submitted for analysis. This was now a simple matter; there were at least three reliable tests for white arsenic. And this is what proved to have been mixed with the salt.

It took the law some time to catch up with her. She lived in Bayreuth a month, then went back to Nuremberg, then tried to persuade her son-in-law in Mainfernheim to take her in. But he was no longer her son-in-law, having divorced the daughter after she had been imprisoned for theft and swindling. Anna went back to Nuremberg, and was arrested on October 18, 1809. In her pockets were found a packet of tartar emetic and a packet of white arsenic.

For six months Anna Zwanziger simply denied everything. But at this point, Frau Glaser's body was exhumed, and the method of Valentine Rose, invented only four years previously, revealed arsenic in the vital organs—arsenic lingers on in the human body (including the hair) for a very long time. When told about this discovery, Zwanziger knew she was trapped; she fell to the floor in convulsions and had to be carried out of court. And a long and detailed confession followed—including the attempted poisoning of fellow servants and guests of her employers, apparently merely for her own entertainment. Sentenced to death, she remarked that it was probably just as well, since it would have been impossible for her to stop poisoning. She was beheaded, by sword, in 1811, more than two years after her arrest.

But such a bare account of her crimes begs the major question: why did she do it? Important clues can be found in Feuerbach's *Remarkable Criminal Trials*. His account of her life throws an entirely new light on the case, and even if we end by feeling no sympathy for the mass murderess, we at least begin to understand why she did it.

Born in Nuremberg in August, 1760, the daughter of an innkeeper, Anna was orphaned by the time she was five. After living for five years with various relatives, she was taken at the age of ten into the house of her guardian, a wealthy merchant, and there received a good education. But when she was fifteen, her guardian decided to marry her to a drunken lawyer named Zwanziger, who was more than twice her age. She objected, but finally had to give way.

Spending most of her days alone, while her husband was out drinking with cronies, she became an avid reader of novels and plays. She was so moved by Goethe's *Sorrows of*

Young Werther—which had caused an epidemic of suicide ten years earlier—that she was also tempted to kill herself. She also read Richardson's novel *Pamela*, about a servant girl whose master tries hard to seduce her, but is finally so overcome by her virtue and goodness that he marries her. This also exercised a powerful influence on her. And she was deeply moved by Lessing's tragedy *Emilia Galotti*, about a girl who is pursued by a wicked prince (who has murdered her fiancé) and ends by persuading her father to kill her to prevent rape.

Her husband soon spent her inheritance—he was capable of drinking ten bottles of wine a day, and was soon a hopeless alcoholic. Anna was now forced to become a high-class prostitute to support her husband and two children—although she claimed she only slept with gentlemen. This, at least, was better than starving; she leaned to use her physical charms to persuade men to support her. She even thought up a brilliant scheme involving a lottery of watches (we would call it a raffle), which once again made them prosperous; but her husband again spent the money. One lover, a lieutenant, persuaded her to leave her husband, but her husband then persuaded her to return. When she divorced him, he persuaded her to remarry him the next day. Clearly, Anna was not the ruthless bitch Feuerbach represents her as. She admits that she ended by feeling very fond of him.

Finally, Zwanziger died, and after eighteen years, Anna was left on her own. There was no national assistance or social security in Bavaria in 1796. She had to find a way to support herself and her children. She tried to set up a sweet-shop in Vienna, but it failed. She became a housekeeper, but had to leave when she had an illegitimate child by a clerk— she put it into a foundlings' home, where it died.

Anna was now 38, still attractive to men. She found a "protector" who installed her in lodgings, and tried to supplement her income with doll making. Tired of being a kept woman, she accepted an excellent job as a housekeeper in the home of a minister, but left after a few months—Feuerbach says because of her dirty habits, but more probably because she gave herself "airs and graces." For, as Feuerbach remarks perceptively, "the insupportable thought of having fallen from her station as mistress of a house and family to the condition of a servant, worked so strongly on her feelings as to cause her to behave like a madwoman." In short, the ups and downs of her life caused her to suffer a mental breakdown. "She laughed, wept and prayed by turns. She received her mistress's orders with a laugh, and went obediently away, but never executed them."

Anna was now definitely insane, and in her misery, she retained one basic obsession: to have a man to look after her and protect her. But her physical charms were fast disappearing. Her old "protector" took her back for a while and got her pregnant again, then left her to chase an actress. She had a miscarriage. After that she attempted suicide by drowning, but was rescued by two fishermen. She was ill with fever for several weeks.

At the age of 44, no longer attractive, Anna was forced to take an ill-paid job as a housemaid; now she was at a kind of rock bottom. She stole a diamond ring and absconded. Her master reacted by placing a notice in the newspaper naming her as a thief, which destroyed any remnants of reputation she still possessed. Her son-in-law, with whom she was staying, threw her out.

In the following year, it looked as if fate had finally smiled on her. Working as a needlework teacher, she attracted an old general and became his mistress. Again she dreamed of security and being in charge of her own household. But he walked out on her, and ignored her letters.

And so, in 1807, after more miserable wandering from

place to place, she found herself in Pegnitz, near Bayreuth, where she was offered a job by Judge Glaser. (To explain her preference for judges, we have to remember that her first husband was a lawyer.) At 50, the craving for security had given her the cunning of a madwoman. She poisoned the wife of Judge Glaser, hoping he would marry her—an insane hope, since she was now skinny, sallow and ugly. She moved on to the home of Judge Grohmann, who was unmarried and twelve years her junior. Now, surely, she had found the man who was destined to bring security to her old age . . . ? Grohmann suffered from gout, and she enjoyed nursing him. She enjoyed nursing him so much that she began slipping small quantities of arsenic and antimony into his food. Eventually, she overdid it—this seems clear, since she can have had no reason to kill her meal ticket—and he died. Feuerbach says she appeared inconsolable, and this is almost certainly because she was.

This raises an interesting possibility. Was Anna herself an arsenic addict? We know that arsenic was widely used in the nineteenth century as a tonic, and that James Maybrick used it as a drug. If Anna used it herself, then it seems possible that she administered it to Grohmann to help his gout—in which case, she would have been devastated when it killed him.

With her security gone, Anna slipped deeper into madness. She had once been a mistress with servants, an attractive woman whom men had desired; now she was an unwanted nobody. Poisoning brought back once more some sense of self-respect and identity, of being in control of her own destiny—or at least, those of other people. In our own society she would have been confined in an asylum after her trial, and so found some kind of security in her final years. As it was, she knelt at the block, and her head fell into the headsman's basket. Perhaps the woman who had identified with Emilia Galeotti and Pamela felt that it was at least more appropriate than dying in a workhouse.

The year 1811, in which Anna Zwanziger was beheaded, was also the year in which England was shocked by one of the most horrific mass slaughters of the nineteenth century, the Ratcliffe Highway murders. Thomas De Quincey wrote a famous—if not completely reliable—account in the appendix to his essay "On Murder Considered as one of the Fine Arts."

Towards midnight on Saturday December 7, 1811, 18-year-old Margaret Jewell, servant to the young Marr family (Timothy Marr ran a hosier's business in the Ratcliffe Highway), was sent out to purchase oysters for supper; diligent but unlucky in her quest at such a late hour, she returned to the Marr establishment at 1 a.m. to find the door locked and the house silent and dark. De Quincey, in his account, describes masterfully the girl's increasing sensation of horror and foreboding, particularly when recalling the sinister stranger she had seen prowling around the house earlier in the evening, and goes on (doubtless with dramatic licence) to relate how stealthy footsteps were heard from within the building, and how the hysterical servant's screams attracted passers-by and neighbors, so leading, within a few minutes, to the finding of the Marr family (Timothy, wife Cecilia, and young baby) together with their 13-year-old apprentice John Goen, all with their skulls smashed and throats cut; nothing had been taken from the premises. The whole of London, in fact, was appalled by the senseless slaughter, and when another family was murdered, obviously by the same hand, on December 19, there was panic. Now the victims were an elderly publican Mr. Williamson, his wife Catherine, and their maidservant, 50-year-old Bridget Harrington; the killer slipped into the inn, the King's Arms, 81 New Gravel Lane, shortly after closing time on 11 p.m.; Mr. Williamson invariably left the front door open to "oblige" the nocturnal imbiber. The Williamsons' lodger, 26-year-old John Turner, alone in his bedroom, and disturbed by unfamiliar sounds, crept downstairs and, himself unseen, saw a stranger, "in creaking shoes," bending over one of the corpses; terrified but resolved to remain alive, he returned to his room and effected an escape by knotting his bedclothes together into a "rope" by which he escaped through the window, dropping on to the local night watchman, George Fox, who immediately broke into the public house and found the corpses.

Even greater ferocity had been employed during the second series of murders; Bridget Harrington was almost decapitated, and Mr. Williamson (who had evidently put up a struggle for life) savagely hacked in every limb. The couple's grandchild, 14-year-old Kitty Stillwell, had escaped the massacre, the killer apparently having been disturbed by the inquiring watchman. A sailor's maul was discovered by one of the bodies; it bore the initials "JP" and was found to belong to a Swedish sailor, John Petersen, who, being then on the high seas, had a perfect alibi; he lodged when in London with a Mrs. Vermiloe, and it was a fellow-lodger, John Williams, whom the police now suspected. Little is known of his interrogation (at Shadwell Police Office) save that he refused to answer several questions, although admitting that he spent much time at Williamson's tavern. He had been seen walking towards the King's Arms late on the evening of the murders, and had returned to his lodging in the early hours of the morning with a bloodied shirt—the result, Williams explained, of a card-game brawl. Arrested and taken to New Prison at Coldbath Fields, he committed suicide on December 28, by hanging himself from a wall-rail in his cell. He was accorded a suicide's burial, being transported by cart on the morning of December 31, through East End crowds to the cross-roads by Cannon Street and New Road (near present-day Cable Street) where he was buried in quicklime and a stake driven through his heart. (Cross-roads were traditionally selected for suicides so as to confuse their restless souls' sense of direction; one assumed that in Williams' case the stake—reminiscent of Bram Stoker—was an added measure taken by uneasy citizens to ensure his "staying put.") De Quincey, in 1854, described Williams as a grotesquely fey, thin, albino-faced creature, but in fact a contemporary print (drawn during the burial procession) showed a stocky, muscular, plebeian laborer-type spreadeagled in death upon a slanting shaft of wood.

The evidence against Williams was circumstantial; the killings terminated, however, upon his death. Popular with women, he had confided to a barmaid friend shortly after the Marr murders: "I am unhappy, and can't remain easy." A syphilitic, it has also been suggested that he killed out of a grudge towards humanity.

There is one point upon which De Quincey is obviously reliable: his account of the terror that spread all over the Home Counties as a result of the murders. There was nothing like it again until the crimes of Jack the Ripper. It underlines the point that although murder was common enough, crimes of real atrocity were rare.

Two decades after the crimes of Anna Zwanziger, another German, Gesina Gottfried, was challenging her supremacy as a mass poisoner. Gesina was born in a small town in North Germany. She seems to have had the temperament of Flaubert's Emma Bovery—desire for excitement, wealth, travel. She was attractive and had several suitors. From these, she chose a businessman named Miltenberg. By the age of twenty she had two children. But her husband was a drunkard, and his business was on the verge of bankruptcy. And, like many working-class husbands of the period, he beat his wife. One day, Gesina saw her mother using a white powder to mix bait for mice and rats. She took some of it, and dropped it into a glass of her husband's beer. He was dead by the next morning. She now pursued a young friend of her husband's called Gottfried, who had displayed signs of being interested in her before Miltenberg's death. But Gottfried was shy and cautious. Her patience soon wore out, and she began to slip small quantities of the white powder, arsenic, into his drink. As he became more ill, he became more reliant on her, and her chances of administering minute doses of poison increased. When her parents got wind of the intimacy with Gottfried, they opposed it. Gesina did not hesitate for a moment; she got herself invited to supper, and dropped arsenic in their beer. Then, carried away with her new-found power, she went on to poison her own two children. Gottfried, now permanently weakened, was persuaded to marry her; a day later, he was dead. His wife succeeded to his property, which had been her central motive all along.

A merchant she met at Gottfried's funeral began to court her. She did not like him, but he had more money than her former lover. She poisoned him with the same patient deliberation that she had already shown in the case of Gottfried. When her brother turned up one day, on leave from the army and drunk, she disposed of him quickly with a glass of poisoned beer—she was not prepared to risk having him around while she poisoned her current lover. The latter was persuaded to make a will in her favor, then he died. It is not known exactly how many more she poisoned. Charles Kingston mentions in *Remarkable Rogues* another lover, a woman to whom she owed five pounds, and an old female acquaintance who tried to borrow money. She moved from place to place during the course of these murders, and ended in Bremen, where she poisoned the wife of her employer, a master wheelwright named Rumf. The wife died shortly after giving birth to a baby, so Gesina was not suspected; it was assumed to be puerperal fever. Rumf's five children died one by one after Gesina took charge of the family. Rumf himself began to feel rather ill after Gesina's meals. One day, when she was away, he tried a meal of pork, and was delighted that it seemed to agree with him. He was so pleased with his pork that he went to look at the joint in the larder when he came home from work the next day. Gesina had sprinkled it with white powder in the meantime, and Rumf knew it had not been there that morning. So he took the leg along to the police, who quickly identified the powder as arsenic. When arrested, Gesina made no attempt to deny her guilt; on the contrary, she confessed to her various crimes with relish. Her execution followed as a matter of course.

A Dutch nurse named van der Linden—of whom, unfortunately, little is known—surpassed Zwanziger and Gottfried by poisoning more than a hundred.

No account of nineteenth-century crime would be complete without at least some reference to the most celebrated of French criminals, Pierre-François Lacenaire. As far as we know, Lacenaire killed only three people, so only just qualifies as a multiple killer. But his attitude of God-defying rebellion, so reminiscent of Sade, and of many serial killers of the late twentieth century, gives him a psychological significance out of all proportion to his crimes.

In December 1834, a widow named Chardon, and her homosexual son—a begging-letter writer—were stabbed and hatcheted to death in Paris. Chief Inspector Louis Canler found no clues to the killer (or killers).

Two weeks later, a young bank messenger was attacked when he went to call at a flat in rue Montorgueil; someone closed the door behind him and someone stabbed him in the back, while someone else tried to grab his throat. The clerk was strongly built, and managed to struggle free; his assailants ran away. The flat, it turned out, had been rented by a man who called himself "Mahossier." Canler searched the registers of dozens of cheap hotels looking for the name—for even if it was an alias, the chances were that the man would use it more than once. He found it at a place called Mother Pageot's. She claimed she was unable to recall Mahossier, but *did* recall his companion, a big, red-headed man. Canler recalled that a big, red-headed man called François was in gaol at the moment, and went to see him. 'Why did you use an alias when you stayed at Mother Pageot's?' he asked, and François replied: 'Because I'd be stupid to use my real name . . .' So François *was* Mahossier's companion.

Mother Pageot now admitted she *did* recall François's companion (the presence of her husband, who hated the police, had made her deny it earlier). He was a courteous man with a high forehead and a silky moustache.

Casual conversation with many criminals finally convinced the detective that this description corresponded to that of a man who also called himself Gaillard. He managed to locate a room in which Gaillard had stayed, and found some republican songs and satirical verses—in Mahossier's handwriting.

Eventually, François broke, and told Canler that a man named Gaillard had murdered the Chardons. Now, for the first time, Canler knew that the murder of the Chardons and the attack on the bank messenger were connected. He also learned that Gaillard had a rich aunt who lived in the rue Bar-du-Bec. This aunt was able to tell Canler that she lived in fear of being murdered by her unsavory nephew, and that his name was Pierre-François Lacenaire.

Lacenaire was soon arrested for trying to pass a forged bill. And when Lacenaire learned that he had been betrayed, he made a full confession, implicating a crook named Avril in the murder of the Chardons, and François in the attack on the bank messenger.

In jail, awaiting his execution, he wrote his memoirs (which Dostoyevsky later printed in a magazine he edited, to increase circulation). They are a remarkable document, and tell us all we need to know of the man. Lacenaire was born in Lyon, the second child of a well-to-do merchant, in 1800. His elder brother was the favorite son; he developed a sense of injustice that soon expressed itself in thieving. One day his father pointed out the scaffold to him and told him he would end on it if he did not change his ways. Lacenaire was a lone wolf; a description in his memoirs is typical: "All night I strode along the Quais. I lived ten years in an hour. I wanted to kill myself, and I sat on the parapet by the Pont des Arts, opposite the graves of those stupid heroes of July . . . Henceforth my life was a drawn-out suicide; I belonged no longer to myself, but to cold steel . . . Society will have my blood, but I, in my turn, shall have the blood of society." He read Rousseau and became a revolutionary. But he had a resentment against life. Failures filled him with a desire to "spite" life. (He did not believe in God, and so could not spite God.) This in turn was rationalized into a hatred of Society. It would have been useless to point out to him that "Society" does not exist, and that even if it did, living the life of a criminal would not spite it.

Somewhat more rationally, he hated the complacent rich; but then, neither of the crimes for which he was hanged was committed against the rich. But he describes in his memoirs how his first murder was a "bourgeois" whom he pushed into the river after stealing his watch.

A point came where he decided to be a criminal in the same way that another man might decide to devote his life to poetry. He observed his own lack of "feeling" about life (like Meursault, the bored hero of Camus' l'Étranger), that he had killed two men in duels without the slightest feeling (did Dostoyevsky borrow some of Stavrogin's character from Lacenaire?). He was basically a poet and a metaphysician; he wanted a meaning in life. He surveyed life and found it inscrutable, revealing no sign of an important destiny for himself. And he craved revenge. But he lacked the discipline to carry out his ideal purpose; if he had possessed literary discipline he might have been an earlier Lautreamont or Rimbaud; perhaps even a Swift or Voltaire. He wanted to be a scourge of Society, its sternest critic. In a sense, he was trying to put into effect the gospel of Shaw's Undershaft, the armament manufacturer in *Major Barbara,* who said "Thou shalt starve ere I starve," and who then used every means in his power to achieve success. (Having achieved it, he became, as he pointed out, a sane and useful member of Society.) But Lacenaire was too much driven by emotion to make a good job of it, and finally brought himself to the guillotine.

The execution was carried out, unannounced, on a cold and foggy January morning. Lacenaire watched Avril's head fall into the basket without flinching; but when he himself knelt under the blade, there was an accident that would have broken another man's nerve; as the blade fell, it stuck halfway, and had to be hauled up again; Lacenaire was looking up at it as it dropped and severed his head.

Here, as in the case of Sade, we encounter the attempt of a man who lacks self-discipline to justify his lack of discipline with a philosophy of revolt. Lacenaire is the first major criminal in whom we encounter the "philosophy of resentment," which was to become so common in serial killers from Panzram to Manson. We shall encounter it many times in the course of this book.

Oddly enough, one of the first attempts to understand the psychology of the serial killer was made by a novelist—

Émile Zola, who was intrigued by the case of Eusebius Pieydagnelle (which we have already encountered) and by the Jack the Ripper murders. Both cases formed the inspiration for his novel *La Bête Humaine* (1890)—the hero of which is named Jack. Jacques Lantier, "the human beast," is possessed by an overpowering urge to kill women. At sixteen he is playing with a young relative when she falls down.

In a flash he had seen her legs revealed to the thigh, and he had flung himself at her. The following year he recalled honing a knife to thrust into another girl's throat. That was a fair-haired little thing whom he saw pass his door every morning. She was very plump-bosomed and very pink, and he had actually selected the spot, a mole directly under her ear. Then came others, and yet others, a succession of nightmares, so many women whose flesh he had touched, to be possessed with that sudden lust for murder . . . One in particular, recently married, who had sat near him at a variety show and laughed loudly. In order not to slit her belly open he had been obliged to run away in the middle of an act . . .

One day he tries to kiss his step-cousin Flora, who lives in the same house—in fact, she finds him very attractive. As he struggles with her, her bodice is torn so her breasts are exposed; then, as she lies there, prepared to yield to him, he seizes a pair of scissors and is about to stab her when he is suddenly overcome with horror, and flees. But later in the novel, he is unable to resist the temptation when he sees his mistress naked, and stabs her to death.

Zola's description of Lantier's torments has remarkable power; no one has ever succeeded in capturing with such realism the urges of a "sex maniac." Yet the sheer force of the writing, the insight with which Zola succeeds in describing a man who feels impelled to stab women, again makes us aware of the question: why? And the answer, surely, is that when sexual desire is raised to this morbid intensity, the mere act of copulation seems insufficient. Lovemaking takes place by mutual consent; his step-cousin Flora is willing to yield and allow herself to be possessed. But Lantier's desire is so violent that lovemaking by mutual consent seems an anticlimax. He wants to possess her—as Zola says—to the point of destruction.

This is, in fact, the mechanism of all sexual "perversion." Even in someone as apparently "normal" as D. H. Lawrence, there are hints—in *Women in Love* and *Lady Chatterley's Lover*—that he finds sodomy a more exciting experience than vaginal sex. And anyone who has read *Sons and Lovers* can easily grasp why this is so. For Lawrence, sex is conquest—the triumphant male being permitted to possess the yielding female. His relation with Frieda was so important because she was also a German aristocrat and another man's wife. Possessing her, persuading her to abandon her husband and children, was an enormous stimulus to the working-class Lawrence's self-esteem. The same is true of the gamekeeper Mellors' relationship with Lady Chatterley. So persuading her to permit sodomy—as Mellors does—is an additional proof of conquest. The sexual urge and the urge to self-esteem are inextricably intertwined.

An equally important clue is offered by Krafft-Ebing when he is discussing fetishism. He speaks of a man who could only make love to a woman who was wearing a silk dress, petticoats and a corset, and comments: "The reason for this phenomenon is apparently to be found in the mental onanism of such individuals. In seeing innumerable clothed forms they have cultivated desires before seeing nudity."

What is interesting here is that there is obviously something not quite-right about Krafft-Ebing's explanation. It is not because such individuals have cultivated desires before seeing nudity—99 per cent of young males experience sexual desire before seeing nudity. It is surely because a nude woman is comparatively easy to get used to. *Consciousness is too feeble; it is quickly taken over by habit.* For the same reason, the normal male is not excited by a woman in a bikini, although he *would* be excited by a glimpse up the skirts of the same woman—even if she happened to be wearing a bikini underneath. This is because a sense of "forbiddenness" is created by the fact that she is clothed, and the excitement is caused by the *contrast* between her skirts and the nakedness underneath. Krafft-Ebing's fetishist needs to make love to a woman in a silk dress, petticoats and a corset (but without knickers) because his first love affair (at fourteen) was with a girl who kept most of her clothes on during lovemaking in case they were interrupted. This naturally produced a feeling of alertness, as well as "wickedness."

In short, the basic answer is that consciousness is always falling into the sleep of habit, and has to be awakened from this sleep by the contrast produced by "forbiddenness." The weaker the individual, the more his consciousness falls asleep, and the more forbiddenness is required to shake it awake.

The habit of novel-reading that was created by *Pamela* meant that gentle, sensitive individuals could compensate for the boredom of everyday life by retreating into a world of daydreams. This was good for the imagination but bad for the ability to cope with the everyday world. "Escapism" leads to the weakening of the crude vital impulse. This is why so many "sensitive plants" in the nineteenth century were killed off by their inability to deal with everyday problems. As Tolstoy points out, the healthy peasant avoids these problems—which is why Tolstoy himself decided to become a healthy peasant, and spent more time chopping wood than writing books.

So the steep increase in sexual perversion in the nineteenth century can be directly linked to the development of imagination which was the nineteenth century's most interesting achievement. Does this mean that the development of imagination should be seen as a doubtful blessing? Clearly not; Tolstoy's woodchopping did no harm to his imagination. The problem lies in the tendency of weak individuals to make imagination an excuse for running away from everyday life—in other words, for excusing their own laziness. This is the essence of the "Outsider" problem.

In short, the rise in sexual perversion and sex crime in the nineteenth century was an unfortunate consequence of its development in the realm of imagination. Krafft-Ebing is correct when he links fetishism with onanism (masturbation). W. B. Yeats admits in his autobiography that the retreat into the fairylands of his early poetry was accompanied by excessive masturbation. And in the original version of *Sons and Lovers*, Lawrence describes becoming sexually excited as he pulls on the stockings of his girlfriend. Once we understand this "compensatory" mechanism, a great deal about the rise of sex crime suddenly becomes clear.

In the year following the trial of Eusebius Pieydagnelle, 1872, Vincent Verzeni was arrested for sadistic sex crimes, as described above. But it was in the following year that Thomas W. Piper, America's first multiple sex killer, committed his first murder. Piper was the sexton in the Warren Avenue Baptist church in Boston. He was 26 years old, had a large black moustache, and was described as a "melancholy young man."

He had apparently been regarded as a quiet and agreeable young man until the 16-year-old daughter of a local minister met him in the vestry one Sunday evening and hurried home to tell her parents that "she thought he was a very bad man indeed, and was afraid of him." What Piper proposed to her is unrecorded, but is not difficult to guess.

The Rev. Mr. Pentecost, the Baptist minister, later described how he had found Piper reading a novel called *Cord and Creese*; the prosecutor, who read it as a preparation for the trial, commented that its publishers "ought to be sent to the House of Correction for the rest of their lives." It also emerged later that Piper kept a bottle with a mixture of whiskey and laudanum in a dark corner under his pew.

On the snowy night of December 5, 1873, a man walking along a lonely road near Dorchester heard a thrashing noise in the bushes, and when he went to investigate, was startled when a cloaked figure jumped up and ran away. By the light of his lantern, the man saw the body of a girl lying at his feet in a clearing, the snow around her head covered in blood. The nakedness of the lower part of her body made it clear that he had interrupted a rape. The man gave chase, but the fugitive disappeared over the railway embankment. The girl was later identified as a domestic servant named Bridget Landregan. Nearby was found a "bat-like" club stained with blood.

A few hours later another unconscious girl was found. This time, it seemed, the rapist had accomplished his purpose. The girl was rushed to the hospital, and eventually survived. Her name was Sullivan, but further details were withheld out of respect for her privacy.

In early January 1874, a prostitute named Mary Tynam was found unconscious in her bed; it looked as if she had been battered unconscious with the back of an axe. She also survived the attack, but was too brain-damaged to describe what had happened. She died a year later in an asylum.

The police actually traced the bat-like club to the shop of

Thomas Piper, and detained him. But they were unable to find conclusive evidence against him, and he was released.

No more was heard of the sexual crime wave for another year. On the afternoon of May 23, 1875, children began to arrive at the Baptist church for Sunday school. Among them was 5-year-old Mabel Young, accompanied by her aunt, Miss Augusta Hobbs. When the class was over, Miss Hobbs went to speak to the Rev. Pentecost. When she had finished, she looked around for her niece, and found that she was nowhere to be seen. She and several other women began to search, and to call Mabel's name.

Up in the room below the belfry, Thomas Piper was standing with the unconscious child at his feet. Her head was bleeding from the blow he had struck with the bat-like club, and he threw a piece of newspaper onto the blood. Then he heard a voice downstairs calling "Mabel." He opened the door and peeped through; a lady named Mrs. Roundy was below. He closed the door and waited. Then, from behind him, he heard the sound of a child crying out. He had been convinced that Mabel was dead—he later admitted that he had heard her "bones crack" as he hit her twice. In a panic, he picked up the body and carried it under his arm up into the belfry, fumbling frantically with the trapdoor; then he startled the pigeons by throwing Mabel among them.

He went downstairs to the gallery and looked out of the window; it was a drop of about twenty feet to the ground. But he was desperate; he climbed out, hung on to the window ledge, then dropped into the street, landing outside the church door. There he encountered a boy who asked if he could see the pigeons; Piper refused brusquely and went into the church. There, in a state of obvious agitation, he began rearranging the chairs, ignoring the excitement of the people who were looking for Mabel Young.

Someone rushed in from outside. "We can hear the cries

of a child from the tower." They ran upstairs, but found the tower door locked. Piper claimed that he had lost the key, which he usually kept in a drawer. Some young men forced open the door, and a few moments later, found the battered child. Mabel was carried to a nearby house. The following day she died—like Mary Tynam, without being able to describe what had happened. But by now the police had found the bloodstained "bat" in the room below the belfry, and Thomas Piper was under arrest.

Before his trial, Piper tried to commit suicide by cutting his wrists with a piece of metal; prompt action saved his life. At his trial in December 1875, the jury was unable to agree. But in a second trial the following January, after evidence about the "evil literature" he read, Piper was sentenced to death.

On May 7, 1876, Piper sent for his attorney, and told him that he had also been guilty of the previous three sex attacks—on Bridget Landregan, on the girl called Sullivan and on Mary Tynam. He described how, after drinking a mixture of whiskey and laudanum, he had followed Bridget Landregan down the street until she reached the lonely lane through the woods, then knocked her down with the club. The rape had been interrupted, so he ran away. Later the same evening he had attacked the other girl.

According to Piper, the murder of Mary Tynam was not a sex crime. He had already spent the night with her, and after leaving, collected the axe, went back to her room, and battered her unconscious, taking back the money.

He had lured Mabel Young to the belfry by asking her if she wanted to see the pigeons, taking her in by another door in the church so as not to be seen. But, he insisted, he had *not* jumped from the window—the witness who claimed he had seen him land in the street was lying. He concluding his confession by sighing: "I am a very bad man."

Piper showed the investigators where he had buried the

axe that killed Mary Tynam. Three days later, he was hanged.

Early accounts of the case—with titles like *The Boston Fiend*—are understandably reticent about the sexual motive. Crime historian Jay Robert Nash makes up for this by adding that Piper also confessed to the rape of several children.[1] Richard Dempewolff's chapter in *Famous Old New England Murders* (1942) is also inclined to reticence, but scatters enough clues to clarify the picture. To begin with, Piper admitted that he made the "bat-like club" three days before attacking Bridget Landregan with the intention of killing someone. This is obviously a euphemism for raping someone. After the interrupted rape, "being dissatisfied, I made another assault on a girl."

Asked about the attack on Mabel, Piper said: "I have not got there yet," then went on to explain that he had a "strange mania for setting fires," and that just over a week after the rape, he had set fire to the Concord Hall, then, when this was blazing, gone to a nearby shop and tried to start another fire—this second one "did not burn well." More than anything else, this makes clear that Piper was a sadistic sex criminal. Pyromania is a well-known form of sexual perversion, and almost without exception, the pyromaniac has an orgasm while watching the fire. Peter Kürten, the Düsseldorf sadist, interspersed murders and violent attacks with setting fire to haystacks and buildings.

The murder of Mary Tynam presents the most interesting puzzle. Piper said he battered her with an axe to get his money back, and this sounds plausible until we look at it more closely. He had spent the night in her room; he crept out in the dawn, and went home for an axe. Would anyone take such a risk—since he was likely to be seen returning

[1] *Bloodletters and Badmen* (M. Evans, Inc., New York, 1973).

and then leaving again—for a few dollars? It sounds far more likely that the same "mania" that led him to batter two other women and to start fires made him return for the axe. Like Pieydagnelle—and Zola's Jacques Lantier—Piper was driven by a desire to cause injury, to batter women insensible.

The murder of Mabel Young was not a matter of sudden impulse. Several witnesses claimed to have seen the "cricket bat" leaning against the wall of the vestibule earlier in the day. He approached Mabel before the Sunday school class to ask her if she would like to look at the pigeons afterwards—probably aware of her aunt's habit of engaging the clergyman in conversation. Here, as in the case of Bridget Landregan, he was interrupted before he could complete the rape. So he hid the body, hoping to return later, then dispose of it. But Mabel recovered consciousness and cried out, and Piper's career as a sex attacker came abruptly to an end.

Also in Boston, in April 1874, a 14-year-old boy named Jesse Pomeroy was questioned about the murder of a 4-year-old named Horace Mullen, whose mutilated body had been found in a marsh near Dorchester. Two years earlier, Pomeroy had been sentenced to reform school for enticing seven young boys to lonely places, where they were stripped and beaten, or sadistically injured with a knife. Pomeroy was a tall, gangling boy with a hare lip and a "white eye." When he was taken into custody, a knife with bloodstains was found on him; mud on his shoes was similar to that of the marsh where the child's body had been discovered. Plaster casts of footprints were taken, and they proved to be Jesse Pomeroy's.

Promeroy lived with his mother, a poor dressmaker. She had moved from a house on Broadway Street, south Boston. When the landlord sold the property in July 1874, laborers digging in the cellar found the remains of a girl of about 10. She proved to be a neighbor of the Pomeroys called Patricia

Curran, and she had vanished in the previous March. Pomeroy finally confessed to her murder, and to that of Horace Mullen. He admitted that he was driven by an overwhelming desire to inflict pain, and that he chose children because they were easy to overpower.

Pomeroy was sentenced to death, but on appeal this was reduced to a life sentence. He spent most of his imprisonment in solitary confinement, and "became a highly educated man" through reading. But he made several attempts to escape. The most ambitious involved gaining access to a gas pipe behind a granite block in the wall of his cell, and filling his cell with gas, after which he struck a match. He was hoping that the explosion would blow open the door; it did, but it also blew Jesse Pomeroy out of it. He was badly injured, but recovered. One newspaper report stated that other prisoners were burned to death in their cells, but this seems unlikely. Pomeroy was finally transferred from the Charleston prison to the Bridgewater State mental hospital. He died there in 1932, after fifty-two years in prison.

In Paris on April 15, 1880, a 4-year-old girl named Louise Dreux vanished from her home in the Grenelle quarter. The following day, neighbors complained of the black smoke pouring from the chimney of a retarded 20-year-old youth named Louis Menesclou, who lived on the top floor of the same building as the Dreux family. When police entered his room they found a child's head and entrails burning in the stove. A forearm was in Menesclou's pocket, and other parts of the body were found in the toilet. In Menesclou's room the police found a poem that contained the lines "I saw her, I took her." Menesclou admitted to strangling the child and sleeping with her corpse under his bed. He indignantly denied raping her, but became embarrassed when asked why the child's genitals were missing. Menesclou had been suffering from convulsions from the age of nine months, and came of a family with a history of insanity and alcoholism; his mother had periods of "mania" when menstruating. He had spent some time in a reformatory, and also in the marines, but proved "lazy and intractable." After his execution, his brain was examined, and found to have various "morbid" abnormalities.

Twenty years after the execution of Boston bellringer Thomas Piper, an oddly similar case achieved nationwide—in fact worldwide—publicity. Again the central character was a respectable young churchgoer. Theodore Durrant was a medical student, and a Sunday school teacher in the Emanuel Baptist church in San Francisco. He was devoting his romantic attentions to an attractive girl called Blanche Lamont, who had some misgivings about him because he had once made immoral proposals to her during a walk in the park—in fact, she had refused to speak to him for several weeks.

On April 3, 1895, at 4:15 in the afternoon, he met Blanche out of her cookery class, and they were seen to enter the Baptist church together—Durrant had a key. Three-quarters of an hour later, the church organist arrived and found the young man looking pale and shaken—he explained that he had accidentally inhaled some gas. Blanche was nowhere to be seen, and Durrant later insisted he had no idea where she was.

Only a week later, Blanche's friend Minnie Williams accompanied Theodore Durrant into the church. The following morning, women who had come to decorate the church for Easter found Minnie, half naked, in the library, whose walls were covered with blood; half a knife blade was still in her breast. Further search revealed Blanche's naked body in the belfry, perfectly preserved by the cold; she had died from strangulation. Durrant was arrested at a militia training camp and swore his innocence of both murders. But at least fifty witnesses had seen him with both girls immediately before they disappeared.

Durrant's clothes proved to be free of bloodstains. But another young lady to whom Durrant had been attracted was able to suggest an explanation. She described how Durrant had taken her into the church library, excused himself for a while, then reappeared naked. She had fled screaming. He had clearly done the same thing with Blanche and Minnie, then killed them.

Durrant was found guilty and sentenced to death; in January 1898, after a series of appeals, he was finally hanged.

The evidence presented in court allows us an insight not only into Durrant' psychology, but into this whole problem of the rise of sex crime. The fact that he had been seen by so many witnesses indicates that the murders were not carefully planned. The number of young ladies who came forward and revealed that Durrant had proposed that they should enter the library for a "physical examination" leaves no doubt that he was a highly sexed and intensely frustrated young man who had a strong desire to expose himself. Even so, it requires a considerable effort of imagination to grasp what it must have been like to be a young man of normal sexual impulses in the San Francisco of the late nineteenth century. Police Captain Thomas S. Duke, who describes the case in *Celebrated Criminal Cases of America*, mentions that he has a photograph of Durrant taken at a picnic when he was sixteen, and that "the position in which he posed proves conclusively that he was a degenerate even as a child." He presumably means that Durrant had his hand in his pocket in a position that suggested he was holding his penis. It seems incredible that, a mere sixty years later, when San Francisco was at the forefront of the movement for sexual freedom, couples openly had sexual intercourse in the Golden Gate Park.

Suddenly, we can begin to understand the social context of the rise in sex crime in the nineteenth century. As late as the 1860s, men and women bathed naked at respectable seaside resorts. Then sex became taboo; young men were expected to spend years wooing a girl and submitting to long engagements before they were permitted to see her naked. The novelist Robert Musil catches something of the frustration that ensued when he writes of the sex murderer Moosbrugger (in *The Man Without Qualities*): "Girls were something that he could only look at . . . Now one must just try what that means. Something that one craves for, just as naturally as one craves for bread or water, is only there to be looked at. After a time, one's desire for it becomes unnatural. It walks past, the skirts swaying around its ankles. It climbs over a stile, becoming visible right up to the knees . . ."

"Something that one craves for, just as naturally as for bread or water . . ." If Durrant had dared to assert that his desire for sex was "natural," he would have been told that, on the contrary, it was sinful. And so, as Musil says, the desire for it became "unnatural"—inflamed by auto-erotic fantasies—until he began to risk his reputation by openly propositioning young ladies of the church. This in itself reveals how "unnatural" the desire had become, since the chance of any of them agreeing to a mutual "examination" was a million to one. But the alternative—picking up a prostitute—almost certainly struck Durrant as unthinkable; his rigid Christian upbringing would probably have made him impotent.

And so eventually, the craving to see a girl naked—and to have her see him naked—becomes so obsessive that he risks everything by inviting her into the library, then takes off his clothes and presents himself to her. Understandably, she screams and runs away—what else did he expect her to do? But now he knows that if he wants to take a girl's virginity—

which he imagines as a supreme ecstasy that will sweep away years of frustration like a flash flood—he will have to compel her to stay in the library, and silence her screams.

When it finally happens, it is unplanned. So many girls have declined to accompany him into the library that he expects Blanche to refuse him too. This explains why he meets her openly, travels on a tram car, and is seen entering the church with her. But this time, when he enters the room naked and she screams, he flings himself on her and chokes her into silence. Ten minutes later, with a naked body at his feet, he is suddenly convinced that he will be interrupted at any moment. He grabs her by the hair and drags her up to the belfry (strands of her hair were found caught in the splintered wood of the stairs). When the organist arrives, Durrant is pale and trembling, but Blanche—and her clothes and school books—have been concealed . . .

Convinced that the body will be found at any moment—particularly when he is told that witnesses saw him with Blanche that afternoon—he prepares for arrest. In fact, nothing happens; days go by and he is still free. But he knows that this cannot go on for ever. Sooner or later, the bell-ringer will notice a smell of decay and will investigate. Now, living in a kind of nightmare, he feels that if he is going to be hanged, he might just as well repeat the pleasure of possessing one of these infinitely desirable young church-goers who seem to embody the allure of the whole female species . . . And so Blanche's best friend is persuaded to enter the library. This time he is so certain that he will be caught that he makes no attempt at concealment; he stabs her to death, rapes her, then leaves the body on the floor. And the next day, as he goes off to the militia camp, he is aware that he has literally traded his life for just two sexual experiences . . . Does he count "the world well lost?" Probably not. But then, as Musil suggests, deprivation-needs have turned a natural desire into something that is so morbid and unnatural that it has become an insane compulsion. Theodore Durrant encapsulates the sexual problem of the whole Victorian era.

The rise of sex crime presented the police with a completely new problem. In the average murder case, there is some connection between the killer and the victim, and the task of the detective is to find it. But in sex murders, the victim is chosen at random. So unless the criminal can be caught in the act, or unless he leaves some obvious clue behind, the chances of catching him are a thousand to one. It was the fiasco of the hunt for Jack the Ripper that suddenly made this obvious.

If the Ripper murders produced dismay at Scotland Yard, the police must have been encouraged by their success in arresting two more mentally disturbed killers, both of whom have been suspected of being Jack the Ripper.[1] Dr. Thomas Neill Cream, who obtained his medical degree in Canada, was a bald-headed, cross-eyed man, who arrived in London in 1891. He picked up young prostitutes in the Waterloo Road area, and persuaded them to take pills containing strychnine, apparently from motives of pure sadism; four of them died in agony. But Cream was undoubtedly insane: he wrote confused letters accusing well-known public men of the murders, and went to Scotland Yard to complain of being followed by the police. A young constable who had followed him from the house where two prostitutes had been poisoned explained why he suspected the cross-eyed doctor, and Cream's arrest followed swiftly. After his arrest, he wrote to a prostitute to tell her that his name would be cleared by a Member of Parliament, who had over 200 witnesses to prove

---

[1] For a comprehensive discussion of the murders and suspects, see *Jack the Ripper: Summing Up and Verdict*; by Colin Wilson and Robin Odell (Transworld, London, 1987).

his innocence. Cream should undoubtedly have been found guilty but insane; he told one prostitute that he lived only for sex, and was probably suffering from tertiary syphilis, with softening of the brain. After his execution in 1892, it was frequently suggested that Cream was Jack the Ripper. This seems unlikely for two reasons. No sex murderer has been known to change his *modus operandi* from stabbing to poisoning, and at the time of the Ripper murders, Cream was serving a term in Joliet penitentiary in Chicago for the murder by poison of his mistress's husband. So although Cream's last words on the scaffold were: "I am Jack the . . . ," there can be no doubt that he is the least likely suspect.

George Chapman, a Pole whose real name was Severin Klossowski, *was* in Whitechapel at the time of the Ripper murders, and was suspected at the time by Detective Inspector Frederick Abberline, one of the officers in charge of the investigation. A doctor named Thomas Dutton suggested to Abberline that he should be looking for a Russian or Pole with a smattering of surgical knowledge—it was often asserted, inaccurately, that the mutilations showed medical skill. Chapman, who was 23 in 1888, practiced the trade of "barber-surgeon"—one writer asserts that he rented a shop in the basement of George Yard Buildings, the slum tenement where Martha Turner was stabbed 39 times. But in 1888, Klossowski had no known criminal record. In 1890, he married (bigamously) and went to America. In 1892 he returned to England, met Annie Chapman, a woman with a private income, and allowed her to set him up in a barber's shop in Hastings. But in 1897, she died after a great deal of vomiting; her death was attributed to consumption. In the following year, Klossowski—who was now a publican—married his barmaid Bessie Taylor; she died in 1901 after a long period of vomiting and diarrhea. He married another barmaid,

Maud Marsh, but his mother-in-law became suspicious when her daughter fell ill, and even more suspicious when she herself almost died after drinking a glass of brandy prepared by Chapman (as he now called himself) for his wife. When Maud Marsh died, an autopsy revealed arsenic poisoning, and Chapman was arrested. A second inquest revealed that the poison was antimony, not arsenic; and when the bodies of the previous two women were exhumed, it was discovered that they had also died from antimony poisoning. Although there was no obvious motive for the murders, the evidence against Chapman was overwhelming, and he was sentenced to death.

Abberline had continued to regard Chapman as a prime suspect in the Ripper murders; he had questioned the woman who was his mistress at the time—Lucy Baderski—and she said that Chapman was often out until four in the morning. When Chapman was arrested by Detective Inspector George Godley, Abberline remarked to Godley: "You've got Jack the Ripper at last." But although Chapman certainly had the opportunity to commit the Whitechapel murders, the same objection applies to him as to Neill Cream: a sadistic killer who has used a knife is not likely to switch to poison.

So although the police had reason to congratulate themselves on the arrest of two multiple murderers, they must also have recognized that detecting a poisoner is far easier than tracking down a sadistic "slasher." It was obvious that the Ripper-type killer was by far the most serious challenge so far to the science of crime detection.

This view was confirmed by a series of murders which began in France in 1894. In May of that year, a 21-year-old mill-girl named Eugénie Delhomme was found behind a hedge near Beaurepaire, south of Lyon; she had been strangled, raped and disemboweled. And during the next three years, the "French Ripper" went on to commit another ten sex murders of the same type. The next two victims were teenage girls; then a 58-year-old widow was murdered and raped in her home. In September 1895, the killer began killing and sodomizing boys, also castrating them: the first victim was a 16-year-old shepherd, Victor Portalier. Later that month, back near the scene of his first crime, he killed a 16-year-old girl, Aline Alise, and a 14-year-old shepherd boy. Soon after this, he was almost caught when he tried to attack an 11-year-old servant girl, Alphonsine-Marie Derouet, and was driven off by a gamekeeper, who was walking not far behind her. A man was stopped by the police, but allowed to go after producing his papers. He was, in fact, the killer—a 26-year-old ex-soldier (and ex-inmate of an asylum) named Joseph Vacher, whose face was paralyzed from a suicide attempt with a revolver.

Imprisonment as a vagrant stopped the murders for six months, but almost as soon as he was released he raped and disemboweled Marie Moussier, the 19-year-old wife of a shepherd; three weeks later, he murdered a shepherdess, Rosine Rodier. In May 1897 he killed a 14-year-old tramp, Claudius Beaupied, in an empty house, and the body was not found for more than six months. The final victim was Pierre Laurent, another 14-year-old shepherd boy, who was sodomized and castrated. On August 4, 1897, he came upon an Amazonian peasant woman named Marie-Eugénie Plantier, who was gathering pine cones in a forest near Tournon, and threw himself on her from behind, clamping a hand over her mouth. She freed herself and screamed; her husband and children, who were nearby, came running, and her husband threw a stone at Vacher, who in turn attacked him with a pair of scissors. Another peasant appeared, Vacher was overcome and dragged off to a nearby inn. There he entertained his captors by playing the accordion while awaiting the police.

The "disemboweler of the south-east" (*l'éventreur du sud-est*) was finally trapped.

There had been a massive manhunt for the disemboweler, and dozens of vagabonds had been arrested on suspicion. An extremely accurate description of Vacher had been circulated, which mentioned his twisted upper lip, the scar across the corner of his mouth, the bloodshot right eye, the black beard and unkempt hair. Yet he committed eleven murders over three years, and if he had not been caught by chance, might well have gone on for another three.

The great pathologist Alexandre Lacassagne spent five months studying Vacher, and concluded that he was only pretending to be insane. Vacher insisted that he had been abnormal since being bitten by a mad dog as a child. Tried for the murder of Victor Portalier, he was sentenced to death in October 1898 and guillotined on December 31. But there seems to be little doubt that Lacassagne was mistaken; Vacher was undoubtedly insane, and his random mode of operation had enabled him to play hide-and-seek with the combined police forces of south-eastern France.

It was a disturbing lesson for the police and the crime scientists; in the 1890s, the random sex killer constituted a virtually insoluble problem.

Yet new scientific discoveries were beginning to provide the police with some of the techniques they needed. In the year of the Ripper murders, Sir Francis Galton went to Paris to study a new method of criminal identification called "Bertillonage" (because it was invented by Alphonse Bertillon) which consisted of a record of the criminal's physical statistics—height, color of eyes, circumference of head, and so on. Galton saw that fingerprinting would be a far simpler method, if only he could devise some method of classifying the prints. He did this over the next three years, and published his results in 1891. Soon after the turn of the century, the new method was being used by Scotland Yard and other police forces in Europe.

So was an equally exciting discovery: the ability to distinguish human from animal bloodstains, developed by a young Viennese doctor named Paul Uhlenhuth. His starting-point was the discovery that blood serum—the colorless liquid that separates out when blood is left to stand—develops "defensive reactions" against various proteins, including other types of blood. If a chicken's blood is injected into a rabbit, the rabbit's blood will develop defenses. If some of the rabbit's blood is then left in a test tube so the serum separates out, and a drop of chicken's blood is added to the serum, it will defend itself by turning cloudy. So if a rabbit is injected with human blood, its serum will turn cloudy when human blood is added. If an unknown bloodstain is dissolved in salt water, and added to the rabbit's serum, it is instantly apparent whether or not it is a human bloodstain.

The first murderer to be trapped by this discovery was a serial sex killer who was driven by the same sadistic impulse as Jack the Ripper.

Around 1 p.m., on September 9, 1898, the mothers of two small girls in the village of Lechtingen, near Osnabrück, became worried when they failed to return home. And when Jadwiga Heidemann and her neighbor Irmgard Langmeier called at the school, they learned that their children had not been to classes that day. The whole village joined in the search, and at dusk, the dismembered body of 7-year-old Hannelore Heidemann was found in nearby woods—some parts had been scattered among the trees. An hour or so later, the remains of 8-year-old Else Langmeier were found hidden in bushes; she had also been mutilated and dismembered.

The police learned that a journeyman carpenter named Ludwig Tessnow had been seen entering Lechtingen from the direction of the woods, and that his clothes seemed to be bloodstained. Tessnow was soon arrested, but insisted that the stains on his clothes were of brown woodstain. A powerful microscope would have revealed that this was a lie, but the Osnabrück police knew nothing of forensic science, and let him go for lack of evidence. But a policeman visited Tessnow in his workshop, and contrived to knock over a tin of woodstain so that it ran down Tessnow's trousers. In fact, it dried exactly like the other stains. And since Tessnow continued to work in the village, his neighbors concluded that he must be innocent. He remained until January 1899, when he went to work elsewhere.

Two and a half years later, a frighteningly similar crime occurred near the village of Göhren, on the Baltic island of Rügen. On Sunday, July 1, 1901, two brothers named Peter and Hermann Stubbe, aged 6 and 8, failed to return home for supper, and parties went into the nearby woods, carrying burning torches and shouting. Shortly after sunrise, the bodies of both children were found in some bushes, their skulls crushed in with a rock and their limbs amputated. Hermann's heart had been removed, and was never found.

The police interviewed a fruit seller who had seen the two boys in the late afternoon; they were talking to a carpenter named Tessnow. Tessnow had recently returned to Rügen, after traveling around Germany, and was regarded as an eccentric recluse. Another neighbor recollected seeing Tessnow returning home in the evening, with dark spots on his Sunday clothes.

Tessnow was arrested and his home searched. Some garments had been thoroughly washed, and were still wet. And a stained pair of boots lay under the stone kitchen sink. Tessnow remained calm under questioning, and seemed to be able to account satisfactorily for his movements on the previous Sunday. Again, he insisted that stains on his clothing were of woodstain.

Three weeks before the murders, seven sheep had been mutilated and disemboweled in a field near Göhren, and their owner had arrived in time to see a man running away; he swore he could recognize him if he saw him again. Brought to the prison yard at Greifswald, the man immediately picked out Tessnow as the butcher of his sheep. Tessnow steadfastly denied it—he was not the sort of man, he said, to kill either sheep or children . . .

The examining magistrate, Johann-Klaus Schmidt, now recalled a case in Osnabrück three years before, and contacted the police there. When they told him that the name of their suspect was Ludwig Tessnow, Schmidt had no doubt that Tessnow was the killer. But how to prove it? At this point, his friend Prosecutor Ernst Hubschmann of Greifswald recollected reading about a new test for human bloodstains. And at the end of July, Uhlenhuth received two parcels containing Tessnow's Sunday clothes, brown-stained working overalls, and various other items, including a bloodstained rock, probably the murder weapon. It took Uhlenhuth and his assistant four days to examine over a hundred spots and stains, dissolving them in distilled water or salt solution. The overalls were, as Tessnow had claimed, stained with wood dye. But they also found 17 stains of human blood and nine of sheep blood. It took the Rügen prosecutor a long time to bring Tessnow to trial—German justice was extremely slow-moving—but when he eventually appeared in court, Uhlenhuth was there to give evidence and explain his methods. Ludwig Tessnow was found guilty of murder and sentenced to death.

3

MASS MURDER IN EUROPE

IN THE FIRST DECADE OF THE TWENTIETH CENTURY, SEX CRIME was still something of a rarity. It seems to have been the triggering mechanism of the First World War that finally released the age of sex crime on Europe. The dubious distinction of being its inaugurator probably goes to the Hungarian Bela Kiss, whose crimes presented an apparently insoluble problem to the police of Budapest.

In 1916, the Hungarian tax authorities noted that it had been a long time since rates had been paid on a house at 17 Rákóczi Street in the village of Cinkota, ten miles north-west of Budapest. It had been empty for two years, and since it seemed impossible to trace the owner, or the man who rented it, the district court of Pest-Pilis decided to sell it. A blacksmith named Istvan Molnar purchased it for a modest sum, and moved in with his wife and family. When tidying-up the workshop, Molnar came upon a number of sealed oil drums behind a mess of rusty pipes and corrugated iron. They had been solidly welded, and for a few days the blacksmith left them alone. Then his wife asked him what was in the drums—it might, for example, be petrol—and he settled down to removing the top of one of them with various tools. And when Molnar finally raised the lid, he clutched his stomach and rushed to the garden privy. His wife came in to see what had upset him; when she peered into the drum she screamed and fainted. It contained the naked body of a woman, in a crouching position, the practically airless drum had preserved it like canned meat.

Six more drums also proved to contain female corpses. Most of the women were middle-aged; none had ever been beautiful. And the police soon realized they had no way of identifying them. They did not even know the name of the man who had placed them there. The previous tenant had gone off to the war in 1914; he had spent little time in the house, and had kept himself to himself, so, nobody knew who he was. The police found it difficult even to get a description. They merely had seven unknown victims of an unknown murderer.

Professor Balazs Kenyeres, of the Police Medical Laboratory, was of the opinion that the women had been dead for more than two years. But at least he was able to take fingerprints; by 1916, fingerprinting had percolated even to the highly conservative Austro-Hungarian Empire. However, at this stage, fingerprinting was unhelpful, since it only told them that the women had no criminal records.

Some three weeks after the discovery, Detective Geza Bialokurszky was placed in charge of the investigation; he was one of the foremost investigators of the Budapest police. He was, in fact, Sir Geza (*lovag*), for he was a nobleman whose family had lost their estates. Now he settled down to the task of identifying the female corpses. If Professor Kenyeres was correct about time of death—and he might easily have been wrong, since few pathologists are asked to determine the age of a canned corpse—the women must have vanished in 1913 or thereabouts. The Missing Persons' Bureau provided him with a list of about 400 women who had vanished between 1912 and 1914. Eventually, Bialokurszky narrowed these down to fifteen. But these women seemed to have no traceable relatives. Eventually, Bialokurszky found the last employer of a 36-year-old cook named Anna Novak, who had left her job abruptly in 1911. Her employer was the widow of a Hussar colonel, and she still had Anna's "servant's book," a kind of identity card that contained a photograph, personal details, and a list of previous employers, as well as their personal comments. The widow assumed that she had simply found a better job or had got married. She still had the woman's trunk in the attic.

This offered Bialokurszky the clue he needed so urgently: a sheet from a newspaper, *Pesti Hirlap*, with an advertisement marked in red pencil "Widower urgently seeks acquaintance of mature, warm-hearted spinster or widow to help assuage loneliness mutually. Send photo and details, Poste Restente Central P.O. Box 717. Marriage possible and even desirable."

Now, at last, fingerprinting came into its own. Back at headquarters, the trunk was examined, and a number of prints were found; these matched those of one of the victims. The Post Office was able to tell Bialokurszky that Box 717 had been rented by a man who had signed for his key in the name of Elemer Nagy, of 14 Kossuth Street, Pestszenterzse-bet, a suburb of Budapest. This proved to be an empty plot. Next, the detective and his team studied the agony column of *Pesti Hirlap* for 1912 and 1913. They found more than twenty requests for "warm-hearted spinsters" which gave the address of Box 717. This was obviously how the unknown killer of Cinkota had contacted his victims. On one occasion he had paid for the advertisement by postal order, and the Post Office was able to trace it. (The Austro-Hungarian Empire at least had a super-efficient bureaucracy.) Elemer Nagy had given an address in Cinkota, where the bodies had been found, but it was not of the house in Rákóczi Street; in fact, it proved to be the address of the undertaker. The killer had a sense of humor.

Bialokurszky gave a press conference, and asked the newspapers to publish the signature of "Elemer Nagy." This quickly brought a letter from a domestic servant named Rosa Diosi, who was 27, and admitted that she had been the mistress of the man in question. His real name was Bela Kiss, and she had last heard from him in 1914, when he had written to her from a Serbian prisoner of war camp. Bialokurszky had not divulged that he was looking for the Cinkota mass murderer, and Rosa Diosi was shocked and incredulous when he told her. She had met Kiss in 1914; he had beautiful brown eyes, a silky moustache, and a deep, manly voice. Sexually, he had apparently been insatiable . . .

Other women contacted the police, and they had identical stories to tell: answering the advertisement, meeting the handsome Kiss, and being quickly invited to become his mistress, with promises of marriage. They were also expected to hand over their life savings, and all had been invited to Cinkota. Some had not gone, some had declined to offer their savings—or had none to offer—and a few had disliked being rushed into sex. Kiss had wasted no further time on them, and simply vanished from their lives.

In July 1914, two years before the discovery of the bodies, Kiss had been conscripted into the Second Regiment of the Third Hungarian Infantry Battalion, and had taken part in the long offensive that led to the fall of Valjevo; but before that city had fallen in November, Kiss had been captured by the Serbs. No one was certain what had become of him after that. But the regiment was able to provide a photograph that showed the soldiers being inspected by the Archduke Joseph; Kiss's face was enlarged, and the detectives at last knew what their quarry looked like. They had also heard that his sexual appetite was awe-inspiring, and this led them to show the photograph in the red-light district around Conti and Magyar Street. Many prostitutes recognized him as a regular customer; all spoke warmly of his generosity and mentioned his sexual prowess. But a waiter who had often served Kiss noticed that the lady with whom he was dining usually paid the bill . . .

Now, at last, Bialokurszky was beginning to piece the story together. Pawn tickets found in the Cinkota house revealed that the motive behind the murders was the cash of the victims. But the ultimate motive had been sex, for Kiss promptly spent the cash in the brothels of Budapest and Vienna. The evidence showed that he was, quite literally, a satyr—a man with a raging and boundless appetite for sex. His profession—of plumber and tinsmith—did not enable him to indulge this appetite, so he took to murder. He had received two legacies when he was 23 (about 1903) but soon spent them. After this, he had taken to seducing middle-aged women and "borrowing" their savings. One of these, a cook named Maria Toth, had become a nuisance, and he killed her. After this he had decided that killing women was the easiest way to make a living as well as indulge his sexual appetites. His favorite reading was true-crime books about conmen and adventurers.

Bialokurszky's investigations suggested that there had been more than seven victims, and just before Christmas 1916, the garden in the house at Cinkota was dug up; it revealed five more bodies, all of middle-aged women, all naked.

But where was Kiss? The War Office thought that he had died of fever in Serbia. He had been in a field hospital, but when Bialokurszky tracked down one of its nurses, she remembered the deceased as a "nice boy" with fair hair and blue eyes, which seemed to suggest that Kiss had changed identity with another soldier, possibly someone called Mackavee; but the new "Mackavee" proved untraceable. And although sightings of Kiss were reported from Budapest in 1919—and even New York as late as 1932—he was never found.

The first decade of the twentieth century also saw the emergence—and decline—of two female mass murderers: Jeanne Weber and Belle Gunness. Belle—whom we shall consider in the next chapter—seems to have killed purely for profit. Jeanne Weber, on the other hand, was undoubtedly a genuine serial killer—that is, one who kills repeatedly with a sexual motive. As in the case of her German predecessor, Anna Zwanziger (whose crimes took place precisely a century earlier), the sexual motive is less obvious than in the case of male serial killers; but no one who studies the case of the "ogress of the Goutte D'Or" can fail to be aware of its existence.

In the Goutte d'Or, a slum passageway in Montmartre, lived four brothers named Weber, one of whose wives, Jeanne Weber, had lost two of her three children, and consoled herself with cheap red wine. Just around the corner lived her brother-in-law Pierre and his wife. On March 2, 1905, Mme Pierre asked her sister-in-law if she would baby-sit with her two children, Suzanne and Georgette, while she went to the public *lavoir*, the 1905 equivalent of a laundromat. Mme Pierre had been there only a short time when a neighbor rushed in and told her that 18-month-old Georgette was ill—she had heard her choking and gasping as she passed. The mother hurried home, and found her child on the bed, her face blue and with foam around her mouth; her aunt Jeanne was massaging the baby's chest. Mme Pierre took the child on her lap and rubbed her back until her breathing became easier, then went back to the laundromat. But when she returned an hour later, with a basket of clean washing, Georgette was dead. The neighbor observed some red marks on the baby's throat, and pointed them out to the father, but he seems to have shrugged it off. Nobody felt any suspicion toward Jeanne Weber, who had behaved admirably and apparently done her best.

Nine days later, when both parents had to be away from home, they again asked Aunt Jeanne to baby-sit. Two-year-old Suzanne was dead when they returned, again with foam around her mouth. The doctor diagnosed the cause of death as convulsions. Aunt Jeanne appeared to be dazed with grief.

Two weeks later, on March 25, Jeanne Weber went to visit another brother-in-law, Leon Weber, and was left with the seven-month-old daughter Germaine while her mother went shopping. The grandmother, who lived on the floor below, heard sudden cries, and hurried upstairs to find Germaine in "convulsions," gasping for breath. After a few minutes of rubbing and patting, the baby recovered, and the grandmother returned to her own room. Minutes later, as she talked with a neighbor, she once more heard the child's cries. Again she hurried upstairs and found the baby choking. The neighbor who had accompanied her noticed red marks on the child's throat. When the parents returned, Germaine had recovered.

The following day, Jeanne Weber came to inquire after the baby. And, incredibly, the mother again left her baby-sitting. When she returned, her child was dead. The doctor diagnosed the cause as diphtheria.

Three days later, on the day of Germaine's funeral, Jeanne Weber stayed at home with her own child Marcel; he suffered the same convulsions, and was dead when the others returned.

A week later, on April 5, Jeanne Weber invited to lunch the wife of Pierre Weber, and the wife of another brother-in-law, Charles. Mme Charles brought her ten-month-old son

Maurice, a delicate child. After lunch, Jeanne baby-sat while her in-laws went shopping. When they returned, Maurice was lying on the bed, blue in the face, with foam around his lips, breathing with difficulty. The hysterical mother accused Jeanne of strangling him—there were marks on his throat—and she furiously denied it. So Mme Charles swept up her child in her arms, and hastened to the Hospital Brétonneau. She was sent immediately to the children's ward, where a Dr. Saillant examined the marks on Maurice's throat. It certainly looked as if someone had tried to choke him. And when he heard the story of the other four deaths in the past month, Dr. Saillant became even more suspicious. So was his colleague Dr. Sevestre, and together they informed the police of this unusual case. Jeanne Weber was brought in for questioning, and Inspector Coiret began to look into her background. When he learned that all three of her children had died in convulsions, and that three years earlier, two other children—Lucie Alexandre and Marcel Poyatos—had died in the same mysterious way when in the care of Jeanne Weber, suspicion turned to certainty. The only thing that amazed him was that the Weber family had continued to ask her to baby-sit; they were either singularly fatalistic or criminally negligent. But then, the death of Jeanne's own son Marcel had dispelled any suspicions that might have been forming. When Examining Magistrate Leydet was informed of this, he found himself wondering whether this was precisely why Marcel had died.

The magistrate decided to call in a medical expert, and asked Dr. Léon Henri Thoinot, one of Paris's most distinguished "expert witnesses," second only to Paul Bouardel, the author of a classic book on strangulation and suffocation. Thoinot began by examining Maurice, who had now fully recovered. The child seemed perfectly healthy, and it was hard to see why he should have choked. Thoinot decided it could have been bronchitis. Next, the bodies of three of the dead children—Georgette, Suzanne and Germaine—were exhumed. Thoinot could find no traces of strangulation on their throats. Finally, Thoinot studied the body of Jeanne Weber's son Marcel; again he decided there was no evidence of strangulation—for example, the hyoid bone, which is easily broken by pressure on the throat, was intact.

The accusations of murder had caused a public sensation; Jeanne Weber was the most hated woman in France. The magistrate, Leydet, had no doubt whatsoever of her guilt. Yet at her trial on January 29, 1906, Thoinot once again stated his opinion that there was no evidence that the children had died by violence, while the defense lawyer Henri Robert—an unscrupulous man—intimidated the prosecution witnesses until they contradicted themselves. The "ogress of the Goutte d'Or"—as public opinion had christened her—was acquitted on all charges. The audience in the courtroom underwent a change of heart and cheered her. And Brouardel and Thoinot collaborated on an article in a medical journal in which they explained once again why Jeanne Weber had been innocent.

The public did not think so. Nor did her husband, who left her. Jeanne Weber decided that she had better move to some place where she was not known. She was a flabby, sallow-faced woman, who had little chance of attracting another male. And at that point, rescue arrived out of the blue. A man named Sylvain Bavouzet wrote to her from a place called Chambon—in the department of Indre—offering her a job as his housekeeper; it seemed he had been touched by her sad tale, and by the injustice that had almost condemned her to death. In the spring of 1907, Jeanne Weber—now calling herself by her unmarried name Moulinet—arrived at the farm of Sylvain Bavouzet, and understood that the offer had not been made entirely out of the goodness of his heart. It was a miserable, poverty-stricken place, and Bavouzet was a widower with three children, the eldest an ugly girl with a hare lip. What he wanted was cheap labor and a female to share his bed. But at least it was a home.

A month later, on April 16, 1907, Bavouzet came home to find that his 9-year-old son Auguste was ill. He had recently eaten a large amount at a local wedding feast, so his discomfort could have been indigestion. The child's sister Louise was sent to the local town Villedieu to ask the doctor to call. But Dr. Papazoglou gave her some indigestion mixture and sent her on her way. Hours later, Sylvain Bavouzet arrived, in a state of agitation, and said the boy was worse. When Papazoglou arrived, Auguste was dead, and the new housekeeper was standing by the bedside. The child was wearing a clean shirt, tightly buttoned at the collar, and when this was opened, the doctor saw a red mark around his neck. This led him to refuse a death certificate. The next day, the coroner, Charles Audiat, decided that, in spite of the red mark, Auguste's death was probably due to meningitis.

The dead boy's elder sister Germaine, the girl with the hare lip, hated the new housekeeper. She had overheard what "Mme Moulinet" had told the doctor, and knew it was mostly lies. Her brother had not vomited just before his death—so requiring a change of shirt. Precisely how Germaine realized that Mme Moulinet was the accused murderess Jeanne Weber is not certain. One account of the case declares that she came upon Jeanne Weber's picture by chance in a magazine given to them by neighbors; another asserts that she searched the housekeeper's bag and found press cuttings about the case. What is certain is that she took her evidence to the police station in Villedieu and accused Mme Moulinet of murdering her brother.

An examining magistrate demanded a new autopsy, and this was performed by Dr. Frédéric Bruneau. He concluded that there *was* evidence that Auguste had been strangled, possibly with a tourniquet. (Doctors had found a scarf wrapped around the throat of Maurice Weber, the child who had survived.) Jeanne Weber was arrested. The new accusation caused a sensation in Paris.

Understandably, Henri Robert, the man who had been responsible for her acquittal, felt that this reflected upon his professional integrity. Thoinot and Brouardel agreed. They decided that the unfortunate woman must once again be saved from public prejudice. Robert agreed to defend her for nothing, while Thoinot demanded another inquest. He carried it out three and a half months after the child's death, by which time decay had made it impossible to determine whether Auguste Bavouzet had been strangled. Predictably, Thoinot decided that Auguste had died of natural causes—intermittent fever. More doctors were called in. They agreed with Thoinot. The latter's prestige was such that Examining Magistrate Belleau decided to drop the charges against Jeanne Weber, although he was personally convinced of her guilt. Henri Robert addressed the Forensic Medicine Society and denounced the ignorance and stupidity of provincial doctors and magistrates. Jeanne Weber was free to kill again.

History repeated itself. A philanthropic doctor named Georges Bonjeau, president of the Society for the Protection of Children, offered her a job in the children's home in Orgeville. There she was caught trying to throttle a child and dismissed. But, like Thoinot and Henri Robert, Bonjeau did not believe in admitting his mistakes and he kept the matter to himself.

She became a tramp, living by prostitution. Arrested for vagrancy, she told M. Hamard, chief of the Sûreté, that she had been responsible for the deaths of her nieces. Then she withdrew the statement, and was sent to an asylum in Nanterre, from which she was quickly released as sane. A man named Joly offered her protection, and she lived with him at Lay-Saint-Remy, near Toul, until he grew tired of her and threw her out. Again she became a prostitute, and finally met a lime-burner named Émile Bouchery, who worked in the quarries of Euville, near Commercy. They lived in a room in a cheap inn run by a couple named Poirot. One evening, "Mme Bouchery" told the Poirots that she was afraid that Bouchery meant to beat her up—as he did periodically when drunk—and asked them if their seven-year-old son Marcel could sleep in her bed. They agreed. At 10 o'clock that evening, a child's screams were heard, and the Poirots broke into Mme Bouchery's room. Marcel was dead, his mouth covered in bloodstained foam. Mme Bouchery was also covered in blood. A hastily summoned doctor realized that the child had been strangled, and had bitten his tongue in his agony. It was the police who discovered a letter from *maître* Henri Robert in Mme Bouchery's pocket, and realized that she was Jeanne Weber.

Once again, the reputations of Thoinot and Robert were at stake (Brouardel having escaped the public outcry by dying in 1906). Incredibly both declined to admit their error. They agreed that the evidence proved unmistakably that Jeanne Weber had killed Marcel Poirot, but this, they insisted, was her first murder, brought about by the stress of years of persecution. It is unnecessary to say that the French press poured scorn on this view. Yet such was the influence of Thoinot that Jeanne Weber was not brought to trial; instead she was moved out of the public gaze to an asylum on the island of Maré, off New Caledonia in the Pacific. There she died in convulsions two years later, her hands locked around her own throat.

In the year of Jeanne Weber's death, another mass murderer had already embarked on a career that would end under the guillotine. Henri Désiré Landru's motives were strictly commercial; after an unsuccessful career as a swindler, which earned him a number of jail terms, Landru decided that dead victims would have no chance to complain. Between 1914 and 1918 he seduced and murdered ten women (as well as the son of one of his victims) for the sake of their property and savings. He was guillotined in 1922, and his nickname—Bluebeard—has since been applied to all mass killers with purely commercial motives.

England's most celebrated Bluebeard had already gone to the gallows seven years earlier. George Joseph Smith was a petty crook with a cockney accent, and he had served two jail sentences for persuading women to steal for him when he decided that murder was less complicated. His method was to marry a lonely spinster or widow, persuade her to make a will in his favor, then drown her in the bath tub by raising her ankles. His first two victims died in seaside resorts, with minimal publicity. Smith's mistake was to move to Highgate, in London, for his third murder, and the resulting publicity in *The News of the World* drew the attention of relatives of previous victims, who informed the police. Smith was tried only for the death of his last victim, but his fate was sealed when the judge ordered that details of the previous "accidents" should be revealed to the jury.

The interest of these two mass murderers, in this particular context, is that women who had escaped with their lives testified that both had curiously hypnotic powers, and that a single penetrating glance could deprive them of their will. By contrast, most serial murderers have clearly failed to master the art of seduction—often because they have been physically repulsive.

Yet there is, nevertheless, a basic similarity. Landru, like Casanova, found seduction the most fascinating of sports. The way women yielded and melted as he gazed into their eyes was a kind of drug. He might be a crook and a failure, but when he saw that yielding look in a woman's eyes, he felt like a god. And so, as in the case of the serial killer, the mass murderer kills out of a form of inadequacy.

At the same time as Landru was pursuing his career as a lady-killer in Paris, another mass murderer of women was operating in Berlin. The full details of Georg Karl Grossmann's crimes will never be known, since he committed suicide before he came to trial. But it is clear that, in terms of the number of victims, he is one of the worst mass murderers of the century.

In August 1921 the owner of a top-story flat in Berlin near the Silesian railway terminus heard sounds of a struggle coming from the kitchen and called the police. They found on Grossmann's kitchen bed (a camp bed) the trussed-up carcass of a recently killed girl, tied as if ready for butchering.

Grossmann had been in the place since the year before the war. He had stipulated for a separate entrance, and had the use of the kitchen, which he never allowed his landlord to enter. He was a big, surly man who kept himself to himself, and lived by peddling. He was not called up during the war (which led the other tenants to assume—rightly—that he had a police record), and lived in self-chosen retirement. He picked up girls with great regularity (in fact, he seldom spent a night alone). He killed many of these sleeping partners and sold the bodies for meat, disposing of the unsaleable parts in the river. (The case became known as *Die Braut auf der Stulle*—"The bread and butter brides," since a companion for a night is known as a "bride" in Germany.) At the time of his arrest, evidence was found which indicated that three women had been killed and dismembered in the past three weeks.

Grossmann was a sexual degenerate and sadist who had served three terms of hard labor for offenses against children, one of which had ended fatally. He also indulged in bestiality. It is of interest that Grossmann was indirectly involved in the famous "Anastasia" case—the Grand Duchess Anastasia who was believed by many to be the last surviving member of the Tsar's family. At one point it was announced that "Anastasia" was really an impostor named Franziska Schamzkovski, a Polish girl from Bütow in Pomerania. Franziska's family were told that their daughter had been murdered by Grossmann on August 13, 1920; an entry in his diary on that date bore the name "Sasnovski." Anastasia's enemies insisted that this was not true, that Franziska and Anastasia were the same person.

Grossmann laughed when he heard the death sentence, and afterwards had fits of manic behavior. He hanged himself in his cell. The number of his victims certainly runs into double figures, since he was "in business" throughout the war.

The defeat of Germany in 1918 brought soaring inflation, which was soon followed by revolution. In October 1918 the sailors at Kiel mutinied when ordered to go to sea and fight the British. In November an independent socialist republic was proclaimed in Bavaria. On November 9, the Kaiser abdicated and a republic was proclaimed in Berlin. Two days later, the Armistice was signed. In January, there was a communist (Spartacist) revolt, which was crushed by the army; two of its leaders, Rosa Luxemburg and Karl Liebknecht, were killed while under arrest. Magnus Hirschfeld described going to the mortuary with a patient in search of her son, and seeing hundreds of bodies, many mutilated or with their throats slit. He also observed some young girls who kept rejoining the queue who filed past the unidentified bodies, obviously fascinated by the sight of naked male bodies, and unable to remove their eyes from genitals that were swollen with hemorrhages and decay.

In the same paragraph, Hirschfeld also describes standing beside the wife of a State Attorney at an execution, and observing her heaving chest and ecstatic groans as the condemned man was dragged to the executioner's block, followed by a convulsion like a sexual orgasm as the axe fell. These two descriptions—in juxtaposition—suddenly afford us one of those flashes of insight into the rise of sex crime. There is no great gulf between bored working girls, inexperienced and sexually frustrated enough to be fascinated by swollen male genitals, and a State Attorney's wife, so morbidly aroused by the thought of a man's execution that horror turns into sexual excitement. Sade once admitted that his senses were too coarse and blunt, so that it required a strong stimulus to arouse them. But there is a sense in which this is true for all human beings. We are all too mechanical, too prone to sink into a state that is akin to hypnotism. Intense sexual stimulus causes a sudden awakening. A man who catches sight of a woman undressing through a lighted window—as Ted Bundy did—is literally "galvanized." This in turn explains why Sade was stimulated by blows; they stirred his jaded senses to sudden attention.

Moreover, having experienced such a sensation once, human beings discover that nature will obligingly reproduce the sexual excitement at the mere thought of the original stimulus—for example, swollen genitals or a man losing his head. The link is created by association of ideas, and persists through habit. And so the straightforward sexual urge—which is, after all, designed simply to ensure the continuation of the species—turns into a kind of monstrous parody of itself.

The mechanism can be seen clearly in the most notorious German sex killer of the post-war period, Fritz Haarmann.

The city of Hanover, in Lower Saxony, was reduced to unparalleled chaos by the poverty and starvation that followed the First World War. It became the center of crime, black marketeering and prostitution—particularly male prostitution.

In the summer of 1924, the city's inhabitants were disturbed by rumors of a mass murderer. Five skulls were found on the banks of the River Leine within a few weeks, and boys playing in marshland found a sack full of human bones. The skulls were those of boys, one as young as eleven. These skulls had been cleanly removed with a sharp instrument. At first it was suggested that they might have been planted as a joke by medical students, but the fact that fragments of flesh were adhering to some of them made this unlikely. Superstitious servant girls began to talk about a "werewolf." Finally, a massive search of the surrounding countryside was organized on Whit Sunday. After more human bones had been found, the river was dammed, and the mud searched by workers. More than five hundred parts of corpses were found. Medical examination revealed that these came from at least twenty-two bodies. And some of the remains were still fresh.

In fact, the police had a suspect—an overweight middle-aged man with a Hitler moustache named Fritz Haarmann, who was known to be homosexual—as the killer obviously was. He was often seen in the company of young men, whom he picked up at the railway station, and witnesses also reported seeing him throw a heavy sack into the river. But the thought that Haarmann might be the "werewolf" caused some embarrassment, since Haarmann had been working for the police for the past five years—in fact, some people knew him as "Detective Haarmann." He mixed freely with the police, and was also a leading member of a patriotic organization called the Black Reichswehr, which was opposed to the French occupation of the Ruhr. He even ran a detective bureau called the Lasso Agency, in partnership with a police official. If Haarmann *was* "the werewolf" there would be a great many red faces.

The police finally decided to try and trap Haarmann by

means of two young policemen from Berlin. But before this could happen, Haarmann fell into their hands by accident. On June 23, 1924, he approached the police and demanded that they arrest a 15-year-old boy called Fromm, who was traveling on forged papers. The boy was taken to the police station at two in the morning. He countered by alleging that he had spent several nights in Haarmann's apartment, and that Haarmann had repeatedly performed homosexual acts on him. He had also held a knife against his throat and asked him if he was afraid to die. The vice squad used this allegation as an excuse to keep Haarmann in custody. The police then hastened to search his room in the Neuerstrasse. There they found many bloodstains, as well as a great deal of clothing that obviously belonged to young men. Confronted with this evidence, Haarmann pointed out that he made a living both as a butcher and an old clothes merchant. And after several days of questioning, the police had to admit that they had no evidence to link Haarmann with the human bones and skulls.

The breakthrough came by chance. A couple named Witzel were the parents of a teenage boy named Robert Witzel, who had disappeared. Robert Witzel's friend had finally admitted to the parents that both he and Robert had been seduced by "Detective Haarmann." Some of Witzel's clothes had been found in Haarmann's room, but Haarmann professed to know nothing about them. Now, as Herr Witzel and his wife sat outside the office of Police Commissioner Ratz, a young man walked past them, and Frau Witzel recognized the jacket he was wearing as belonging to her son. When the young man—named Kahlmeyer—was asked where he had obtained the jacket, he acknowledged that he had been given it by Haarmann, who had also given him a pair of trousers in which he had found an identification card belonging to Robert Witzel.

Confronted with this evidence, Fritz Haarmann suddenly broke down, and admitted that he had murdered young men in the act of sexual intercourse; he said that he would suddenly be overcome with an insane desire to bite their throats and strangle them.

Even now, Haarmann refused to make a full confession. When pressed, he burst into tears or violent rages. It took seven days of non-stop interrogation finally to wear him down. Finally, his resistance collapsed, and he took the police to a site where he had hidden the skull of a youth of 16—his last victim, Eric de Vries, killed only a week before his arrest. He now claimed that he had asked the police to take young Fromm into custody because he knew that he would be unable to resist the urge to kill him that night.

There was something oddly childish about Haarmann; it was clear that, in spite of considerable cunning and impudence, he was in some ways mentally retarded. His confession also made it clear that he was—like Zola's *bête humaine*—in the grip of a sadistic obsession that swept him away and made him kill his sex partners.

Haarmann was also known to be intimate with a young man called Hans Grans, who had not been present at Haarmann's arrest, since he was in prison for stealing a watch. Haarmann's confession soon made it clear that Grans knew about his strange sexual habits, and had often procured murder victims for him. Two weeks after Haarmann's arrest, Grans was also taken into custody.

A psychologist named Theodore Lessing was fascinated by the case. Lessing was also a philosopher—strongly influenced by Schopenhauer and Nietzsche—and a pacifist. He was struck by the parallel between Haarmann's crimes and the carnage of the recent world war. He received permission to interview Haarmann, and got to know him well. This is what he learned.

Friedrich Heinrich Karl Haarmann was born on October 25, 1879, the youngest of six children. His father was a retired railway worker, cantankerous, miserly and inclined to drunkenness. He had married a woman seven years his senior, who brought him a small fortune in property; even so, he remained an indefatigable satyr, even bringing his mistresses into the home. In later life he contracted syphilis.

Haarmann senior seems to have detested the gentle, rather effeminate Fritz, who was pampered by his mother. Fritz, in turn, hated his father. And although he loved to play with dolls, he also had a morbid streak—he liked to tie up his sisters so they looked like bodies, and to tap on windows at night, pretending to be a ghost.

He seems to have suffered from meningitis as a child, and after his death, examination of his skull revealed that the brain touched it in several places, probably as a result of the illness. Again, when he was a 16-year-old recruit in the army, he began to show signs of mental illness and was admitted to the hospital. Haarmann blamed a blow on the head which had occurred during bar exercises in the gymnasium, and sunstroke. In fact, both probably reactivated the problems due to the meningitis. Many murderers have changed character after a blow on the head.

This may also explain Haarmann's lifelong record as a child molester. Lessing learned that he had been seduced at school when he was 7 years old—Lessing does not say by whom—and that the offences against children began after a sexual experience with a "mannish woman," who lured him into her room when he was 16. It seems possible that the experience suddenly convinced Haarmann that he was not heterosexual, and that the attempts to seduce children resulted from a kind of revulsion.

At 17 he was charged with acts of indecency performed with children he had lured into doorways or cellars. He was found to be suffering from "congenital mental deficiency" (in fact, probably a result of the meningitis) and placed in an asylum at Hildesheim. Because he was regarded as dangerous, he was transferred for a while into a Hanover hospital—presumably with better security—then back to Hildesheim. He developed a kind of terror of mental hospitals, and often said to Lessing: "Hang me, do whatever you like with me, but don't send me back to the loony bin." After several escapes, he succeeded in escaping to Switzerland, where he worked in a shipyard near Zurich. By the time he returned to Hanover, his escape seems to have been forgotten.

He quarreled endlessly with his father, mostly about Haarmann's refusal to take a regular job—even in his own father's cigar factory. He became engaged to a girl called Erna, who became pregnant by him a few years later. But they were to drift apart.

In 1900, at the age of 21, Haarmann enlisted for his military service, and for a while was an excellent soldier. But on a strenuous route march, he collapsed with dizzy spells—a recurrence of the old trouble with his head. He was dismissed from the army after a diagnosis of mental deficiency, and granted a small pension. This meant that for the rest of his life he was never destitute.

His mother had died while he was in the army. Back in Hanover, Haarmann again quarreled continuously with his father, who tried to have him committed to a mental home. But a doctor who examined him declared that although he was "morally inferior, of low intelligence, idle, coarse, irritable and totally egotistical, he is not mentally ill as such . . . "

Haarmann had gonorrhea for a while, which seems to have confirmed his indifference to women. At this point—in his early twenties—he met a 40-year-old homosexual, Adolf Meil, who picked him up at a fair and invited him back to his room. "He kissed me. I was shy . . . He said: 'It's late, stay with me.' I did. He did things I'd never imagined . . ." The affair lasted for many years—possibly until Meil's death in 1916.

In 1904 he applied for a job as an invoice clerk in a paint factory, although he had no idea of what this involved. He persuaded an apprentice in the office to do his work, so his own duties were relatively light. He presented invoices to customers in which the price was deliberately low, so they paid in cash, which Haarmann then pocketed. He also became friendly with the factory cleaner, Frau Guhlisch, who had a 10-year old son who was already an accomplished thief. The three of them removed large quantities of paint from the factory, which they sold. They also burgled homes and robbed graveyards, often digging up recently buried corpses . . . Eventually Haarmann was caught and received his first prison sentence—the first of many. Released from jail, he pretended to be an official from the municipal "disinfection service," calling at homes in which someone had recently died of disease and advising the family to have the place disinfected; he used the opportunity to steal.

He spent the First World War in prison for burglary. Back in Hanover in 1918, he found himself in a Germany suffering from galloping inflation and acute food shortages. It was just the kind of environment in which he was fitted to thrive. He soon discovered that the railway station was the center of the black market, and it became virtually his headquarters. He also discovered that the police were understaffed and overworked, and were glad of any tip-offs he could offer. Within months, Haarmann was accepted by the police and railway officials as a kind of unofficial policeman. His friendship with crooks, pimps and prostitutes meant that he often got wind of big "jobs" before they happened; in one case he was instrumental in catching a gang of counterfeiters.

But for a man of Haarmann's sexual tastes, the railway

station represented a non-stop temptation. Homeless young men flocked in from the countryside. Haarmann often demanded to see their papers, and even questioned them in the stationmaster's office. The young men he liked were invited back to his room for food and a bed. They soon learned that the price was to spend the night in bed with Haarmann, engaged in mutual oral sex which often went on for hours before Haarmann reached orgasm. He claimed to be impotent—perhaps as a result of the gonorrhea—and in any case was not inclined towards sodomy. But he had one disconcerting peculiarity. As he reached sexual ecstasy, he experienced an overpowering desire to bite the windpipe of his sexual partner. If the youth was young or slightly built, he stood no chance against the well-built Haarmann. The result—Haarmann confessed to Lessing—was that his partners often died from lack of air; in some cases, he actually bit through the windpipe.

One of the major shortages in post-war Germany was of meat. Haarmann dealt in the meat of horses and other illegally slaughtered animals. His landlady became accustomed to the sound of chopping and banging from his room, and on one occasion met him coming downstairs with a covered bucket; the cloth slipped aside and she saw that it contained blood. The woman next door received a bag of fresh bones from Haarmann, from which she made brawn. Then she decided that the bones looked too white, and decided not to eat the meat. To Haarmann, the cheerful opportunist, it would probably have seemed sinful to waste the body parts of his victims when they could be sold as meat. Haarmann never actually confessed to this—but then, he made a habit of confessing only to crimes that could actually be proved against him.

Some time in 1919, Haarmann was approached by a "pretty" youth named Hans Grans. His father was a bookbinder, and Hans was an obsessive reader. But he was less than honest, and already had a varied career of petty crime behind him when he met Haarmann. A friend at the railway station told him that "that queer over there gave a pretty boy 20 marks the other day." Grans lost no time in approaching Haarmann and fluttering his eyelashes. Although not specifically homosexual—in fact, he was something of a womanizer—Grans had no objection to selling his body.

What he saw was a plump little man with a full-moon face and a broad and reassuring peasant accent. As he walked he moved his behind in a feminine manner, and his hands were soft and white. The rather high voice quavered like that of an old woman. His teeth were very white, and he had a habit of licking his lips with his fleshy tongue.

Haarmann was fascinated, and lost no time in inviting Hans back to his room and persuading him to undress. But when naked, Hans ceased to be attractive; his body was covered with hair like a monkey. It was not until he shaved it off that Haarmann was able to experience desire.

There was something about Hans that arrested Haarmann's murderous impulses—the mixture of charm, dishonesty and total unscrupulousness. Haarmann became the teacher, Hans the pupil. Haarmann gave him cigarettes and meat to sell, and lent him money which Hans often spent on girls. Hans soon became aware of Haarmann's sexual peculiarities, and often procured boys for him. He discovered what happened to some of the boys when he walked into Haarmann's room one day and found a corpse in the bed. Haarmann told him to go away; the next day, the corpse had gone. It was not difficult for Haarmann to dispose of a body: the river ran past the wall of his lodgings in the Neuestresse. Provided he dismembered the corpse and carried it down in a bucket, chances of detection were virtually non-existent.

The two of them remained together until Haarmann's arrest—although often separated when one or the other of them was in prison. They sometimes quarreled violently, on one occasion brandishing knives at one another and shouting "Murderer!" More than once, Haarmann ordered Hans to leave—then found himself unable to exist without him, and begged him to return. When Haarmann became angry and violent—as he was prone to—Hans would put his arms around his waist and slip his tongue into his mouth, whereupon Haarmann would melt. Hans always made sure that he held his lover's arms as he did this, knowing that when sexually excited, he would bite the throat. (Later, Haarmann became sentimentally attached to his lawyer, and on one occasion, hugged him enthusiastically; when the lawyer looked anxious, Haarmann assured him: "Don't worry—I won't bite.")

Oddly enough, there was a third member of this partnership, another good-looking boy named Hugo Wittkowski, who was Grans's closest friend. Unlike Grans, Hugo was completely heterosexual, and often brought women to Haarmann's apartment. When Haarmann was in prison for six months, Hugo and Hans allowed young prostitutes to move in, and took a share of their earnings. Haarmann hated Wittkowski, and on one occasion planned to murder the two young men and then commit suicide. Haarmann suffered from the odd delusion that young men found him irresistible, and once shouted at Hugo: "You've offered yourself to me hundreds of times, but I didn't want you. You weren't good enough for me"—to which Wittkowski replied simply: "I only like women."

Within a few weeks of Haarmann's arrest, the prosecutors had enough evidence to charge him with twenty-seven murders, beginning with a schoolboy called Fritz Rothe in 1918. When asked how many boys he had killed, Haarmann would shrug and say: "I forget. Perhaps thirty, perhaps forty . . ." Grans was charged as an accessory in at least one murder.

His trial began at the Hanover Assizes on December 4, 1924. It lasted fourteen days and 130 witnesses were called. The public prosecutor was Oberstaatsanwalt Dr. Wilde, assisted by Dr. Wagenschiefer; the defense was conducted by Justizrat Philipp Benfey and Rechtsanwalt Oz Lotzen. Haarmann was allowed remarkable freedom; he was usually gay and irresponsible, frequently interrupting the proceedings. At one point he demanded indignantly why there were so many women in court: the judge answered apologetically that he had no power to keep them out. When a woman witness was too distraught to give her evidence about her son with clarity, Haarmann got bored and asked to be allowed to smoke a cigar; permission was immediately granted.

He persisted to the end in his explanation of how he had killed his victims—biting them through the throat. Some boys he denied killing—for example, a boy named Hermann Wolf, whose photograph showed an ugly and ill-dressed youth; like Oscar Wilde, Haarmann declared that the boy was far too ugly to interest him.

Haarmann was sentenced to death by decapitation; Grans to twelve years in jail. Haarmann later produced a confession which has much in common with that of Mme De Brinvilliers or Gilles de Rais; it is full of accounts of sexual perversion and the pleasure he took in committing murders that were all inspired by his sexual perversion.

In his account of Haarmann, Theodore Lessing also mentions another case that caused a sensation at the time: that of Karl Denke. On December 21, 1924, a few days after Haarmann had been sentenced to death, a traveling journeyman named Vincenz Oliver called at the home of 54-year-old Denke to beg for food. Denke was known as a recluse—although he was a good churchgoer, and blew the organ in the local church. A retired farmer, he lived in an apartment block which he owned near Munsterberg, in Silesia.

Denke invited the journeyman in and told him to sit down. But instead of bringing him food, he attacked him with a hatchet. Oliver struggled and called out, and the noise was heard by a coachman named Gabriel, who lived in the flat above. Thinking his landlord was in trouble, Gabriel rushed downstairs—to find Oliver almost unconscious. The journeyman was able to gasp out that Denke had tried to kill him. Gabriel called the police and Denke was arrested. A search of the house revealed identity papers belonging to twelve traveling journeymen, as well as clothing. Two tubs proved to contain human meat pickled in brine, and there were also pots of fat and bones. Medical examination revealed that these belonged to thirty victims. A ledger was found in which Denke recorded the dates on which he had pickled the carcases, and the weight. The earliest murder had been in 1921, and the victims were mostly tramps, beggar women and journeymen.

Denke never came to trial; he hanged himself with his braces a few days later. It is assumed that he was a cannibal, who had found this ingenious way of overcoming Germany's meat shortage.

German schoolchildren were soon repeating a riddle that went: "Who is Germany's greatest mass murderer?" The child was instructed to answer: "Haarmann, ich denke" (Haarmann, I think), which also sounded like a confession of guilt (Haarmann, I, Denke)."

They also sang a nursery rhyme that went:

> Warte, warte, nur ein weilchen,
> Dann kommt Haarmann auch zu dir,
> Mit dem kleinen Hackenbeilchen,
> Und macht Hackefleisch aus dir.

*   *   *

Wait, wait, a little while
Then Haarmann will come to you,
And with his little chopper
Will make mincemeat out of you.

(The English "mincemeat" misses the sheer gruesomeness of the German *Hackefleish*—hacked flesh.)

Four years after Haarmann's execution, Germany again became the subject of worldwide news coverage as another "monster" committed a series of sadistic crimes in Düsseldorf. Peter Kürten is Germany's Jack the Ripper, and the book about him, *The Sadist*, by Karl Berg, Professor of Forensic Medicine in the Düsseldorf Academy, is—like Lessing's book on Haarmann—one of the great classics of criminology. Since the English translation (by Olga Illnerr and George Godwin) has been out of print for nearly half a century, I shall allow Berg to introduce the case in his own words:

In the whole history of crime there is to be found no record comparable in circumstances of frightfulness with the long series of crimes perpetrated in our own time by the Düsseldorf murderer, Peter Kürten.

The epidemic of sexual outrages and murders which took place in the town of Düsseldorf between the months of February and November in the year 1929, caused a wave of horror and indignation to sweep, not only through Düsseldorf, but through all Germany and, it may be said without exaggeration, throughout the whole world.

As one outrage succeeded another and always in circumstances of grim drama; as one type of crime was followed by yet another, public consternation reached the point of stupefaction.

Kürten, however, has been judged; he now belongs to criminal history.

Kürten's crimes were not merely the subject of exhaustive judicial examination; justice went deeper in his case and sought to probe the soul of this strange and enigmatic man.

In so doing Justice has placed us in a position to understand the nature both of the crimes and of the perpetrator of them. Here, for the medico-jurist, is truly absorbing material for study, for Kürten is a clinical subject who yields, in exchange for a careful analysis, a real enlargement of our knowledge of the abnormal operating in the sphere of crime.

Here is Berg's account of Kürten's first murder of 1929:

On the 9th of February, 1929, about 9 o'clock in the morning, workmen going to work found in the vicinity of the building upon which they were employed in the Kettwiger-strasse, in the Flingern district, the body of an eight-year-old girl lying under a hedge. The ground at that point sloped slightly towards the hedge, and as the hedge faced a wide open space, it was only by chance that the body was discovered.

The body was completely clothed and clad in a cloak. The clothing, however, was partially burnt and the underclothing still smoldered. The body, which smelled strongly of petroleum, was not in any sort of disorder, for even the openings of the dress and the knickers were not disarranged. A closer examination of the clothing revealed bloodstains from multiple wounds in the breast, wounds made, quite obviously, through the clothing. On the inner part of the knickers near the external genitalia were two small bloodstains. Microscopic examination revealed the presence hereabouts of seminal fluid. In the vagina there was fluid blood which had flowed from a wound 1 cm. in length, at the entrance of the vaginal cavity.

The autopsy showed that the burning had affected practically only the clothing, injuring the skin surface nowhere but on the upper part of the thighs, the neck and chin, over which area the skin was blackened and discolored, while the hair of the head was a black. charred mass, here and there completely burned off. On the left breast there was a group of thirteen wounds, the face was bloated and livid. The stabs about the left breast were grouped over an area rather smaller than a hand. Five of the wounds had penetrated the heart, three had pierced the left and right pleuræ; three had penetrated the liver. In the pleural cavities I found 750 cc. of blood. Death must have been swift through internal hemorrhage. The scene of the crime was without trace of blood. The criminal had attempted to burn the clothing of the body only. There were no traces to suggest that soot had been inhaled, and the burning was without vital reaction. In the tissues of the lumbar region there was some 4 cm. of blood infiltration.

In the stomach was found a mass of chyme, partially digested white cabbage, and remains of meat.

The essential factors to be considered, from the medico-legal standpoint, for a diagnosis of the cause of death and for a theory as to the time of it, as well as for the motive of the murderer, were the characteristic stabs, the congestion of blood which was found in the head, the exact nature of the wounds and the condition of the contents of the stomach, and, last, the injury to the genitalia. So far as the congestion of blood in the head is concerned, one can only suggest that it indicated a forcible strangulation.

The judicial autopsy of the Ohliger child established the time of death, the contents of the stomach assisting to that end.

Death must have occurred very quickly through the heart wounds. There were no visible marks where the strangling grip had been applied, but some manner of strangulation must have initiated the attack though leaving no traces on the skin of the neck. No calls for help were heard in the rather populous neighborhood where the crime was committed.

The mother deposed that the murdered child had eaten sauerkraut about 2 p.m. and had then set out to visit a friend. At 6 o'clock the friend had advised the child to hurry home before dark. There was a public footpath which she could take and which offered her a short cut.

Bearing in mind the fact that in six hours the stomach could normally complete the work of digestion, then the scarcely digested food found in the stomach indicates that death took place between 6 and 7 o'clock in the evening. The autopsy indicated that the child had been waylaid while on her homeward way.

The condition of the genitals revealed an injury of little consequence on the mucous membrane of the vagina. The hymen was torn about 1 cm. Only slight traces of seminal fluid were found on the child's underclothing. It was clear that an ejaculation could not have taken place into the vagina.

From these considerations I arrived at the conclusion that the criminal's objective had not been coitus, but that he must have inserted a finger smeared with semen under the unopened knickers of the child and thus inserted it, into the vagina. This must have been done with force, for in addition to the scratch at the entrance of the vagina, there was also a trace of bruising of the pelvis.

The stabs in the skin of the breast were all together and parallel. Some of these showed that the knife had been held with the cutting edge of the blade upward. I concluded from the position of these wounds that the criminal had done the stabbing in the breast as the child lay unconscious on the ground, delivering the blows in swift succession. Otherwise one would have expected that the stabbings inflicted on a person still conscious would have been placed irregularly. In addition one would expect to find defensive wounds on the hands.

That my conclusions were correct is borne out by the attack which took place on an elderly woman and of which I learned only later. This attack took place five days before the murder of Rosa Ohliger. I attributed it immediately to the same criminal, an assumption which was to be confirmed by later events.

In April 1929 it seemed that the "monster" had been caught. Following two more attacks on women, an idiot named Strausberg was arrested and confessed to the murders. He had a cleft palate and hare lip. The police were soon convinced that, although he was undoubtedly responsible for the latest attacks, he had not committed the murders. He was sent to a mental home.

For three months, Kürten satisfied himself with affairs with servant girls, whom he attempted to strangle "playfully." (All this emerged at the trial.) On July 30, a prostitute named Emma Gross was found strangled in her room, but it seems that Kürten was not responsible for this.

In August, Kürten strangled a girl he referred to as "Anni," and pushed her body into the river; but the body was not recovered, so it is not certain whether this story was Kürten's invention. Also in late August, a young woman, Frau Mantel, was stabbed in the back as she walked in the western suburb of Lierenfeld, where a fair was being held. Her wound was not serious. In the same month a girl, Anna Goldhausen, and a man, Gustav Kornblum (who was sitting in the park), were stabbed in the back. In neither case were the injuries fatal. Then, on August 24, a double murder horrified the city. The bodies of two children, 5-year-old Gertrude Hamacher and 14-year-old Louise Lenzen, were found on an allotment near their home. Both had been strangled, and then had their throats cut. Neither had been raped.

The same Sunday afternoon, a servant girl named Gertrude Schulte was on her way to a fair at Neuss, and was spoken to by a man who called himself Fritz Baumgart. In a wood he attempted sexual intercourse, and the girl said, "I'd rather die." "Baumgart" replied, "Well die then," and stabbed her several times. But she did not die, and was eventually able to give the police a description of her assailant.

This episode strengthened the police suspicion that there were two maniacs at work, since it seemed unlikely that the same man would kill two children on Saturday, and be out looking for further victims on Sunday.

In September, Kürten attacked three more girls and threw one of them into the river after his attempted strangulation. But these events caused little sensation in comparison with the next murder, which occurred in late September. Another servant girl, Ida Reuter, set out for her Sunday afternoon walk and never returned; the next day she was found in a field near the Rhine meadows. Her head had been battered with a heavy instrument (which turned out to be a hammer), and her handbag and knickers were missing; she was found in a position that indicated sexual assault.

The next case took place a few weeks later, in October. Again the victim was a servant girl, Elizabeth Dorrier. Again she was found (on October 12) near the River Düssel at Grafenberg. Her death was also due to hammer blows on the head, and her hat and coat were missing.

On October 25, a Frau Meurer was accosted by a man in Flingern, who asked, "Aren't you afraid to be out alone?" She woke up in the hospital, her skin having been broken by a hammer, which had not, however, cracked the skull. Later the same evening, in the center of the city, a Frau Wanders, who was seeking an escort, was accosted and knocked unconscious with a hammer, which had struck her four blows.

On November 7, a 5-year-old child, Gertrude Albermann, was missing from her home. Two days later her body was found near a factory yard, among nettles and brick rubble; she had been strangled and stabbed thirty-six times.

At this point Kürten imitated the "Ripper's" tactics by sending a letter to a newspaper, stating where the body could be found, and mentioning the whereabouts of another body. (Kürten had a great admiration for the Ripper, and had studied the case carefully.) A spot in the meadows at Papendelle was mentioned. This letter led to the discovery of the body of Maria Hahn, who had been dead since August. Her body was dug up, after some days of searching, on November 14, and was found to be completely naked. She had twenty stab wounds. Thousands of spectators streamed out to the spot where the body was found.

Berg comments:

No other crime is more significant for an understanding of the personality of Kürten than this. Kürten himself has told about it in all its details, and even confessed to the examining magistrate the sexual motive. Here is his statement:

"On the 8th of August, 1929, I was strolling in the Zoo district. I hadn't any intention of committing any offense on a girl at the time. On the Hansaplatz a girl was sitting on a bench. She accosted me. I sat down beside her and we talked pleasantly together and made a date for an excursion to the Neanderthal the next Sunday. On Sunday, punctually at 1:30 in the afternoon, I found myself in the Hansaplatz where the girl was already waiting. We went to the Neanderthal, visited a beer garden and then on to the Stinter mill. We stayed there for three hours, drank a glass of red wine each. There also I bought her a slab of chocolate. Towards 7 o'clock we went to Erkrath where we had supper with beer. We then strolled past the house of the Morps, and along by the river. Here we decided to have sexual intercourse. After sexual intercourse we left the bank of the river and went into the meadow. Here I decided to kill her. I led Hahn to a big bush near a ditch and there we settled down. It was half-past nine. Suddenly I strangled her until she became unconscious, but she came to herself quickly again. Again I strangled her. After a bit I stabbed her in the throat with the scissors. She lost a lot of blood but regained consciousness, repeatedly asking me in a feeble voice to spare her life. I stabbed her in the breast a blow that probably pierced the heart. I then gave her repeated stabs in the breast and head. The process of dying probably took an hour. I let the body roll into the ditch and threw branches over it. Then I crossed the meadow and came to the road that runs from Morp-Papendell highway. I had taken the handbag of Hahn with me. From it I took the watch of the dead girl. I made a gift of it to somebody later on. The bag with the keys I threw into an oatfield.

"When I got home my wife was already in bed. Next morning we had a row, because she was suspicious about the night before. She became so excited about it that I made up my mind that I would have to find some way of seeing that the body of Hahn wasn't discovered, otherwise my wife would connect the blood stains on my clothes with it. So I went again on Monday after finishing work to the scene of the crime and pondered where I could bury the body. I went back to the flat and fetched a shovel, inventing an excuse to give my wife. Near the scene of the crime, in the corner of the wood, I dug a deep hole in a fallow field, and carried the body along the footpath, avoiding the oatfield. By the hole I put the body down. I got into the hole and dragged the body down to me. Here I laid it on its back as one buries a body. A shoe had slipped off when the body was dragged down and I laid it beside it. Then I filled the hole. During the whole of this funeral ceremony a sentimental feeling possessed me. I caressed the hair and the first shovelful of earth I strewed thinly and gently on the body. I stamped the earth down and smoothed the soil as it was before. As my shirt had become bloody in carrying the body I took it off and washed it in the river and put it on again still wet. I hid the shovel near the river, then I went home and arrived there about 6 o'clock. My wife began reproaching me, asked me where I had been wandering all the night. I had cleaned my shoes thoroughly in the grass, using the cleaning rag which I always carried with me. I then drank coffee and went to work in the same clothes. After I had put the body of Hahn in the grave I removed her wristwatch. Four weeks later I gave the watch to Kaete W . . . W . . . lives in the same house where I live. She often came into my room and we repeatedly had sexual intercourse."

(The witness W . . . vehemently denied this assertion. I found, as a matter of fact, that she was a virgin with enlarged introitus of the vagina.)

The shovel was in fact found at the place indicated. Frau Kürten confirms the hour at which her husband left her on the 12th of August, namely, about 11 o'clock p.m., when he gave as explanation that he was on night work. Between 5 and 6 o'clock he had come back with dirty shoes and blood on his clothes. Later Kürten admitted that he had not given the wristwatch to the witness W . . . The first assertion that he had done so was an act of vengeance for the trouble she had given him and the part she had taken in bringing about his capture.

The murders were, of course, causing a panic in the Düsseldorf area that can only be compared to that caused by the Ripper in 1888 or by the Ratfcliffe Highway murderer in 1811. Inspector Gennat, of the Berlin police, was assigned to the case. He had once had to follow up eight hundred clues to track down a murderer, and was noted for his thoroughness.

The German underworld was also greatly disturbed by the murders (as Fritz Lang showed in his film version of the crimes, *M*), and police raids made the criminals of the Rhine as anxious as the general public to see the murderer taken.

A tailor's dummy, dressed in Dorrier's clothes, was taken around the dance halls of Düsseldorf, in the hope that one of the dancers would recognize the clothes and remember the girl's companion on the day of her death.

But although no one knew it, the murders had come to an end, although the attacks would continue for six months more. There had been eight murders in ten months, and fourteen attacks.

In 1929, there were several attacks on girls walking alone, and Kürten also continued playfully to strangle his girl-friends, some of whom did not seem to object to the treatment. (Evidence of these girls figures largely in the trial.)

Let Berg tell the story of Kürten's capture:

Suddenly all these uncertainties and perplexities were ended by the capture of the criminal and his confession. This totally unforeseen outcome was not due to the efforts of the police, but to a sheer coincidence, coupled with the criminal's lack of caution.

It was the famous Butlies affair which resulted in the discovery. For that reason I propose to describe it here, and do so in Kürten's own words.

"On the 14th of May, 1930, I saw a man accost a young girl at the railway station and go off with her. Out of curiosity I followed the couple along the Graf-Adolf-strasse, the Karlstrasse, Klosterstrasse, Kölner Strasse, Stoffeler Strasse to the Volksgarten. When the man wanted to go into the dark park with the girl, she resisted him. I seized the opportunity to approach the couple.

"I asked him what he meant to do with the girl. He replied that the girl had no lodging and that he proposed to take her to his sister. At this point the girl asked me whether the Achenbachstrasse was in that neighborhood—it was there the man's sister was supposed to live. When I assured her very convincingly that the street was in an entirely different neighborhood, she stepped to my side, and the man made off very quickly. We returned. The girl told me that she was out of work and had nowhere to go. She agreed to come with me to

THE KILLERS AMONG US BOOK II   129

my room in the Mettmanner Strasse 71. Round about 11 o'clock we got to my room which is on the third floor. Then she suddenly said she didn't want any sexual intercourse and asked me whether I couldn't find her some other place to sleep. I agreed. We went by tram to Worringerplatz and on towards the Grafenberger Wald, going along the Wolfschlucht until we came to the last of the houses. Here I seized Butlies with one hand by the neck, pressing her head back very hard and kissing her. I asked her to let me have her. I thought that under the circumstances she would agree, and my opinion was right. Afterwards I asked whether I had hurt her, which she denied. I wanted to take her back to the tram, but I did not accompany her right to it because I was afraid that she might inform the police officer who was standing there. I had no intention of killing Butlies. She had offered no resistance. We had sexual intercourse standing, after I had pulled down her knickers. There was another reason why I could not do anything to her—I had been seen by a friend in the tram. I did not think that Butlies would be able to find her way back again to my apartment in the rather obscure Mettmanner Strasse. So much the more was I surprised when on Wednesday, the 21st of May, I saw Butlies again in my house."

Butlies supplements this statement thus:

On the 14th of May she had come from Cologne to Düsseldorf. There on the railway station she got into contact with a "Frau Brückner," and made an appointment with her for 8 o'clock in the evening of that day. She had then waited in vain on the railway station for the woman and in the end had been accosted by a man who wanted to put her up.

Her statement corroborates Kürten's. After her adventure Butlies took the tram from Grafenberger Wald

back to the town. Then she walked the streets of Düsseldorf. At last she went to the *Gertrudishaus,* where she
told the Sisters about the attack. On the 17th of May she
wrote to her new acquaintance, Frau Brückner, in Düsseldorf—Bilker Allee—a letter in which she hinted that
she had fallen into the hands of a murderer. The recipi-
ent of the letter, Frau Brügmann, suspected the connection with the Düsseldorf murderer, and took the letter to
the criminal police department. The writer of the letter
was interrogated and eventually succeeded in finding
the house of the unknown man. On her own account she
had already made inquiries in different houses in the
Mettmanner Strasse for a man of a certain type and, at
last, she had heard from the inhabitants of No. 71 that a
crying girl had once come in the same way asking for a
man of the same description. Her description fitted
Peter Kürten, who lodged there. That was on the 21st of
May.

Kürten continues his Narrative

"On Wednesday, the 21st of May, I happened to look
over the bannisters and saw Butlies and recognized her.
She can be recognized easily. She has very fair hair, is
slant-eyed and bow-legged. She left the house again. I
saw her stand in the entrance door and speak to the
landlady. Then in the afternoon she came again to the
house, this time coming up to our floor. She entered the
flat of the Wimmers and she saw me. She was startled. I
think it is likely that she recognized me then. I knew
what would happen after that!

"That same evening I fetched my wife from the place
where she worked: 'I must get out of the flat,' I said. I
explained the Butlies case to her. But I only mentioned
the attempt at sexual intercourse, saying that as it could
be called 'rape', along with my previous convictions, it

was enough to get me fifteen years' penal servitude. Therefore I had to get out. I changed. Throughout the night I walked about. On Thursday, the 22nd of May, I saw my wife in the morning in the flat. I fetched my things away in a bag and rented a room in the Adlerstrasse. I slept quietly until Friday morning."

The events of this Friday were described to me by Kürten in writing.

"It was at nine in the morning when I went to my flat. Shortly before I reached No. 71 two men came out of it. I found out afterwards they were detectives. I thought right away that they were that. When I went into the flat my wife was still there. When I asked her why she had not gone to work to-day she answered: 'I did, but I was taken away from it by two detectives who brought me home.' Both these men had searched the place and a few moments before they had gone down the staircase. Then my wife asked me to leave the house saying she did not want me to be arrested there. I did as she asked and later met her—she had gone back to the place where she was employed. I then asked her to come with me for a little while. Two days before I had told her about the Butlies affair. To-day, the 23rd, in the morning, I told my wife that I was also responsible for the Schulte affair, adding my usual remark that it would mean at least ten years' or more separation for us— probably for ever. At that my wife was inconsolable. She spoke of age, unemployment, lack of means and starvation in old age. When the lunch hour approached I had not even then succeeded in calming my wife down. She raved that I should take my life. Then she would do the same, since her future was completely without hope. Then in the late afternoon I told my wife that I could help her. That I could still do something for her. I told her that I was the Düsseldorf murderer. Of course, she didn't think it possible and didn't want to believe it. But then I disclosed everything to her, naming myself the murderer in each case. When she asked me how this could help her, I hinted that a high reward had been offered for the discovery as well as for the capture of the criminal; that she could get hold of that reward, or at least some part of it, if she would report my confession and denounce me to the police. Of course, it wasn't easy for me to convince her that this ought not to be considered as treason, but that, on the contrary, she was doing a good deed to humanity as well as to justice. It was not until late in the evening that she promised me to carry out my request, and also that she would not commit suicide. I then accompanied her almost to the door. It was 11 o'clock when we separated. Back in my lodging I went to bed and fell asleep at once. What happened the next morning, the 24th of May, is known.

"First a bath, then several times around the neighborhood of the Kortzingens' flat [Kürten had planned a robbery here]. Lunch, a hair-cut, and then, at 3 o'clock I met my wife according to the arrangement and there the arrest took place. As a matter of fact, my wife had carried out my order a bit too quickly for me. I want to point out again that I never collapsed on the 23rd or 24th of May, but kept steadily before me my purpose to the very end."

Thus Kürten. I now contrast his statement with that of his wife:

"In the morning, after the detectives had brought me from the place where I work, my husband came to the flat. 'You must have done something awful!' I said. 'Yes,' he replied. 'I did it. I did everything.' Then, with that he left the flat. We then met by arrangement at

11:30 in the morning in the Hofgarten. We had dinner in a restaurant in the Duisberger Strasse. I could not eat anything, but he ate up the lot, my portion, too.

"At 2 o'clock we were walking over the Rhine Bridge back and forwards. In the late afternoon I asked him what he meant with his words: 'I have done everything.' 'If you promise solemnly that you won't give me away I'll tell you something,' he said. I promised. 'I have done everything that has happened here in Düsseldorf!' 'What do you mean by that?' I asked. 'Everything—the murders and the attacks.' 'What, those innocent children, too?' I asked. 'Yes,' he said. 'Why did you do that?' I asked him. 'I don't know myself,' he replied, 'it just came over me.'

"Then all the big cases were talked over, including that of Mülheim. When I got terribly excited about it all, he said, 'I've done something very silly. I ought not to have told you.' That afternoon Kürten was very depressed and in a way I had never seen before. He told me that he had not cried once in his whole life, but yesterday evening, when he was alone, he had cried bitterly. In the afternoon while we spoke only about the fact that the detectives were after him, he was quiet and self-possessed, But towards the evening when I wanted to go home he was as I have never seen him in his life before. He was very cast down. He could not look into my eyes. All the indifference had disappeared. He burst out with it all, telling of the murders and the attacks as if some power forced him to it. I thought he had gone crazy. Nothing had been said about any reward."

Who could not understand Frau Kürten—who would reproach her that she was not able to carry alone the weight of this ghastly secret—but that she gave it away to the police when pressed by them?

She had a last meeting with her husband near the Rochus Church, for the following day, the 24th.

That, too, the woman, who was quite distraught, reported to the police. The church square was quietly surrounded and Kürten was arrested as he walked towards his wife. He was quite composed. Subsequently, he often told me how he smilingly calmed the detective who advanced excitedly towards him, the revolver leveled at him.

When Kürten was questioned by the police he not only told of the attacks of 1929, but he gave also an account of a long chain of crimes without being questioned. For reasons to which I will return presently he lengthened this chain with some imaginary links, but he soon brought it back again to the facts.

TABLE I
THE SEQUENCE OF THE CRIMES
ACCORDING TO KÜRTEN'S OWN STATEMENT

Born 1883 in Köln-Mülheim. Passed his childhood there. Left for Düsseldorf 1894; 1897 apprenticed as a molder. In 1899 first convicted for theft.

TABLE OF OFFENSES

Nov. 1899	Attempted strangulation	18-year-old girl unknown

FROM 1900 TO 1904 IN PRISON

1904	Arson	Barn after harvest
1904	Arson	Hay loft
1904	Arson	Two hay-ricks

1905 TO 1913 IN PRISON

1913	Attempted strangulation	Margarete Schäfer
1913	Murder by strangulation and throat-cutting	Christine Klein, Mülheim
1913	Axe blow	Unknown man
1913	Axe blow	Unknown woman
1913	Axe blow attempt	Hermes, sleeping girl
1913	Strangulation	Gertrud Franken
1913	Arson	Hay-rick and hay wagon

1913 TO 1921 IN PRISON

1921	Strangulation	War widow
1925	Strangulation	Tiede
1925	Strangulation	Mech
1925	Strangulation	Kiefer
1926	Strangulation	Wack
1927	Arson	Three hay-ricks
1927	Arson	Shock of sheaves
1927	Arson	Two barns
1927	Attempted strangulation	Anni Ist
1927	Arson	Two barns
1927	Arson	Plantation
1928	Arson	Barn
1928	Arson	Farmyard
1928	Arson	Shock of sheaves (twice)
1928	Arson	Hay-rick
1928	Arson	Hay wagon
1928	Arson	House
1928	Arson	House
1928	Arson	Shed

1928	Arson	Forest fire
1928	Arson	Sheds
1929	Arson	Stacks
1929	Arson	Barns, sheds, stacks, (ten cases)

1929

Feb 3	Attack with scissors	Frau Kühn
Feb. 13	Stabbed and killed	Rudolf Scheer
Mar. 8	Strangled and stabbed after death	Child—Rose Ohliger
March	Attempted strangulation	Edit Boukorn
July	Attempted strangulation	Maria Witt
July	Attempted strangulation	Maria Mass
July	Attempted strangulation	Unknown domestic servant
August	Strangled and stabbed to death	Maria Hahn
August	Strangled and drowned	"Anni," a housemaid
August	Stabbed with dagger	Anna Goldhausen
August	Stabbed with dagger	Frau Mantel
August	Stabbed with dagger	Kornblum
August	Strangled and throat cut	Child—Hamacher
August	Strangled and stabbed	Child—Lenzen
August	Stabbed with dagger	Gertrud Schulte
August	Attempted strangulation and thrown into river	Heer
Sept.	Blow with tool	Rückl
Sept.	Attempted strangulation	Maria Rad
Sept.	Killed by hammer blows	Ida Reuter
October	Killed by hammer blows	Elisabeth Dörrier
October	Attack with hammer	Frau Meurer
October	Attack with hammer	Frau Wanders

| November | Strangled and stabbed with scissors | Child—Albermann |

1930

February	Attempted strangulation	Hilde
March	Attempted strangulation	Maria del Sant
March	Attempted strangulation	Irma
April	Attempted strangulation	Sibille
April	Attempted strangulation	Unknown girl from Herne
April	Attempted strangulation	Young woman, Hau
April	Attacks	Several girls
April	Attack with hammer	Charlotte Ulrich
May	Attempted strangulation	Maria Butlies
May	Attempted murder	Gertrud Bell

The way in which Kürten enumerated all his offences, tabulated here in a sequence chronologically accurate, and the way in which he dictated it with every detail, is quite extraordinary. He was not accused of these crimes one by one, but reeled off on his own account, beginning with No. 1 and ending with No. 79, every single case, dictating them, in fact, to the stenographer and even showing enjoyment at the horrified faces of the many police officers who listened to his recital, day by day.

Kürten was born in Köln-Mulheim in 1883, the son of a molder, a violent man, boastful and given to drunkenness. The family of thirteen were very poor, and lived for a time in a single room. The environment was heavily charged with sex. According to Kürten, all his sisters were oversexed, and one made sexual advances to him. Kürten was apparently not attracted by her, but he attempted incest with another sister—a sister whom his father attempted to rape, and on whose account the molder served a term in prison. Kürten senior was in the habit of forcing his wife to have intercourse when he came home drunk, and Kürten frequently witnessed his mother being "raped." At the age of 8 he ran away from home for a short time, sleeping in furniture vans. He also admitted to Berg that his taste for sadism had first been awakened by a sadistic dog-catcher who lived in the same house, and who taught Kürten to masturbate the dogs. Kürten often watched him torturing the dogs.

Kürten was the third of thirteen children. His grandfather had served sentences for theft, and cases of delirium tremens, feeble-mindedness and paralysis abound in his family connexions on his father's side. (His mother's side of the family were normal and hard-working people.)

When Kürten was 12, the family moved to Düsseldorf. But according to his own confession, he had already committed his first murder. At the age of 9, he pushed a boy off a raft on the banks of the Rhine, and when another boy dived in to help the first one, he managed to push him under the raft, so that both were drowned.

In his early teens he ran away from home again and lived as a vagabond and robber—attacking mostly girls and women. His adolescent sexuality was abnormal. He attempted intercourse with schoolgirls and with his sister, and masturbated excessively. From his thirteenth year onward he practiced bestiality with sheep, pigs and goats. He discovered that he received a powerful sexual sensation when having intercourse with a sheep in the Düsseldorf meadows and stabbing it simultaneously. He did this many times between his thirteenth and sixteenth years. At 16 he became an apprentice molder, and received much ill-treatment; finally he stole money and ran away to Coblenz. There he lived with a prostitute who allowed him to ill-treat her. Finally, he was arrested for theft, and received the first of the seventeen sentences that were to take up twenty-seven years of his life. He was then 15. Released from prison two years later in 1899, he discovered that his mother was divorced from his father, and so decided to keep living a vagrant life. He lived with a prostitute of twice his age who enjoyed being maltreated, and this developed his sadistic propensities further.

In November 1899, according to Kürten's own account, he committed what he supposed to be his first adult murder: strangling a girl while having sexual intercourse with her, he thought she had died, and left her in the Grafenberger Wald. But no body was reported in that month, so it seems likely that the girl woke up and went home, saying nothing to anyone.

His first prison period, according to himself, made a real criminal of him; in the cells at the Berger Gate he met hardened criminals, and wanted to rival them. He had himself tattooed.

He served two brief sentences about 1900 for minor fraud, and then attempted to shoot a girl with a rifle, and was given two more years. Together with another sentence for theft, this brought his period of jail up to 1904. During this time, Kürten admitted, he used to dream of revenge, and found that his fantasies of killing excited him sexually. He deliberately committed minor infringements of prison regulations to get solitary confinement, so that he could indulge these fantasies freely. On his release he was called up as a conscript to Metz, but soon deserted. He also committed his first cases of arson, setting fire to barns and hay-ricks. The sight of fire caused him sexual excitement, and he also hoped that tramps might be sleeping in the hay. In 1905 he received seven years in jail for theft (he had been living with another woman who also lived by thieving). He served the term in Münster prison, and had an attack of "prison psychosis," rolling himself in a bundle of silk and lying under the table, claiming to be a silkworm. He also claimed later that he was able to poison some prisoners in the prison hospital. He nursed fantasies of revenge on society, and dreamed of "compensatory justice"—that is, that he could get his own back on his tormentors by tormenting someone who was completely innocent. This kind of illogicality is typical of murderers and psychopaths.

As soon as he was released from prison in 1912, he maltreated a servant girl during intercourse, and was soon back in prison for discharging fire arms in a restaurant when he tried to accost a woman and was interrupted by the waiter. For this he received a year in jail.

On May 25, 1913 he committed his first sexual murder. He had become a specialist in robbing business premises. He entered a pub in the Wolfstrasse, Köln-Mulheim, on an evening when the family were out at a fair. In one of the bedrooms he found 13-year-old Christine Klein asleep. He strangled her, cut her throat with a penknife, and penetrated her sexual organs with his fingers. He dropped a handkerchief with his initials on it. But it happened that the child's father was called Peter Klein, and his brother Otto had quarreled with him on the night of the murder and threatened to do something that Peter "would remember all his life." Otto Klein was arrested and tried, but released for lack of evidence. Public opinion was against him, and he was killed in the war, still under the shadow of the murder. Kürten later claimed that it was the memory of his sufferings in jail that prompted the murder. A few weeks after this crime, Kürten was again about to attack a sleeping girl when someone woke up and frightened him off. He also attacked an unknown man and an unknown woman with a hatchet, securing sexual orgasms by knocking them unconscious and seeing their blood. (Since the sadistic dog-catcher, blood had always been Kürten's major sexual stimulant.) He also burned another hay wagon, and attempted to strangle two women. Then, luckily, he spent the next eight years in prison.

In 1921 Kürten returned to Altenberg, declaring that he had been a prisoner of war in Russia. Here he met the woman who became his wife, at the home of his sister. She had had her own misfortunes; she had been engaged to a gardener for eight years and had been his mistress; then he refused to marry her and she shot him. For this she served a five-year jail sentence. When Kürten met her she was a rawboned, broad-shouldered, prematurely aged woman. It is difficult to know why Kürten was attracted by her; perhaps because she seemed "solid" and reliable, or perhaps because she had suffered. Until the end of his life, ten years later, she continued to be the only human being for whom he felt normal feelings of affection and attachment. At first, she refused to marry him, but when Kürten threatened to murder her, she consented. Then, for two years, he lived a fairly respectable life, working as a molder in Altenberg, and becoming active in trade union circles and in a political club. But his sadistic activities persisted and he was twice charged with maltreating servant girls. In 1925 he returned to Düsseldorf, and was delighted that the sunset was blood-red on the evening of his return. Then began Düsseldorf's "Reign of Terror." But it began quietly enough. Like many maniacs of a similar type, Kürten began with a few widely spaced attacks; these became steadily more frequent and more violent, until, in the year 1929, they finally reached a climax. Between 1925 and 1928 Kürten admitted four cases of attempted strangulation of women, and seventeen cases of arson. On two occasions he set houses on fire.

The year 1929 began with six more cases of arson of barns

and stacks. Then, on February 3, a Frau Kuhn was walking home late at night when she was suddenly attacked by a man with a knife. She received twenty-four stab wounds, and was in the hospital for many months.

A few days later, on February 13, a 45-year-old mechanic named Scheer was found dead in the roadway in Flingern; he had been drunk when attacked, and had been stabbed twenty times.

On March 9, workmen discovered the body of 8-year-old Rose Ohliger lying behind a fence on a building site. She had been stabbed thirteen times; there had been some attempt at sexual assault, and an attempt to burn the body with paraffin.

And so began the series of murders that made the "monster of Düsseldorf" as notorious as Jack the Ripper, and which finally ended with his arrest on May 24, 1930.

It is not surprising that Kürten was not an obvious suspect. Even after his arrest, most of his neighbors and work mates considered that it was a mistake. He was known as a quiet, well-behaved man, a dandy in his dress, intelligent, and a good worker.

Kürten made a full confession of the murders, although he later withdrew it. Gertrude Schulte picked him out of a number of men paraded in front of her. Professor Berg was introduced to Kürten, and remarked that Kürten proved to be an intelligent truthful man, interested in his own case, and anxious to help the psychiatrist to understand the strange urges that had led to his crimes.

Some of the things Kürten revealed to Berg are terrifying. On one occasion when he could not find a victim in the Hofgarten, he seized a sleeping swan, cut off its head, and drank the blood. The swan was found the next morning. On another occasion, he saw a horse involved in a street accident, and had an orgasm. At first he tried to convince Berg that he killed for "revenge on society," but was later frank in admitting the sexual origin of his crimes. The horror caused by his crimes gave him deep satisfaction. It was for this reason that he had gone back to the body of Rose Ohliger many hours after he had killed her, and poured paraffin on the body. Later still, he had lingered on the edge of the crowd, and had an orgasm provoked by the horror of the spectators.

The following is typical of Kürten's statements about his attacks:

> In March 1930, I went out with my scissors. At the station a girl spoke to me. I took her to have a glass of beer, and we then walked towards the Grafenberg woods. She said her name was Irma. She was about 22. Near the middle of the woods, I seized her by the throat and I held on for a bit. She struggled violently, and screamed. I threw her down the ravine that runs down to the Wolf's Glen and went away.

Many young women gave evidence of similar experiences. One servant girl whom Kürten attempted to strangle complained that he was rough. He told her "that was what love was." She met him on several occasions after this! Another believed he was a single man and was going to marry her; one day she inquired at his home and was told he was married; this experience made her particularly bitter against Kürten. On another occasion, Kürten's wife caught him out with a woman and slapped her face. Kürten brushed her cheek with a rose and turned and walked off, leaving the two women together.

Kürten's wife never suspected his perversions; he had sexual intercourse with her periodically, but admitted that he had to imagine sadistic violence in order to go through with the love-making.

With respect to his crimes, Kürten's memory was of astonishing accuracy; seventeen years after the murder of Christine Klein, he was able to describe her bedroom in detail. On other points, his memory was average; it was obvious that he took such intense pleasure in his crimes that every detail remained in his mind. He admitted to dwelling on them afterwards and having sexual orgasms as he recalled their details. He also told Berg that he used to walk through the streets of Düsseldorf and daydream of blowing up the whole city with dynamite. Hitler lost a talented lieutenant in Kürten, one who might have outshone Eichmann or Heydrich in mass murder.

The Hahn case revealed a curious aspect of Kürten's sadism—an element of necrophilia. The naked body had been sexually assaulted, both vaginally and anally; leaves and earthmold were found in the anus. Kürten admitted how, after killing her, he had buried her roughly. Later he decided to alter the location of her grave; he also had an idea that it would be exciting to crucify her body on two trees and leave it to be found. However, the body was too heavy; nevertheless, Kürten changed the location of the grave, and admitted to kissing and fondling the victim when he had dug her up. He returned often to the site of the grave and masturbated on it.

And yet one of Kürten's favorite dream fantasies was of saving Düsseldorf from the "monster," and having torchlight processions in his honor. He would be nominated police commissioner for his service. (Perhaps Kürten had read the life of Vidocq.)

Kürten's trial opened on April 13, 1931. In accordance with the German custom, it took place in front of three judges. Kürten's counsel was Dr. Wehner, a young lawyer; the prosecution was led by the police prosecutor, Dr. Jansen. Dr. Jansen asked several times that the press and public be excluded—no doubt because he wanted to reveal evidence

THE KILLERS AMONG US BOOK II   145

that would leave no room for any but the death sentence—but his pleas were unsuccessful. Professor Berg gave evidence, describing Kürten as a "king of sexual perverts." Professor Sioli gave psychiatric evidence for the prosecution, and Professor Rather for the defense. The defense was of insanity at the time of the murders. The case closed on April 23rd. Kürten's final remarks are of some interest:

> As I now see the crimes committed by me, they are so ghastly that I do not want to attempt any sort of excuse for them. Still, I feel some bitterness when I think of the physician and the lady physician in Stuttgart who have been encouraged by a section of the community to murder and who have stained their hands with human blood to the extent of fifteen hundred murders.[1] I do not want to accuse, all I want to do is to let you see what passes in my soul. I cannot refrain from reproaching you, Professor Sioli, for saying that the conditions of my home were not the decisive factor. On the contrary, you may well assume that youthful surroundings are decisive for the development of character. With silent longing I have sometimes in my early days glimpsed other families and asked myself why it could not be like that with us.
>
> I contradict the Chief Public Prosecutor when he asserts that it was out of cowardice that I revoked my confession. The very day that I opened up to my wife I well knew the consequences of the confession; I felt liberated in a certain way and I had the firm intention of sticking to my confession so that I could do a last good turn to my wife. But the real reason was that there arrives for every criminal that moment beyond which he cannot go. And I was in due course subject to this psy-

[1] A reference to the case of certain abortionists

chic collapse. As I have related already, I followed the reports in the newspapers then and, of course, later, very thoroughly. I convinced myself that on the whole the newspaper reports had been moderate. I may say that I used to intoxicate myself with the sensational press, it was the poison which must bear part of the responsibility of my poisoned life. By being moderate now, it has done a great deal to prevent the public from being poisoned. I feel urged to make one more statement: some victims made it rather easy for me to overpower them.

I do not want to forget to mention what I frequently said before—that I detest the crimes and feel deep sorrow for the relatives. I even dare to ask those relatives to forgive me, as far as that may be possible for them. Furthermore, I want to point out emphatically that, contrary to the version of the Chief Public Prosecutor, I never tortured a victim. I do not attempt to excuse my crimes. I have already pointed out that I am prepared to bear the consequences of my misdeeds. I hope that thus I will atone for a large part of what I have done.

Although I can suffer capital punishment only once, you may rest assured that it is one of the many unknown tortures to endure the time before the execution of the sentence, and dozens of times I have lived through the moment of the execution. And when you consider this and recognize my goodwill to atone for all my crimes. I should think that the terrible desire for revenge and hatred against me cannot endure. And I want to ask you to forgive me.

The jury was out for an hour and a half, and Kürten was sentenced to death nine times for murder.

For a while there seemed some hope that Kürten might not suffer the death penalty, which had not been carried out since a man named Böttcher had been executed in 1928 for the murder of a woman and a child in a wood near Berlin. It is indicative of the extreme liberalism in Germany in the early 1930s that there was something of a storm at the death penalty on Kürten, and the German Humanitarian League protested. Kürten appealed, but the appeal was rejected. Kürten himself was calm and well-behaved. He was bombarded with letters, love letters and letters describing sadistic punishments arriving in equal quantities. Many people asked for his autograph. (A girl who had been assaulted by Kürten when he was 16 described how he stood one day in front of the waxworks of murderers and burglars and said, "One day I shall be as famous as they are.")

He was executed at six o'clock on the morning of July 2nd, 1931. He enjoyed his last meal—of Wiener schnitzel, chips, and white wine—so much that he asked for it again. He told Berg that his one hope was that he would hear the sound of his own blood running into the basket, which would give him intense pleasure. (He also admitted to wanting to throttle Berg's stenographer because of her slim, white throat.) He was guillotined, and seemed cheerful and unconcerned at the last.

4

MASS MURDER IN AMERICA, 1890–1920

THE MOST NOTABLE AMEIRCAN MULTIPLE MURDERER OF THE nineteenth century was a man named Herman Webster Mudgett, who (understandably) preferred to call himself Harry Howard Holmes. He belongs to the history of mass murder, but the fact that many of his murders were motivated by sex, and that he was an obsessive seducer, warrants a brief description of his career in this volume. Like so many conmen—Landru, Petiot, Heath, Haigh—Holmes seems to have been one of those born crooks who, from the beginning, looked for a way to do down his fellow human beings. He provides a powerful argument for the belief that certain people are just born bad—in fact, downright rotten. Born in 1860 in Gilmanton, New Hampshire, son of a postmaster, he studied medicine, and was practicing his first swindle in his early twenties—involving the faked death of a patient and the theft of a corpse. When he abandoned his wife and child to move to Chicago in 1886, he soon married a girl from a wealthy family and tried forging the signature of a rich uncle. Then he became the assistant of a Mrs. Holden, who ran a drugstore; within three years she had vanished, and

Holmes was the new owner. He did so well that he built himself a large boarding house opposite the store—which has been christened "Murder Castle" and "Nightmare House." It had chutes leading from most rooms to the basement—where there was a large furnace—and gas pipes so arranged that he could flood any room with gas. It is not known how many "guests" vanished during the Chicago World's Fair of 1893, but it probably ran into double figures. Meanwhile, he had seduced the wife of a jeweler named Conner who rented space in the drugstore; when Conner moved out, both the wife, Julia, and her 18-year-old sister Gertie became his mistresses. Then Gertie became pregnant, and vanished. So did a pretty 16-year-old girl named Emily Van Tassell, who often came into the shop with her mother. If, as seems probable, Holmes killed her in order to posses her, then he certainly qualifies as a sex-killer. When Julia objected to Holmes's new secretary, Emily Cigrand, Julia and her daughter disappeared. Soon after that, so did Emily Cigrand. The following year, so did another mistress—Minnie Williams—and her sister Nannie.

After the World's Fair was over, Holmes was hoist with his own petard when he fell in love with a girl called Georgiana Yoke and married her. In jail for fraud, Holmes met a famous train robber called Marion Hedgepeth, and asked his advice on acquiring a crooked lawyer, offering to cut him in on an insurance fraud.

The "fraud" was actually planned as a mass murder of a family of seven. A fellow crook named Pitezel was supposed to die in a laboratory explosion; Holmes would substitute a corpse bought from a medical school, and would share Pitezel's insurance money with Pitezel's wife. In fact, Pitezel's death was all too real, as was that of three of Pitezel's children who were allowed by their mother to accompany Holmes on a flight around various cities in America and Canada.

Marion Hedgepeth, angered by Holmes's failure to pay him his share of the insurance money, told his story to the insurance company and Holmes was arrested before he could complete the murder plan; a policeman named Geyer followed Holmes's trail around the country and located the remains of the three children—two daughters, aged 11 and 15, and a 9-year-old boy. Holmes was found guilty, and wrote a confession in which he admitted twenty-seven murders; he was hanged in 1895, choking slowly to death on the end of a rope that had been tied by an inefficient hangman.

Was Holmes a serial killer in the modern sense of the word? If we are speaking of obsessive sex killers like Jack the Ripper and the Boston Strangler, the answer is probably no. But if we mean a man who is in the grip of a sexual fever, and who kills repeatedly and obsessively, then the answer must be yes. We are once again confronting the problem of the dividing line between the serial killer—whose motive is rape—and the mass murderer, who kills for gain. There are some cases of mass murder—like Joseph Smith, the "Brides in the Bath" killer, or Marcel Petiot, the French doctor who offered to help Jewish refugees to escape and then killed them for their money—where there can be no possible doubt that the motive was simply financial gain. But in Holmes, as in Landru, we confront a man in whom the criminal urge and the sexual urge are so closely linked that it is impossible to separate them. Crime itself has become sexualized.

The first decade of the twentieth century was remarkable for the detection of two "bluebeard" killers, one male, one female.

Johann Hoch—born Schmidt—was a native of Horweiler,

Germany; born in 1860, he was destined for the ministry—his father and two brothers were already in the church. In 1887 he abandoned his wife and three children and sailed for America. In Wheeling, West Virginia, he opened a saloon, and married a widow named Caroline Hoch. The minister who performed the ceremony saw Hoch giving his wife some white powder, and hours later she died in agony. Hoch quickly sold the house, claimed on his wife's insurance policy, then faked a suicide by leaving his clothes on a riverbank; after this he disappeared. Later in the same year he married two more women, Martha Steinbucher and Mary Rankin; the first also died in agony, but the second was luckier: Hoch only deserted her.

During the course of the next eight years he married an unknown number of women—ten is a conservative estimate—abandoning some and burying others.

In December 1904, Hoch (as he now called himself) advertised in a Chicago newspaper published in German, claiming to be a wealthy widower in search of a wife. Soon he married a woman named Marie Walcker, who owned a sweet shop. His wife presented him with her entire savings. But she also made the mistake of mentioning that her sister, Mrs. Julia Fischer, also had $800 or so deposited in a savings bank. It sealed her fate. A week later she became seriously ill, and the doctor diagnosed the trouble as nephritis. Mrs. Fischer was sent for to nurse her sister, and soon Hoch was flirting with her. Mrs. Walcker died on January 12, 1905, and Hoch immediately proposed to her sister. Julia protested that it was too soon to think of such things, but nevertheless married him three days later.

They moved to a flat in Wells Street, but there Hoch was upset to learn that he was being denounced as a murderer and a swindler by one of the tenants—a friend of his late bride, and the woman who had drafted the letter in reply to Hoch's advertisement. While Julia was trying to placate this lady, Hoch vanished, taking $750 he had borrowed from Julia.

Julia notified the Chicago police. The man who was placed in charge of the case, Inspector George Shippy, already had some knowledge of Hoch—in fact, had been instrumental in jailing him six years earlier. Shippy had investigated Hoch on a charge of swindling a furniture dealer by selling furniture that was on hire-purchase, and Hoch had received a twelve-month sentence. The clergyman who had seen Hoch slip a white powder into the food of Caroline Hoch, the Rev. Hermann Haas, learned that Hoch was in jail, and contacted Shippy to tell him of his suspicions. Shippy had Mrs. Hoch's body exhumed, but it proved that Hoch had been too clever for him. The vital organs (presumably the stomach and liver) were missing. Shippy investigated Hoch and learned of a trail of abandoned wives from New York to San Francisco. Unfortunately, Hoch had already been released from jail and had vanished.

Shippy immediately requested that the body of Marie Walcker should be exhumed. The post-mortem revealed 7.6 grains of arsenic in the stomach, and 1.25 in the liver. Shippy handed over a picture of Hoch to the press, and requested nationwide publicity.

This quickly produced results. A Mrs. Catherine Kimmerle, who ran a boarding house in West Forty-seventh Street in New York, recognized the photograph as that of a recently arrived boarder named Bartella, who had proposed to her within twenty minutes of entering the house. His ardent manner had frightened her and she had declined.

"Bartella" was quickly arrested, and admitted that he was Hoch. A fountain pen in his possession proved to contain arsenic—which Hoch declared he had bought to commit suicide. The New York police returned him to Chicago.

There Shippy was waiting for him, with a list of a dozen

women whom he had married since 1896, five of whom had died soon after the marriage. Five wives whom he had deserted were brought to Chicago to identify him, and the police had difficulty restraining them from attacking the prisoner.

Tried for the murder of Marie Walcker, he was found guilty and sentenced to death. A lady named Cora Wilson, who had never met Hoch, advanced the money for an appeal, declaring that she was convinced of his innocence; this appeal was rejected, and Hoch was hanged on February 23, 1906.

The number of Hoch's victims is a matter for speculation. In the *Encyclopedia of World Crime*, Jay Robert Nash speaks of "dozens," but the brides who are known to have died soon after marrying him amount only to six. On the other hand Hoch was in America for nine years before he poisoned Caroline Hoch—listed by Thomas S. Duke as the first known victim—so it is highly probable that there were more.

Belle Gunness, America's most notorious murderess, (there was even a Laurel and Hardy film about her) was luckier than Hoch; she escaped before her misdeeds were found out. At least, we think she did.

The end came on the night of April 27, 1908, near the small town of La Porte, Indiana. Earlier that day, Belle Gunness had been to a local lawyer to make her will, leaving her property to her three children, or, if they failed to survive, to the local Norwegian orphanage. She told the lawyer that she was being bothered by her ex-hired man, Ray Lamphere, and that she suspected that he intended to burn down her farm. Just before dawn the next day, the new hired man, Joe Maxson, woke up and smelled burning; when he looked out of the window he saw that flames were bursting out of the windows of the kitchen below. He tried to break into the bed-

room in which Belle Gunness should have been asleep with
her three children; the door was locked. As Maxson rushed
outside, the fire took hold. Neighbors began to arrive, and
Maxson harnessed the horse and drove off for the sheriff. By
the time the volunteer fire brigade arrived, the farmhouse
was little more than a heap of embers. Late that afternoon,
investigation of the cellar disclosed the charred corpses of
the three children, and the headless corpse of a woman. Ray
Lamphere was immediately arrested.

A week later, a man with a Norwegian accent walked into
the office of Sheriff Al Smutzer and introduced himself as
Asle Helgelian. He was in search of his younger brother Andrew, who had left his home in Mansfield, South Dakota, to
marry a rich widow who signed her letters Bella Gunness.
Mrs. Gunness had advertised for a husband in a Norwegian
newspaper, Andrew had replied, and they had been in regular
weekly correspondence for sixteen months before he left for
Indiana the previous January. There he had drawn out all his
money from the local bank, with Mrs. Gunness at his elbow.
But when his brother wrote to Mrs. Gunness to ask about
Andrew, she had answered that Andrew had gone off looking for a friend in Chicago. It was the cashier of the local
bank who had sent Asle Helgelian newspaper cuttings about
the burning down of the farm. Now he was convinced that
his brother was dead—probably buried somewhere on the
farm.

Sheriff Smutzer did not seem to take Asle Helgelian seriously. He made sympathetic noises and recommended that
he go and stay with a fellow Norwegian who lived close to
the Gunness farm. And it was due to Asle Helgelian's urging
that Joe Maxson and a neighbor called Daniel Hutson—who
had been paid to dig in the ruins—transferred their attention
to a "hog pen" where Mrs. Gunness buried rubbish. There all
three men began to dig. Soon there was an unpleasant smell

like rotten fish, and minutes later they uncovered a dismembered body covered with oilcloth. Asle Helgelian identified it as his brother Andrew. The wrist of the left arm had a defensive cut as if he had been trying to wield off the blow of a hatchet, and the fingers of his right hand were also missing. There was still a tuft of brown curly hair in the hand, presumably torn from the head of his murderer. Medical examination would later reveal strychnine in his stomach.

Four feet down, under rubbish, they uncovered the hacked-up remains of four more victims. The topmost body was that of a blonde girl; this was identified as Belle Gunness's adopted daughter Jennie—who according to Mrs. Gunness, had left for school in California eighteen months earlier.

Told about the discovery, Ray Lamphere gasped, and said he had always suspected it. Mrs. Gunness had asked him to buy rat poison and chloroform . . .

A few days later they found more graves. One contained the disjointed skeleton of a young man whose head had been split open with an axe. In another grave were the bones of three men. Two days later they found another grave containing a woman's shoes, the remains of a purse, and the skeleton of a youth. That made fourteen bodies so far.

Slowly, most of the bodies were identified. One was Ole Budsberg, who had sold up his home in Iola, Wisconsin, in March 1907, and moved in with Mrs. Gunness. Soon after, his sons opened a letter addressed to him; it proved to be from Mrs. Gunness and said that she hoped he was not offended that she had refused him, and hoped he would get settled out west. Other relatives identified the remains of Olaf Lindboe, Henry Gurholt and John Moe (or Moo).

Now it was clear that Belle was a mass murderess, doubts began to arise about the headless body in the cellar. There was evidence that the children had also been poisoned—

although a careless mix-up of the stomachs of all four corpses left some doubt about this. The small skulls certainly had holes in them, suggesting that they had been killed by hammer blows. The headless woman's body seemed too small for Belle. Was it not conceivable that she had killed another woman in her place, and removed the head to make sure she was not identified through her teeth?

A number of witnesses soon came forward to state that they had seen Belle on the evening of the fire, driving in a buggy with a dark-haired woman, whom she had apparently fetched from the station . . .

But this theory was also undermined when, after "sluicing" the ashes as if searching for gold, an ex-miner found Belle's false teeth, and also two of her real teeth, to which the set was anchored. The dentist who made the false teeth had no doubt they were Belle's.

The story was now on every front page in America. Journalists soon ferreted out the life story of Belle Gunness, and it confirmed everyone's worst suspicions.

She had been born Brynhild Poulsdatter Pedersen on November 11, 1859, in the fishing hamlet of Innbygde, on the west coat of Norway. Her father was a poverty-stricken farmer. In 1883, she followed her eldest sister Nellie to Chicago, and in the following year married a watchman named Mads Sorenson. Money was scarce, and Belle supplemented their meager income by taking in lodgers, and at one point running a candy store. She was living in Chicago during the 1893 World's Fair when H. H. Holmes was running a rather more expensive—and successful—boarding house. But after twelve years of marriage, Mads was still earning only $15 a week. Belle (as she now called herself) hated poverty—her sister Nellie remarked, "My sister was crazy for money."

She seems to have learned to supplement her income with

insurance fraud. In 1896, the candy store she owned was burned down, and in 1898, their home in the suburb of Austin was damaged by fire. Their daughter Caroline died in 1896, and her son Axel in 1898. Both had symptoms of acute colitis, and both were insured. And in July 1900, the day that two insurance policies on her husband happened to overlap, Mads Sorenson died of a similar illness. The young doctor who was summoned to the deathbed noted the arched body, and suspected strychnine poisoning. But an older colleague told him that he had diagnosed an enlarged heart, and advised him to sign the death certificate. The young doctor later regretted that he had not insisted on a post mortem.

In fact, a post mortem *was* later held, at the request of the dead man's brother, but when it was discovered that the heart *was* enlarged, the coroner did not bother to examine the stomach.

With the $8,500 in insurance money, Belle purchased the farm a mile north of La Porte, a pleasant, small community a dozen miles from Lake Michigan. The farm had been a sporting house, and was a stately-looking building, half brick and half wood, with a large garden, an orchard and numerous outbuildings. It came complete with the brothel's impressive furniture—heavy sideboards, massive chairs and comfortable beds.

Belle now decided to captivate a Wisconsin farmer named Frederickson, but when Frederickson's housekeeper frustrated her plans, married instead the housekeeper's recently widowed son, Peter Gunness. He moved in with Belle in April 1902. Less than a week after their marriage, his baby died suddenly. The doctor who signed the certificate suspected smothering, but he kept his suspicions to himself until many years later.

Eight months later, her husband was the victim of a curious accident. Peter Gunness died on the kitchen floor,

scalded with hot brine, and apparently struck down by a
heavy meat grinder which, according to his wife, had fallen
from the shelf above the stove. His widow explained that she
always kept the meat grinder on the shelf, and that Gunness
must have dislodged it so it struck the bowl of brine on the
stove, then hit him on the head. She did not explain how
the meat grinder jumped off the shelf, struck the brine on the
stove, then jumped up again to strike the fatal blow. But her
12-year-old adopted daughter Jennie corroborated the main
part of the story, and the coroner brought in a reluctant verdict of accidental death.

Six years later, not long before the farm burnt down, her
youngest daughter Myrtle told a school friend: "Mamma
killed my papa—she hit him with a meat cleaver." A more
likely weapon was the back of a chopper.

Belle had adopted Jennie when she was a baby, soon after
her mother's death. Her father, Anton Olsen, had later invited his daughter for a visit to Chicago, hoping she would
want to stay, but Jennie had pined for the farm and gone
back. A young hired man named Emile Greening had been in
love with her, and had been deeply hurt when Jennie—now
sixteen—had departed for California without saying good-
bye, just after Christmas 1906. Significantly, Belle had been
due to pay Jennie a legacy of $1,800 when she was eighteen.
Emile later identified Jennie's skull.

When Peter Gunness died, Belle was pregnant again; she
called the baby Philip.

Over the next few years Belle had a series of hired men,
and most of them seem to have been her lovers. Now in her
mid-forties, she was not particularly attractive—a massive
woman with high cheekbones and stern eyes—but the few
men who slept with her and survived recorded that she had a
natural talent for sex that soon made them her slaves. Regrettably, most of them soon began to think of themselves as

Belle's husband and the master of the house, and she seems to have disliked this intensely—as far as she was concerned, she was the mistress and they were employees. Many of these hired men left suddenly and unexpectedly—so unexpectedly that Belle was left to finish the plowing. Relatives later identified some of them in Belle's home-made cemetery.

Belle also introduced a number of suitors to her neighbors—one from Minnesota, one from Wisconsin, one from South Dakota. She later explained that they had changed their minds and left.

In June 1907, Belle approached a young odd-job man named Ray Lamphere and told him she was looking for a man about the house. Ray was a weak-chinned individual with a droopy moustache and eyes like an anxious koala bear. The first evening he spent at the Gunness farm, he experienced the delights of Belle's excellent—if somewhat heavy—Norwegian cuisine, then retired to a comfortable bed in the spare room. Later that night Belle joined him, and proved that she was as skilled in the arts of lovemaking as of cooking. When she left in the early morning, Lamphere could hardly believe his luck. This magnificent woman, with her comfortable home and equally comfortable income, had chosen him as her mate. It seemed too good to be true.

Six months later he learned that it *was* too good to be true. Just before Christmas 1907, a man arrived at the farm, and Belle explained they were engaged. For the next week Ray was in a frenzy of jealousy; then, to his relief, the man disappeared.

But not long after, in early January, another man appeared; this was Andrew Helgelian, who (as his brother later revealed) had spent ten years in jail for post office robbery. Realizing that his mistress was now spending her nights in Helgelian's bed, Ray was again tormented by jealousy.

On the cold, snowy night of January 14, 1908, Belle ordered him to drive to Michigan City to pick up a horse that was being sent by her cousin Mr. Moe. But when Lamphere. together with a friend he took along for company, arrived at his destination, there was no horse. The two men went drinking, then to a vaudeville show. Finally, on the way home, the spurned lover announced that he was going to the farm to see what "the old woman" was up to. The following afternoon, he saw his friend, and told a strange story. He had, he claimed, bored a hole in the floorboards so he could overhear what Belle and Helgelian were talking about. And, he claimed, they were discussing how to poison him . . .

Whatever happened that night, it made Lamphere morose and jumpy. He declined to sleep under Belle's roof, and on February 3, she discharged him, and hired Joe Maxson in his place. And although she was not sexually interested in Joe, or vice versa, Lamphere continued to haunt the farm. He muttered to friends that he had information that would place Belle behind bars. But if he was really trying to blackmail her, she took it remarkably coolly; in fact, she sued him for trespass, and he was fined. She also alleged that he had stolen a silver watch; but Ray insisted that she had given it to him. And since he had displayed it to friends at the time he and Belle were lovers, the sheriff chose to take his word. (The silver watch later proved to be the property of John Moe, one of the vanished suitors.)

And so Ray Lamphere continued to pester his ex-mistress until that afternoon in April when she went to see a solicitor about her will, and told him that she expected Lamphere to burn down her house . . .

This, then was the situation when Ray Lamphere's trial opened on November 9, 1908, accused of murdering Belle and her children by setting fire to the house. The defense, led by Wirt Worden, based its case on the argument that Belle

Gunness was still alive. A witness was produced who claimed to have seen Belle driving to the farm with another woman—and this woman, said Worden, was the headless body found in the ruins. Belle had a long scar on her thigh, and the corpse had no such scar. Moreover, Belle's neighbor Daniel Hutson claimed that he had actually *seen* Belle in her orchard three months after the fire. Worden's case was that Belle had killed her own children, then escaped. Lamphere had told him—Worden—that he had helped Belle to escape on the night of the fire. The implication was that Ray had set fire to the house, believing it to be empty . . .

The prosecution case was that Lamphere had started the fire to revenge himself on his ex-mistress. The body found in the fire *was* that of Belle Gunness, and the head was missing because it had been burnt off. The false teeth—attached to a real tooth from Belle's head—proved it. Lamphere had admitted to getting up at three on the morning of the fire, and leaving the house twenty minutes later. He had admitted passing the farm on his way to work, and telling his new employer that Belle's house was on fire. Lamphere, said the prosecution, had started that fire. A neighboring boy stated that Lamphere had seen him hiding in the bushes, and had threatened to kill him if he did not go away. Not long after that—just before the first signs of the fire were noticed—he had seen Lamphere running away.

All the same, Worden succeeded in sowing many doubts in the mind of the jury. A doctor stated in court that there was poison in the bodies of the children and the female corpse. The injuries to the skulls were mentioned as proof that the children were murdered. By the end of the trial on Thanksgiving Day (November 26) the jury was confused and divided. But eventually, after many ballots, the foreman announced the verdict. Ray Lamphere *was* guilty of setting fire to the farm. But Belle, the jury believed, had taken her own life with strychnine . . .

Ray Lamphere was sentenced to from two to twenty-one years' imprisonment. His comment, as he approached the penitentiary, was that he felt he was lucky to be alive when he might have ended up in "the old woman's" chicken run.

Just over a year later, he died of consumption. Shortly before his death, he told a strange story to a fellow prisoner. Belle, he insisted, was alive; he had taken her away, disguised as a man, in a hired rig, and handed her over to an accomplice. That accomplice, he implied, was the local sheriff, who was in Belle's pay. Then he had returned and set fire to the house. Belle later sent back her false teeth—plus the real ones—for him to place in the ashes after charring them in a fire.

According to Lamphere, he had been Belle's accomplice for the past year or so, and had helped her dispose of several of the bodies. Belle had killed and dissected them, he had buried them. But he had come to suspect that she intended to kill him, and had refused to sleep on the property. They had quarreled and he left. He was in no position to denounce her because he had been an accomplice. But when she decided it was time to disappear, she offered Ray $500 to help her. She had hired a woman she had seen sitting on a stairway in Chicago, and brought her back to the farm two days before the fire. But the woman had a full set of teeth, and her nose was quite different from Belle's. So her head had to be removed—Ray buried it, together with three other heads, in a rye field. Then he had driven Belle away, handed her to an accomplice, and then set the house on fire early the next morning.

At first sight this sounds by far the likeliest story. But there are strong objections to it. If Lamphere was her accomplice, then presumably he helped her to bury her last victim,

Andrew Helgelian. But if he knew that Helgelian was going to die, why was he so frantic with jealousy? And why did he go back to the farm that night to see what the "old lady" was doing? He should have known what she was doing.

His story of Belle and Helgelian planning to poison him sounds equally unlikely. If Belle wanted to poison Lamphere, she certainly did not need an accomplice. The likeliest explanation is probably that he hung around the farm with a masochistic craving to find out if Belle was in bed with Helgelian. But she had taken care to draw all the curtains and lock all the doors—as a murderess would when she intends to dispose of another victim.

Lillian de la Torre, the author of the best book on the case, *The Truth about Belle Gunness* (1955) has provided a possible solution to the mystery. She is convinced that Lamphere was telling the truth about one thing: that the "accomplice" in the case was Sheriff Al Smutzer himself, and that he had been in the pay of Belle Gunness from the beginning. He was the man to whom Lamphere handed Belle over after driving her away from the farm that night. But what Belle had not anticipated was Smutzer's treachery. He knew she was carrying a large sum of money (usually estimated at $30,000). There was nothing to prevent him from killing Belle and helping himself. A few weeks later, when it was necessary to prove that it was indeed Belle's body in the ruins, he had returned to the corpse and taken out the dentures, which he planted in the ashes after placing them in a fire to char them.

De la Torre points out that Sheriff Smutzer went to Texas in the course of his investigation—a man there had falsely confessed to being implicated in the case—and that this would be an ideal opportunity to open a bank account and deposit the $30,000. In fact, Smutzer made a habit of going to Texas in the years that followed, and finally stayed there for thirty years, before he returned to Laporte, where he died penniless.

The main objection to this theory is that there is not a scrap of evidence that Mutzer was corrupt. Yet we also have to admit that it is hard to fault Lillian de la Torre's logic. Either it was Belle in the burnt-out farmhouse or it was not. And if it was Belle, then either she killed herself, or she was murdered—probably by Lamphere. But there was no time for Lamphere to walk out to the farm, kill Belle and the children, set fire to the house, and hurry on to his other job, all in the space of an hour. In any case, Lamphere was hardly the type—he was too weak. Besides, there was poison in the bodies—we are not sure which because the stomachs were accidentally put in the same jar—which suggests that Belle administered it the night before.

So if the headless corpse was Belle, she committed suicide. That, it might be argued, is just conceivable. Although she may have poisoned two of her children in Chicago, we may assume that she felt attachment to the children she had brought up in La Porte, particularly to baby Philip. Maxson spoke of her love of playing games with the children—they were playing just before the last time he saw them—and everyone agreed that she seemed to be a good mother. But now, at last, after at least eight years of murder, her crimes looked as if they were catching up with her. Relatives of the victims were asking questions, and any day might arrive and make trouble. If they did, that fool Lamphere might tell all he knew, and although it was not much, it might be enough to bring the sheriff with a search warrant of her property. She may have felt that the end was close. And for all we know, she was running out of money. It was true that she had collected many sums of a thousand dollars or so over the years, but with a farm to run and children to bring up, she might well be coming close to the end of her resources. (There was only $700 in her account when she died.) And it was too risky to advertise for yet another husband. So Belle may have decided it was time to die, and to take her children with her, as many suicides do. She also may have decided to take Lamphere with her—which is why, after she made her will, she remarked that she expected him to burn down the house.

Against this hypothesis we have to place what we know of Belle's psychology. She was a survivor. She had killed two husbands, and possibly as many as twenty other men (there were twenty watches found in the ruins). She had murdered her own adopted daughter and possibly two of her children. If it meant killing her own family to save her neck, Belle would not have hesitated. The headless body seemed too small for Belle, and the suggestion—made by a doctor at the trial—that it had shrunk by two-thirds in the heat sounds unlikely.

Yet the most convincing evidence that Belle died in the fire—the evidence that convinced the coroner—is the teeth. When a reporter asked the sheriff whether Belle could not simply have removed her teeth before she fled, the sheriff shook his head, and pointed to the real tooth the false teeth were attached to. This tooth had a gold cap, and a dentist in court said that it would have been impossible to pull out the tooth without splitting this cap.

But if Belle was lying dead and buried, then her killer could have removed her teeth by digging them out of her gums. So we are faced with the unavoidable conclusion: either Belle committed suicide, or someone else killed her—the accomplice to whom Lamphere claimed he delivered her. And we know enough of Belle to know that it is highly unlikely that she committed suicide.

Lillian de la Torre suggests that Jennie was killed because she suspected that Peter Gunness had been murdered. That is unlikely. She gave her evidence in Belle's favor at the inquest, and the coroner signed a certificate of accidental death. That was old history. From what we know of Belle's psychology, Jennie was murdered because Belle was due to pay her $1,800 on her eighteenth birthday, and Belle hated to part with money. A secondary motive may have been the fact that having a 16-year-old girl around the house robbed her of the privacy necessary for murdering and dismembering husbands.

There is one other point on which we might take issue with Lillian de la Torre. That accomplice may not, after all, have been Sheriff Smutzer. Clutched in Andrew Helgelian's hand was a bunch of hair torn from the head of his killer. It was not Belle's hair, or Ray Lamphere's. We do not know if it belonged to Sheriff Smutzer, but it seems unlikely—surely someone would have recollected that Smutzer looked as if he had been in a fight four months earlier, with a lock of his hair torn out by the roots? Belle had had a number of lovers over the years, including a hired man named Peter Colson, who was never under suspicion. That lock of hair in Helgelian's hand certainly belonged to *somebody*, and that somebody was not Belle.

One other person seems to have known the truth. Ray Lamphere's best friend, a woman known as Nigger Liz, claimed to know exactly what happened, and told Wirt Worden that she would send for him and reveal it on her death bed. Unfortunately, Worden was out of town when Nigger Liz sent for him, and by the time he got back, she was dead.

How *do* we explain a woman who can murder husbands and children, and dismember lovers? The key undoubtedly lies in Nellie's remark: "My sister was crazy for money." Belle went to America to escape the poverty of the Norwegian farm; it was the land of opportunity, and she hoped to become—at the very least—a comfortable, middle-class housewife with a home to be proud of. But marriage to Mads

Sorenson proved a mistake; it soon became obvious that he was never going to rise in the world. Then, after twelve years of uphill struggle, the candy store caught fire, and she received the insurance money. It may well be that the fire was accidental. At all events, it taught her that there *were* ways of making large sums of money without slaving like a dirt farmer. Significantly, it was at this point that they moved to the comfortable Chicago suburb of Austin, and at last Belle had the kind of home she wanted. (Nellie quoted her as saying: "I would never remain with this man if it was not for the nice home he has.") Mads was still earning only $15 a week, but fortunately there were a few more insurance windfalls on fires, and on the death of two children from colic. And finally, on July 30, 1900, Belle made a killing in both senses of the word when Mads died in convulsions on the day two insurance policies overlapped, and she received the huge sum of $8,500.

Now, at last, she was able to buy the home of her dreams. The sporting house that had belonged to Mattie Altic was a kind of mansion. At last, she was living in the surroundings she felt she had always deserved. But more insurance fraud was out of the question—it would have raised too much suspicion. She had to find new ways of increasing her wealth. And she did it with a boldness that in a businessman would have been a guarantee of success. The truth is that Belle shared the sense of enterprise that turned Andrew Carnegie and Cornelius Vanderbilt into millionaires. It is not surprising that Americans feel ambivalent about her.

A quarter of a century after the Jack the Ripper murders, New Orleans had its own spectacular series of apparently unsolved murders; the killer became known as the Mad Axeman. But in this case, they seem to have been inspired by the same deep resentment against Italians that the Ripper felt against prostitutes.

On the morning of May 24, 1918, an Italian cobbler named Jake Maggio was awakened by a groaning sound coming from the next room, where his brother Joe slept with his wife. As he entered the room, he saw a woman lying on the floor, her head almost severed from her body; Joe lay in bed groaning. Nearby lay a bloodstained axe and a cut-throat razor, which had been used to slash Joe's throat. He died soon after.

By the time the police arrived, Jake and his second brother Andrew had found how the intruder entered—through a panel chiseled out of the back door. Jake and Andrew were arrested as suspects, but soon released.

On the pavement two streets away someone had chalked on the pavement: "Mrs. Maggio is going to sit up tonight, just like Mrs. Toney." It reminded the police that seven years earlier there had been four axe murders of Italian grocers including a Mrs. Tony Schiambra. They had been attributed to the criminal organization, "the Black Hand," which was rife in New Orleans.

Five weeks after the Maggio killings, a bread delivery man found a back door with a panel chiseled out. When he knocked the door was opened by a man covered in blood. He was a Pole named Besumer, and inside lay a woman who was known as his wife. She was still alive, and told of being struck by a big white man wielding a hatchet. She died later, and Besumer was charged with her murder.

But that night the axeman struck again—a young married man, Edward Schneider, returned home to find his pregnant wife lying in bed covered in blood. Rushed to hospital she survived, and gave birth a week later. The attacker seemed to have entered by an open window.

Five days later, a barber named Romano became the next

victim. His niece heard noises in his bedroom, and went in to find him being attacked by a big man wearing a black slouch hat. As she screamed, the man "vanished as if he had wings." A panel had been chipped out of the door.

New Orleans was in a panic reminiscent of that which had swept London in the days of Jack the Ripper. There were several false alarms, and one man found an axe and chisel outside his back door . . . On August 30, 1918, a man named Nick Asunto heard a noise, and went to investigate; he saw a heavily built man with an axe, who fled as he shouted. All New Orleans began taking elaborate precautions against the Axeman.

For the time being, the attacks ceased, and the ending of the war in 1918 gave people other things to think about. But in March 1919, a grocer named Jordano heard screams from a house across the street, and found another grocer, Charles Cortimiglia, unconscious on the floor, while his wife—a dead baby in her arms—sat on the floor with blood streaming from her head. She said she had awakened to see a man attacking her husband with an axe, and when she snatched up her baby, he killed the child with a blow, then struck her . . . The door panel had been chiseled out. Yet when Mrs. Cortimiglia began to recover, she accused Jordano, the man who had found her, of being the killer, and although her husband (now also recovering) insisted that this was untrue, Jordano and his son were arrested.

Three days after the attack, the local newspaper received a letter signed "The Axeman," datelined "From hell" (as in the case of a Jack the Ripper letter), and declaring that he would be coming to New Orleans next Tuesday at 12:15, but would spare any house playing jazz music. The following Tuesday, the streets of New Orleans rocked with jazz, and the Axeman failed to appear . . . Someone even wrote a "Mysterious Axeman Jazz."

Besumer, who had been in custody since his arrest, was tried and acquitted. But the Jordanos, to everyone's amazement, were found guilty, although Charles Cortimiglia repeated that they were innocent.

And the attacks went on—although there was to be only one further death. On August 10, 1919, a grocer named Steve Boca woke to find a shadowy figure holding an axe beside the bed. When he woke again, he was bleeding from a skull wound. He managed to stagger down to the home of a friend, Frank Genusa, and the frantic police arrested Genusa—then shamefacedly released him.

On September 2, a druggist named Carlson heard scratching noises from the back door, and fired his revolver through the panel. The intruder fled, leaving behind a chisel.

The next day, neighbors found 19-year-old Sarah Lauman unconscious; she had been attacked with an axe and three teeth knocked out. She could remember nothing when she recovered.

The last attack was on a grocer named Mike Pepitone. His wife—in a separate bedroom—heard sounds of a struggle, and entered his room in time to see a man vanishing. Her husband had been killed with an axe blow so violent that it spattered blood up the wall. Again, a chiseled door panel revealed how the axeman had gained entry.

Then the murders ceased. The Jordanos were finally released when Mrs. Cortimiglia confessed that she had lied because she hated them. Now, she said, her husband had left her, and she had smallpox—Saint Joseph had appeared to her and told her to confess. The Jordanos were released.

But Mrs. Pepitone, widow of the last victim, was to enter the story again. On December 7, 1920, in Los Angeles, she had shot and killed a man named Joseph Mumfre, from New Orleans, in the street. She claimed he was the axeman. She was sentenced to ten years in prison, but released after three.

Was Mumfre the Axeman? He could well have been. He had been released from prison just before the 1911 murders, then sent back for the next seven years. Released again just before the first of the 1918 murders, he had been back in prison during the "lull" between August 1918 and March 1919, when they began again. He left New Orleans shortly after the murder of Mike Pepitone.

What was his motive? Almost certainly, he was a sadist who wanted to attack women, not men. Joe Maggio was left alive; his wife was killed. Besumer was only knocked unconscious; his attractive wife died of her injuries. Many of the later victims were women, and it seems likely that he attacked the men when in search of women victims.

Why Italian grocers? In fact, many of the victims were not Italians. *But all kept small shops.* And a small shop is a place where an attractive wife can be seen serving behind the counter. Mrs. Pepitone never revealed how she tracked down Mumfre, but it seems likely that he was a customer, and she recognized him and followed his trail to Los Angeles.

5

MASS MURDER IN AMERICA, 1920–1940

H. H. HOLMES MAY OR MAY NOT BE CLASSIFIED AS A SERIAL killer, depending on our view of whether his crimes were pathological or purely commercial. Johann Hoch and Belle Gunness were undoubtedly mass murderers and not serial killers. Earle Nelson, also known as "the Dark Strangler" and "the Gorilla Murderer," was undoubtedly a serial killer in our modern sense of the word.

On February 24, 1926, a man named Richard Newman went to call on his aunt, who advertised rooms to let in San Francisco; he found the naked body of the 60-year-old woman in an upstairs toilet. She had been strangled with her pearl necklace, then repeatedly raped. Clara Newman was the first of twenty-two victims of a man who became known as "the Gorilla Murderer." The killer made a habit of calling at houses with a "Room to Let" notice in the window; if the landlady was alone, he strangled and raped her. His victims included a 14-year-old girl and an 8-month-old baby. And as he traveled around from San Francisco to San Jose, from Portland, Oregon, to Council Bluffs, Iowa, from Philadelphia to Buffalo, from Detroit to Chicago, the police found him as elusive as the French police had found Joseph Vacher thirty years earlier. Their problem was simply that the women who could identify "the Dark Strangler" (as the newspapers had christened him) were dead, and they had no idea of what he looked like. But when the Portland police had the idea of asking newspapers to publish descriptions of jewelry that had been stolen from some of the strangler's victims, three old ladies in a South Portland lodging-house recalled that they had bought a few items of jewelry from a pleasant young man who had stayed with them for a few days. They decided—purely as a precaution—to take it to the police. It proved to belong to a Seattle landlady, Mrs. Florence Monks, who had been strangled and raped on November 24, 1926. And the old ladies were able to tell the police that the Dark Strangler was a short, blue-eyed young man with a round face and slightly simian mouth and jaw. He was quietly spoken, and claimed to be deeply religious.

On June 8, 1927, the strangler crossed the Canadian border, and rented a room in Winnipeg from a Mrs. Catherine Hill. He stayed for three nights. But on June 9th, a couple named Cowan, who lived in the house, reported that their 14-year-old daughter Lola had vanished. That same evening, a man named William Patterson returned home to find his wife absent. After making supper and putting the children to bed, he rang the police. Then he dropped on his knees beside the bed to pray; as he did so, he saw his wife's hand sticking out. Her naked body lay under the bed.

The Winnipeg police recognized the *modus operandi* of the Gorilla Murderer. A check on boarding-house landladies brought them to Mrs. Hill's establishment. She assured them that she had taken in no suspicious characters recently—her last lodger had been a Roger Wilson, who had been carrying a Bible and been highly religious. When she told them that Roger Wilson was short, with piercing blue eyes and a dark complexion, they asked to see the room he had stayed in. They were greeted by the stench of decay. The body of Lola Cowan lay under the bed, mutilated as if by Jack the Ripper. The murderer had slept with it in his room for three days.

From the Patterson household, the strangler had taken some of the husband's clothes, leaving his own behind. But he changed these at a second-hand shop, leaving behind a fountain pen belonging to Patterson, and paying in $10 bills stolen from his house. So the police now had a good description not only of the killer, but of the clothes he was wearing, including corduroy trousers and a plaid shirt.

The next sighting came from Regina, 200 miles west; a landlady heard the screams of a pretty girl who worked for the telephone company, and interrupted the man who had been trying to throttle her; he ran away. The police guessed that he might be heading back towards the American border, which would take him across prairie country with few towns; there was a good chance that a lone hitch-hiker would be noticed. Descriptions of the wanted man were sent out to all police stations and post offices. Five days later, two constables saw a man wearing corduroys and a plaid shirt walking down a road near Killarney, 12 miles from the border. He gave his name as Virgil Wilson and said he was a farmworker; he seemed quite unperturbed when the police told him they were looking for a mass murderer, and would have to take him in on suspicion. His behavior was so unalarmed they were convinced he was innocent. But when they telephoned the Winnipeg chief of police, and described Virgil Wilson, he told them that the man was undoubtedly "Roger Wilson," the Dark Strangler. They hurried back to the jail—to find that their prisoner had picked the lock of his handcuffs and escaped.

Detectives were rushed to the town by airplane, and posses spread out over the area. "Wilson" had slept in a barn close to the jail, and the next morning broke into a house and stole a change of clothing. The first man he spoke to that morning noticed his disheveled appearance and asked if he had spent the night in the open; the man admitted that he had. When told that police were on their way to Killarney by train to look for the strangler, he ran away towards the railway. At that moment, a police car appeared; after a short chase, the fugitive was captured.

He was identified as Earle Leonard Nelson, born in Philadelphia in 1897; his mother had died of venereal disease contracted from his father. At the age of 10, Nelson was knocked down by a streetcar and was unconscious with a concussion for six days. From then on, he experienced violent periodic headaches. He began to make a habit of peering through the keyhole of his cousin Rachel's bedroom when she was getting undressed. At 21, he was arrested after trying to rape a girl in a basement. Sent to a penal farm, he soon escaped, and was recaptured peering in through the window of his cousin as she undressed for bed. A marriage was unsuccessful; when his wife had a nervous breakdown, Nelson visited her in the hospital and tried to rape her in bed. Nothing is known of Nelson's whereabouts for the next three years, until the evening in February 1926, when he knocked on the door of Mrs. Clara Newman in San Francisco, and asked if he could see the room she had to let . . .

Like Earle Nelson, Albert Fish had also suffered a blow on the head in childhood. But Fish, unlike Nelson and most other serial killers, was at large for an unusually long time, so that we have no idea of how many murders he committed over the years. The case is certainly one of the strangest in the bizarre history of serial murder.

On May 28, 1928 a mild-looking old man called on the family of a doorman named Albert Budd in a basement in

Manhattan. He explained he had come in answer to a job advertisement placed in a New York newspaper by Budd's 18-year-old son Edward. His name, he said, was Frank Howard, and he owned a farm on Long Island. The old man so charmed the Budds that the following day they allowed him to take their 10-year-old daughter Grace to a party; she left in a white confirmation dress, holding Howard's hand. The Budds never saw Grace again; the address at which the party was supposed to be held proved fictitious, and no farmer by the name of Frank Howard could be traced on Long Island. The kidnap received wide publicity, and the police investigated hundreds of tips. Detective Will King of the Missing Persons Bureau became particularly obsessed with the crime and traveled thousands of miles in search of "Frank Howard."

Six years later, the Budds received an unsigned letter that was clearly from the kidnapper. He stated that he had taken Grace Budd to an empty house in Westchester, then left her picking flowers while he went inside and stripped off his clothes; then he leaned out of the upstairs window and called her in. Confronted by this skinny naked man, Grace began to cry and tried to run away; he seized her and strangled her. Then he cut her in half, and took the body back home, where he ate parts of it. "How sweet her little ass was, roasted in the oven. It took me nine days to eat her entire body. I did not fuck her tho I could of had I wished." (In fact, Fish was to admit to his attorney that this was untrue.) Finally, he took the bones back to the cottage and buried them in the garden.

With a brilliant piece of detective work, Will King traced the writer—the letter had arrived in an envelope with the inked-out logo of a chauffeurs' benevolent association on the flap. One of the chauffeurs finally admitted that he had taken some of the association's stationery and left it in a room he used to rent on East 52nd Street. This now proved to be rented by a tenant who called himself A. H. Fish, and his handwriting in the boarding house register was identical with that of the letter writer. King kept watch on the room for three weeks before Albert Fish—the mild little old man—returned. He agreed unhesitatingly to go to headquarters for questioning, but at the street door, suddenly lunged at King with a razor in each hand. King disarmed and handcuffed him. Back at police headquarters, Fish made no attempt to deny the murder of Grace Budd. He had gone to her home, he explained, with the intention of killing her brother Edward, but when Grace had sat on his knee during dinner, had decided that he wanted to eat her.

He took the police to the cottage in Westchester, where they unearthed the bones of Grace Budd. Later, under intensive questioning, he admitted to killing about four hundred children since 1910. (The figure has never been confirmed, and a judge involved in the case placed the true figure at sixteen.)

Soon after his arrest, Fish was visited by a psychiatrist named Fredrick Wertham, who would appear for the defense. "He looked," wrote Wertham, "like a meek and innocuous little old man, gentle and benevolent, friendly and polite. If you wanted someone to entrust your children to, he would be the one you would choose." When Fish realized that Wertham really wanted to understand him, he became completely open and forthcoming.

Fish was a strange paradox of a man. His face lit up when he talked of his 12-year-old grandchild, and he was obviously sincere when he said: "I love children and was always soft-hearted." He was also deeply religious, and read his Bible continuously. The answer to the paradox, Wertham soon concluded, was that Fish was insane. He genuinely believed that God told him to murder children.

Albert Hamilton Fish had been born in Washington, D.C.,

in 1870; his father, a riverboat captain, was 75 at the time. Various members of the family had mental problems and one suffered from religious mania. One brother was feeble-minded and another an alcoholic. The father had died when Fish was five years old, and he was placed in an orphanage, from which he regularly ran away. On leaving school he was apprenticed to a house painter, and this remained his profession for the rest of his life. Access to other people's homes also gave him access to children. He was 28 when he first married, but his wife eloped with the lodger. Later, there were three more marriages, all bigamous.

Fish talked with complete frankness about his sex life—he had always enjoyed writing obscene letters, and no doubt confessing to Wertham gave him the same kind of pleasure. Wertham wrote:

> Fish's sexual life was of unparalleled perversity . . . I found no published case that would even nearly compare with his . . . There was no known perversion that he did not practice and practice frequently.
>
> Sado-masochism directed against children, particularly boys, took the lead in his sexual regressive development. "I have always had a desire to inflict pain on others and to have others inflict pain on me. I always seemed to enjoy anything that hurt. The desire to inflict pain, that is all that is uppermost." Experiences with excreta of every imaginable kind were practiced by him, actively and passively. He took bits of cotton wool, saturated them with alcohol, inserted them in his rectum and set fire to them. He also did this to his child victims. Finally, and clearly also on a sexual basis, he developed a craving going back to one of the arch-crimes of humanity—cannibalism.

I elicited from him a long history of how he preyed on children. In many instances—I stated under oath later "at least a hundred"—he seduced them or bribed them with small sums of money or forced them and attacked them. He often worked in public buildings and had an excuse for spending times in cellars and basements and even garrets. He would put on his painters' overalls over his nude body, and that permitted him to undress in a moment ...

Most, if not all, of his victims came from the poorer classes. He told me that he selected colored children especially, because the authorities didn't pay much attention when they were hurt or missing. For example, he once paid a small colored girl five dollars regularly to bring him little colored boys. Frequently after a particularly brutal episode he would change his address completely ... Altogether he roamed over twenty-three states, from New York to Montana. "And I have had children in every state." He also made a habit of writing letters to women, trying to persuade them to join him in whipping boys.

Fish told me that for years he had been sticking needles into his body in the region near his genitals, in the area between the rectum and the scrotum. He told me of doing it to other people too, especially to children. At first, he said, he had only stuck these needles in and pulled them out again. They were needles of assorted sizes, some of them big sail needles. Then he had stuck others in so far that he was unable to get them out, and they stayed there. "They're in there now," he said. "I put them up under the spine ... I did put one in the scrotum too; but I couldn't stand the pain."

I checked this strange story on a series of X-rays of his pelvic and abdominal region. They showed plainly twenty-nine needles inside his body. One X-ray of the pelvic region showed twenty-seven. They were easily recognizable as needles ... Some of them must have been years in his body, for they were eroded to an extent that would have taken at least seven years. Some of the needles were fragmented by this erosion so that only bits of steel remained in the tissue."

In his middle fifties, says Wertham, Fish began to develop psychosis with delusions and hallucinations. (He was 58 when he murdered Grace Budd.)

At times he identified himself with God and felt that he should sacrifice his own son. He tried to stick needles under his fingernails but could not stand the pain. He made the poignant remark: "If only pain were not so painful!"

He had visions of Christ and his angels ... He heard them saying words like "stripes," "rewardeth" and "delighteth." And he connected these words with verses from the Bible and elaborated them delusionally with his sadistic wishes. "Stripes means to lash them, you know."

He felt driven to torment and kill children. Sometimes he would gag them, tie them up and beat them, although he preferred not to gag them, circumstances permitting, for he liked to hear their cries. He felt that he was ordered by God to castrate little boys ... "I am not insane. I am just queer." After murdering Grace Budd he had cooked parts of the body with carrots and onions and strips of bacon, and ate them over a period of nine days. During all this time he was in a state of sexual excitement.

His state of mind while he described these things in minute detail was a peculiar mixture. He spoke in a matter-of-fact way, like a housewife describing her favorite methods of cooking. You had to remind yourself that this was a little girl that he was talking about. But at times his tone of voice and facial expression indicated a kind of satisfaction and ecstatic thrill. However you define the medical and legal borders of sanity, this certainly is beyond that border.

It became apparent that Fish was a wanted killer who had become known as "the Brooklyn Vampire," who committed four child murders in 1933 and 1934, luring little girls to a basement, flogging them, then garrotting them with a rope. In 1932, a 16-year-old girl had been killed and mutilated near Massapequa, Long Island, where Fish was painting a house. Other murders almost certainly committed by Fish were those of 7-year-old Francis X. McDonnell on Staten Island in 1924, 4-year-old Billy Gaffney in Brooklyn in 1927, and 11-year-old Yetta Abramowitz, who was strangled and mutilated in the Bronx in 1927. (Billy Gaffney's mother subsequently had a series of nervous breakdowns from grief.) Detective Will King, who investigated these murders, was not allowed to introduce them as evidence, since the D.A. was anxious to prove that Fish was sane, and too many murders might throw doubt on this.

To Fish's delight, he was sentenced to death—he remarked with unconscious humor that being electrocuted would be "the supreme thrill of my life." When he was on Death Row, the prison chaplain had to ask him not to "holler and howl" so loud as he masturbated during services. In the execution chamber on January 16, 1936 he mumbled "I don't know why I'm here" just before the switch was thrown.

Wertham records that he tried hard to get Fish's sentence

commuted. "To execute a sick man is like burning witches," he told the prison governor. He went on to make this important observation—even more relevant today than it was in 1936: "Science is prediction. The science of psychiatry is advanced enough that with proper examination such a man as Fish can be detected and confined before the perpetration of these outrages, instead of inflicting extreme penalties afterwards. The authorities had this man, but the records show that they paid no attention." Understandably, the governor was unmoved. Like the D.A., he probably recognized that Fish was legally insane, but felt that it made no difference—that there was no point in burdening society with the keep of such a man. What Wertham had failed to recognize is that the execution of a murderer like Fish actually serves a ritual function. The public wants to see sadistic killers executed, in the same way that children want fairy stories to end with the defeat of the wicked giant. It serves the purpose of exorcising the horror.

What turns a man into a sado-masochist? In the case of Albert Fish, fortunately, we know the answer. In 1875, his father suffered a heart attack in the Pennsylvania Station. Unable to provide for twelve children, Ellen Fish was forced to consign most of them to an orphanage. The 5-year-old boy had no idea why he had been suddenly abandoned; he was deeply miserable, and at first ran away repeatedly. Discipline in the St. John's Refuge was rigid and severe; the matron made them pray for hours every day and made them memorize chapters from the Bible. The slightest infringement of discipline was punished by flogging, administered by the matron. Fish discovered that he enjoyed being whipped on his naked bottom. His fellow orphans teased him because punishment always gave him an erection. What they did not know was that watching other boys being whipped also produced sexual excitement in him. Since it was a co-educational institution (although the boys and girls were kept strictly segregated outside class) there was naturally a great deal of sex talk. After a while, the young Fish was initiated into masturbation and other sex games. By the time his mother took him away from the orphanage two years later—she had obtained a government job—sado-masochism had been firmly "imprinted" in the 7-year-old boy. He told Wertham of an occasion when he and some friends had soaked a horse's tail in kerosene and set it on fire.

He was a sickly and introverted child, and a fall from a cherry tree produced a concussion; thereafter he suffered severe headaches, dizzy spells and a severe stutter. (It has been pointed out that a large number of serial killers have suffered head injuries in childhood.) He continued to wet the bed for many years, and his companions taunted him about it. Fish's reaction to the jeers was to retreat into a world of daydreams. At about this time he insisted on being called Albert (the name of a dead younger brother) rather than Hamilton because his schoolmates called him Ham and Eggs. He began to suffer from convulsive fits.

The daydreams were often of being beaten or watching others being beaten. When his elder brother Walter came home from the Navy and showed Albert books with pictures of naked men and women, and told him stories of cannibalism which he claimed to have witnessed, more sado-masochistic traits were "imprinted." His favorite reading was Poe's story "The Pit and the Pendulum," with its details of mental torture, and this led him on to study everything he could find about the Spanish Inquisition. He became a devotee of true murder cases, and began carrying newspaper clippings in his pockets until they disintegrated. (He was carrying an account of the Hanover "butcher" Fritz Haarmann when he was arrested.) Yet at the same time he continued to be a devoted student of the Bible, and to dream of becoming a clergyman. Having become habituated to sexual and religious fantasy from an early age, he saw no contradiction between them.

When he was 12, Fish began a homosexual relationship with a telegraph boy who excited him by describing what he had seen in brothels. This youth also introduced to Fish peculiar practices such as drinking urine and tasting excreta. By his late teens, Fish was tormented with a violent and permanent sexual appetite that never left him alone. (But this is less unusual than it sounds; the majority of teenagers could tell a similar story.) When he moved to New York at the age of 20, he quickly became a male prostitute, and spent much of his weekends at public baths where he could watch boys. It was at this time that he began raping small boys. By now the pattern was set, and even a marriage—arranged by his mother—failed to change it. A period in Sing Sing—for embezzlement—virtually ended the marriage, and he returned to homosexuality. After his wife's desertion, he began to show signs of mental disturbance; he heard voices, and on one occasion wrapped himself up in a carpet and explained that he was following the instructions of St. John. Then began his period of wandering around the United States and working as a painter and decorator; during this time, he told Wetham, he raped more than a hundred children, mostly boys under six.

When he was 28, a male lover took him to see the waxworks gallery in a museum; there he was fascinated by a medical display showing the bisection of a penis. He returned to see it many times, and "imprinting" occurred again, leading to a new obsession with castration. During a relationship with a mentally defective homosexual, Fish tied him up and tried to castrate him. The rush of blood frightened him and he fled. Now he began adding castration to his rapes, on one occasion severing a child's penis with a pair of scissors. He began going to brothels where he could be spanked and whipped. He committed his first murder—of a male homosexual—in Wilmington in 1910. In 1919 he mutilated and tortured to death a mentally retarded boy. From now on, murder also became a part of his pattern of perversion.

Here, then, we are able to study in unusual detail the development of a sado-masochistic obsession. It is impossible to doubt that it began in the St. John's Refuge in 1875, when he was first whipped by the matron of the Episcopal Sisterhood. It is possible to say with some degree of confidence that if Fish had not been sent to an orphanage at the age of five, he would never have developed into one of the most remarkable examples of "polymorphous perversion" in the history of sexual abnormality.

Then why did his fellow-orphans never achieve the same dubious notoriety? Presumably because they lacked his intensely introverted temperament, the tendency to brood and daydream about sex and pain. In short, they lacked the ability to retreat so totally into a world of fantasy. It is difficult to avoid the conclusion that what turned Fish into a dangerous pervert was precisely the same tendency to morbid brooding and fantasy that turned Edgar Allan Poe into a writer of genius.

How far does this enable us to understand the serial killer? It enables us, at least, to grasp that there is a link between his abnormality and what we recognize as normality. Fish was turned into a serial killer by a kind of "hothouse" conditioning that led him to spend most of his childhood brooding about sex. We must bear in mind that he was born in 1870, at a time when sex crime was almost non-existent. By the time of the Jack the Ripper murders, Fish was 18—old enough, in theory, to have committed them himself. But he was still living in a world of Victorian morality and Victorian behavior, where "dirty books" were still banned—most of the "obscenity" prosecutions of that period now strike us as incomprehensible—and prostitution regarded with deep disapproval. Fish became a fully-fledged pervert by accident, starting with the accident of being sent to an orphanage at the age of 5. If Fish had been alive today, he would have had no difficulty finding material to feed his fantasies, from hard porn magazines to "snuff videos." In most large American cities he would have found streets lined with male and female "hookers" willing to cater to every perversion. It becomes possible to see why, some twenty-five years after the relaxation of the laws governing pornography, serial crime suddenly began to develop into an epidemic.

Earle Nelson and Albert Fish were undoubtedly psychopaths; in our own time, they would probably have been found guilty but insane. Carl Panzram is an entirely different matter; he belongs to a breed of killer that we shall not encounter again for another three decades: the highly intelligent, highly articulate "resentment killer."

When Carl Panzram was locked into his cell in the Washington District Jail on August 16, 1928, no one even guessed that he was one of the world's most brutal mass murderers. It is just possible that no one ever *would* have known—except for a fortunate coincidence. That same week, a young guard named Henry Lesser also arrived in the jail.

Washington, D.C. is a hot city in August—the temperature often soars into the 90s—and the first thing Lesser noticed was the stench of human sweat and disinfectant. The prison was basically a long box, with tier upon tier of barred doors facing each other down either side. The sun entered through tall, dirty windows covered in bars. As Lesser climbed the iron stairs, he noticed the silhouette of a man framed against the afternoon sunlight—a big man with massive shoulders and a round, almost hairless head. There was something about the prisoner that made an immediate impression—

Lesser declared later: "There was a kind of stillness about him." He noticed the name outside the cell door: "C. Panzram." And as he started to walk away, an odd feeling made him turn round. The man was watching him, his huge hands gripping the bars of the door. Lesser asked him when his case came up in court.

"November eleventh." The face was so hard, the eyes so flat and stony, that Lesser assumed he must be a gangster.

"What's your racket?" he asked.

Panzram gave an odd smile. "I reform people."

The two other prisoners in the cell gave a snort of laughter.

Lesser checked on why the big man was in jail. To his surprise it was not violence or extortion—merely burgling the home of a dentist. A fence had been caught selling a radio, and had admitted that Panzram had asked him to dispose of it. The police went along to a room in a cheap rooming house, and found a "bearlike man with a limp, a heavy black moustache and agate-hard eyes." They handcuffed him and asked his occupation; Panzram replied indifferently that he was a thief, then suddenly grinned. When the policeman asked why he was smiling, Panzram said: "Because a charge of stealing a radio is a joke."

"What do you mean?"

Panzram said evenly: "I've killed too many people to worry about a charge like that."

The police assumed this was boasting, and the District Attorney took the same view when they told him about it. Panzram, he said, was a "chiseler," a man who tried to waste time by getting extradition to another state—claiming to have committed crimes that could never be proved against him. Panzram had a long prison record, but it was mostly for burglary and vagrancy.

Henry Lesser soon became well liked among the prisoners. A young Jew from a poor background, he was more liberal and humane than the other guards. Panzram seemed perfectly willing to engage in conversation, although he never initiated it. A few days later Lesser asked him what he meant by "reforming people." Panzram said without expression:

"The only way to reform people is to kill them."

Lesser hurried away. What he had just heard disturbed him profoundly. Yet there was something about Panzram that aroused a curious feeling of response.

The prison governor, William L. Peak, would have found that attitude incomprehensible. He was a tough man who regarded the prisoners as dangerous subhuman creatures who had broken the laws of society, and had to take their punishment. Sympathizing with them would be as pointless as rewarding naughty children. Panzram made no secret of the fact that he hated Peak, and would welcome a chance to get his hands round his throat.

Later that day, the guards were ordered to do a "shake-down" of Panzram's tier, searching for weapons or illegal substances. Two guards entered Panzram's cell, one of them holding a short iron rod with which he tapped the window bars, while the other one watched the prisoners. One of the bars gave a dull sound instead of a clear, metallic ring. The guards looked at one another and left immediately. Ten minutes later, they were back with handcuffs, which they clicked on to Panzram. They knew better than to bother with his cellmates; only Panzram's immense hands would have had the strength to gradually loosen the bar in its cement setting.

Panzram was taken down to the basement of the jail. The iron beams of the ceiling were supported by thick pillars. Panzram's hands were passed around one of these pillars, and then re-handcuffed. Then a rope was passed through the chain of the cuffs and thrown over a beam; Panzram was heaved up until only his toes touched the floor. The angle of his arms around the pillar almost dislocated his shoulders, and the pain was agonizing. For the next twelve hours he was left in this position, the prison doctor periodically checking with a stethoscope to make sure his heart was holding out.

The next morning, Lesser saw him lying on the floor of the isolation cell, the skin of his wrists in ribbons, and his arms covered with bruises where the guards had beaten him with saps. He only muttered when Lesser asked if he was all right. But when one of the other guards looked into the cell, Panzram stirred himself enough to call him a son of a bitch. Soon after, four guards entered the cell; when Panzram resisted, he was knocked unconscious with a blackjack. When he woke up, he was once again standing on his toes in the basement, his arms chained around the pillar. All night he cursed and shrieked defiance at the guards; blows seemed to make no difference. One of the "trusties"—a convict trusted by the guards—told Lesser that, in his agony, Panzram had roared that he had killed dozens of people and would kill more if he got the chance.

The next day, when Panzram was back in his own cell, Lesser handed the trusty a dollar to give Panzram. He knew that a dollar meant extra food and cigarettes.

When the trusty passed on the dollar, Panzram obviously thought it was a joke. When the trusty assured him that it was no joke, Panzram's eyes filled with tears.

Later, when Lesser passed his cell, Panzram limped to the bars and thanked him. "That's the first time a screw has ever done me a favor." He told Lesser that reporters had been asking to see him since word of his "confessions" had leaked out, but he had refused to see them.

"But if you'll get me a pencil and paper, I'll write you the story of my life."

This was strictly against the rules; prisoners were only allowed to write a limited number of censored letters. But Lesser decided to break the rules. The next morning, he smuggled the pencil and paper through the bars, and Panzram hid them under his mattress. That evening, after midnight, Lesser slipped up to Panzram's cell and was handed a batch of manuscript. They had time for a short conversation, and for the first time, Lesser realized that Panzram had a powerful if uncultivated mind. He was startled, for example, when the prisoner told him that he had read the German philosopher Schopenhauer, and he agreed entirely that human life was a trap and a delusion.

Panzram's autobiography began: "This is a true statement of my actions, including the times and places and my reasons for doing these things, written by me of my own free will at the District Jail, Washington, D.C., November 4, 1928."

As he began reading the account of Panzram's childhood, Lesser had no idea that "these things" would include twenty brutal and violent murders.

Just over a week later, Panzram limped into court. With his record of previous convictions, it was likely that the burglary charge would earn him a five-year sentence. In such circumstances, most prisoners would have done their best to seem harmless and repentant. But Panzram seemed to be in the grip of a demon. Having told the judge that he would represent himself, he sat in the witness chair and faced the jury, staring at them with his cold, baleful eyes.

"You people got me here charged with housebreaking and larceny. I'm guilty . . . What I didn't steal I smashed. If the owner had come in I would have knocked his brains out."

This man was obviously a raging psychopath. The jurors looked pale and shaken. Panzram went on evenly:

"While you were trying me here, I was trying all of you too. I've found you guilty. Some of you I've executed. If I live I'll execute some more of you. I hate the whole human race . . . I believe the whole human race should be exterminated. I'll do my best to do it every chance I get. Now, I've done my duty, you do yours."

Not surprisingly, the jury took less than a minute to find him guilty. The judge sentenced him to twenty-five years in Leavenworth, one of America's toughest jails.

Lesser was shocked when he heard of the sentence. But, unlike the other occupants of the Washington Jail, he knew exactly why Panzram had done it. He had been reading Panzram's autobiography, and it revealed a man whose bitterness was so deep that he would have cheerfully destroyed the world. Lesser's own childhood, while poverty-stricken, had been full of family warmth and affection. Now he read with horror and fascination the story of a man who had never received any kind of love, and therefore never learned to give it.

Carl Panzram had been a tramp and a jailbird since he was 14. He had been born one year before the worst depression in American history so far. His father was a poor German immigrant, an ex-soldier who had hoped to make his fortune in America. Instead, he was forced to work as a farm laborer until he scraped together the money to buy a small farm in Minnesota. A man with a violent temper and a brooding disposition, John Panzram saw his investment wasting away through drought and hard times. Carl, their fourth child, was born on June 28, 1891. By now his overworked wife was suffering from high blood pressure and dizzy spells. One day, John Panzram walked out and the family never saw him again.

Carl was a difficult child. He longed for attention, but no one had any time to give it to him. So he behaved badly to gain attention, and was only spanked and then ignored. His first appearance in court was at the age of 8, on a charge of being drunk. At school he had further beatings with a strap—

on his hands, because at this stage he was sickly and often
ill. One day he decided to run away out west to be a cowboy;
he broke into the home of a rich neighbor and stole some
cake and apples, and a revolver. But before he had traveled
more than a few miles he was caught. At the age of 11 he
was sent to his firm reform school. "Right there and then I
began to learn about man's inhumanity to man." He was
often tied naked to a wooden block, and salty water allowed
to dry on his back. The strap with which he was beaten had
holes punched in it, so the skin came up through them as it
struck the flesh, causing small blisters; when these soon
burst, the salt caused agony.

Panzram was a strong-minded boy. "I began to hate those
who abused me. Then I began to think I would have my revenge as often as I could injure someone else. Anyone at all
would do. If I couldn't injure those who had injured me, then
I would injure someone else."

Back home after two years, he was sent to a Lutheran
school whose preacher-teacher detested him on sight and
often beat him. One day Panzram stole a revolver, and when
the preacher began to hit him, pulled it out and pulled the
trigger. It misfired. Before he could be sent back to reform
school, he jumped into an empty car on a freight train and
went west.

Back in detention for robbery, he escaped with another
youth, and they teamed up. "He showed me how to work the
stick-up racket and how to rob the poor box in churches. I in
turn taught him how to set fire to a church after we robbed
it." They enjoyed destruction for its own sake—even boring
holes in the floor of wagons full of wheat so the grain would
run away along the tracks, and emptying sand into the oil
boxes of the freight cars so they would seize up.

A brief period in the army ended in court-martial for in-
subordination, and a three-year sentence in a military jail.

The sentence was signed by the Secretary of War Howard Taft; thirteen years later, Panzram burgled Taft's home and stole $3,000. He never forgave or forgot.

Panzram served his three years, together with an extra month for trying to escape. But he succeeded in burning down the prison workshop. "Another hundred thousand dollars to my credit." He wrote later: "I was discharged from that prison in 1910. I was the spirit of meanness personified." During the next five years his only honest employment was as a strikebreaker—which ended when he was beaten unconscious by strikers. There were also several spells in prison for burglary. But the episode that had turned him into an enemy of society had happened in 1915, when he was 23. In San Francisco, he had been arrested for burgling the home of a bank president. The District Attorney offered him a deal; if he would confess where he had hidden the loot, they would "go easy" on him and give him a minimum sentence. The law broke its word; Panzram was sentenced to seven years.

In an insane rage, Panzram succeeded in breaking out of his cell, plugging all the locks so no guards could get in, then set about wrecking the jail. He tore radiators and pipes off the walls, piled up everything that would burn, and set fire to it. The guards finally broke in and "knocked his block off." Then Panzram was shackled and sent off to the Oregon State Penitentiary, one of the most inhumane in America.

He swore that he would not complete his sentence; the warden, a brutal man named Minto, swore that he would. One of Panzram's first acts was to hurl his chamberpot in a guard's face; he was beaten, then handcuffed to the door of a dark cell known as "the Hole" for thirty days. A few weeks later he was flogged and thrown in again when he was caught trying to hack a hole in the prison roof. When released, he was made to wear a uniform of red and black stripes, recently designed for dangerous troublemakers. The "punishment" misfired; prisoners wearing the "hornet suit" were regarded by other convicts as heroes.

When Warden Minto was shot to death in a hunt for an escaped convict, his brother—who was equally brutal—took over the job. He set out to make Panzram's life difficult; Panzram set out to make Minto's life difficult. He broke into the storeroom and stole bottles of lemon extract—which contained alcohol—and got a crowd of prisoners drunk; they started a riot, while Panzram, who remained sober, sat back and grinned. Next Panzram burned down the prison workshops—but was caught and thrown back into the Hole. Then he was confined in a specially built isolation block called the Bullpen.

Panzram won this round. He roared and cursed all night, beating his slop bucket on the door. The other prisoners joined in. Tension was already high because the warden had cut wages from a dollar to twenty-five cents a day. The warden decided it would be wiser to release Panzram, and assigned him to a job in the kitchen. Panzram went berserk with an axe, causing everyone to flee, and had smashed all the locks in an empty block of cells before he was clubbed unconscious.

Tension mounted until guards refused to go into the yard alone. When two convicts escaped, Minto ordered that Panzram and another suspected plotter should be "fire-hosed"—punishment outlawed by the state. The two prisoners were "water-hammered" until they were battered and bruised all over. But the news reached the state governor, who sent for Minto and ordered him to resign.

The new warden, a man named Murphy, believed that prisoners would respond to kindness. When told that Panzram had been caught sawing the bars of his cell, he asked how many times Panzram had been thrown into the

Hole; the guard said eight. "Then it doesn't seem to be working, does it?" said Murphy, and ordered that Panzram should have extra rations and given books to read. When, a few weeks later, Panzram was again caught with a hacksaw that someone had dropped into his cell, the warden sent for him. Murphy told Panzram that he had heard he was the wickedest man in the jail. Panzram said he quite agreed. And then Murphy gave Panzram the greatest shock of his life. He told him that he could walk out of the prison and go anywhere he liked—provided he gave his word of honor to return by supper time. Panzram gave his word—without the slightest intention of keeping it—and when supper time came, found that some curious inner compulsion made him go back.

Gradually, Murphy increased his freedom and that of the other prisoners. He revived the honors system, and Panzram became virtually a "trusty." But one night when he was "on leave" in the local hospital, Panzram got drunk with a pretty nurse and stayed out too late. He decided to abscond. It took a week to catch him, and then he made a determined attempt to kill the deputies who cornered him. Murphy's critics had a field day and the honors system was undermined. Panzram was given an extra ten years and thrown back into solitary confinement. But soon after that, he succeeded in escaping. At least he had won his bet with the deceased Warden Minto.

The experience of Murphy seems to have been a turning-point in Panzram's life. So far he had hated the world, but not himself. His betrayal of Murphy's trust seems to have undermined his certainty that his hatred and violence were justified. It was after his escape, in May 1918, that he began his career of murder.

In New York Panzram obtained seaman's papers and sailed for South America. He and another sailor planned to hijack a small schooner and murder everybody on board; but the sailor got drunk and tried to carry out the plan alone. In fact, he killed six men, but was caught. Panzram sailed for Europe, where he spent some time in Barlinnie Jail in Glasgow—as usual, for theft . . .

Back in New York he burgled the home of Howard Taft, the man who had confirmed his earlier sentence. He bought himself a yacht with the $3,000 in cash that he found.

"Then I figured it would be a good plan to hire a few sailors to work for me, get them out to my yacht, get them drunk, commit sodomy on them, rob them and then kill them. This I done . . ."

He explained how he would hire two sailors, take them to his yacht and wine and dine them, then blow out their brains in the middle of the night with a revolver he had stolen. Then he would drop their weighted bodies into the sea from a rowboat. "They are there yet, ten of 'em."

He hired two more sailors and sailed down the coast, robbing other yachts. It had been his intention to murder his latest two helpers, but the yacht went on to rocks and sank. Instead of killing them, Panzram paid them off.

A second attempt to become rich through burglary ended in a six-month jail sentence. Once again, Panzram signed on as a sailor, and this time went to the Belgian Congo. A job with an oil company came to an end when he sodomized the boy who waited at table—Panzram observes ironically that the youth did not appreciate the benefits of civilization. Shortly after, Panzram picked up another black boy, raped him, then battered in his skull.

"Then I went to town, bought a ticket on the Belgian steamer to Lobito Bay down the coast. There I hired a canoe and six niggers and went out hunting in the bay and backwaters. I was looking for crocodiles. I found them, plenty. They were all hungry. I fed them. I shot all six of those niggers and dumped 'em in."(Panzram explains that he shot them in the back.) "The crocks done the rest. I stole their canoe and went back to town, tied the canoe to the dock, and that night someone stole the canoe from me."

Back in America in 1920, Panzram returned to burglary and stick-ups. He also raped and murdered another boy. After taking a job as a caretaker at a yacht club in New Haven, he stole a yacht and sailed it down the coast. A man who offered to buy it tried to hold him up at gunpoint, but Panzram was ready for him; he shot him to death and dumped his body overboard.

The police soon caught up with him, but this time a good lawyer succeeded in getting him acquitted, in exchange for the yacht. When the lawyer tried to register the yacht, it was promptly reclaimed by its owner. By that time, Panzram was back in New Haven, where he committed his last rape murder, bringing the total up to twenty.

He now signed on as a sailor to go to China, but was fired the same day for getting drunk and fighting. The next day he was caught as he was burgling the express office in Larchmont, N.Y. Once again, the prosecution offered a deal; if he would plead guilty, he would receive a light sentence. History repeated itself; he received the maximum sentence: five years.

This time he was sent to America's toughest prison: Dannemora, N.Y. Enraged again by sheer brutality, he attempted to escape, but fell thirty feet on to concrete and broke both ankles. There was no attempt to set them; he was simply left alone for months until they healed. "I was so full of hate that there was no room in me for such feelings as love, pity, kindness or honor or decency. I hated everybody I saw." One day he jumped from a high gallery, fracturing a leg; he walked for the rest of his life with a limp. He spent his days dreaming of revenge, planning how to destroy a passenger train by setting a bomb in a tunnel, or poisoning a whole city's water supply.

Within a short time of being released from Dannemora, Panzram burgled a house in Washington and stole a radio. And it was in Washington District Jail that he wrote his story of murder and vandalism for Henry Lesser . . .

On January 30, 1929, Carl Panzram and thirty-one other prisoners were chained together and placed on a train for Leavenworth Penitentiary, Kansas. Henry Lesser was sent along as one of the escorts; they hoped that his presence would calm the "dingbat," as Panzram was known. It was a strange experience for Lesser—to look at this man "under his care," and to know that he had committed more than a dozen sex murders, and that no one but he and Panzram knew the whole truth.

Panzram was in a bad mood. He made a grab for Warden Peak's personal "trusty," but only had time to spit on him before he was manhandled back into line. But he was heard to mutter that he intended to "get" Peak—who was traveling with them—and hoped to wreck the train. Peak had somehow found out that Panzram hoped to pull the emergency cord when the train was at top speed, to try to derail it; accordingly, the emergency cord had been disconnected.

Harris Berman, the doctor who had tested Panzram's heart while he was being flogged, sat up all night watching the "dingbat." He had heard that Panzram was planning to break loose, and would try to kill Peak—or possibly himself. Panzram eyed the doctor with contempt, and made jeering accusations of sodomy with his assistant. He shouted the same accusations at Warden Peak whenever he showed his face.

When Lesser saw Panzram staring at two small boys who were peering in through the window at a station, he shuddered as he imagined what might be going through Panzram's mind.

When the train finally pulled up in the grey stone walls of Leavenworth, the ground was covered with dirty snow. The Leavenworth rule book contained no fewer than ninety rules—including total silence during meals; breaking any single one of them entailed harsh punishment.

While Lesser and his fellow guards were taken on a tour of the five-story cell blocks—all jammed to capacity—Warden Peak paid a call on Warden T.B. White, and warned him that the most dangerous man in the new batch was Carl Panzram. He advised White to keep him in solitary. But White, a lanky Texan, had his own ideas of reform—or perhaps he felt that Panzram was only one of dozens of dangerous prisoners. He decided to ignore the warning, and assigned Panzram to the laundry. Warden Peak and his contingent of guards returned to Washington.

When Deputy Warden Zerbst gave Panzram the regulation lecture on what was expected of him, Panzram only shrugged, then said levelly: "I'll kill the first man that bothers me."

Like so many before him, Zerbst thought this was bluff.

The laundry was one of the worst assignments in the prison: damp, badly ventilated and either too hot or too cold. The man in charge, Robert Warnke, was a short, plump civilian who was a member of the local Ku Klux Klan. He had been warned that Panzram was dangerous, but seems to have felt no misgivings as he directed him to work on a machine with a skinny burglar named Marty Rako.

Years later, in a tape-recorded interview, Rako described his impressions of Panzram. The big prisoner was a loner, seldom speaking to others. But he read throughout his spare time, including volumes of Schopenhauer and Nietzsche. And when he took a dislike to his dirty and illiterate cellmate, he ordered him to apply for a "transfer." (One of the few privileges the prisoners were allowed was to move out of a cell if they disliked their cellmate.)

Panzram received regular letters from Henry Lesser, although many of these failed to get through—the authorities were naturally obstructive concerning anything that gave prisoners pleasure. Lesser told Panzram that he had shown the autobiography to the famous literary critic H. L. Mencken, and Mencken had been impressed by the keenness of Panzram's mind. But he thought the confessions were too horrific to publish. Mencken had told Lesser: "This is one of the most amazing documents I have ever read."

Panzram was flattered, but he had other things on his mind. He hated the laundry, and its plump foreman. But he had thought of a way out. If a prisoner was punished—by being thrown in the Hole—he was seldom sent back to his previous work; most supervisors had no desire to work with a man they had punished.

Accordingly, Panzram made no real attempt to hide the fact that he was breaking the rules by laundering extra handkerchiefs. Many prisoners were wealthy men who were serving sentences for fraud; these were willing to pay for good food and for special services. When Warnke found out, he had Panzram demoted—which meant loss of wages—and sent to the Hole.

So far, Panzram's scheme was working. But when he came out of the Hole, he learned that the second part had misfired. He was being sent back to the laundry. Possibly Warnke felt he would lose face by allowing Panzram to be transferred, since Panzram was known to hate him. Or possibly he simply saw through Panzram's scheme and decided to frustrate it. He also turned down Panzram's direct request for a transfer.

The weather was becoming stifling, and new batches of

prisoners made the jail intolerably overcrowded. There were so many that there were no fewer than nine sittings in the dining hall. The main meal of the day consisted of boiled rice with tomato sauce.

Thursday, June 20, 1929 looked like being another blazingly hot day as foreman Warnke walked into the laundry, and prepared to check on the prisoners. He walked down the aisle towards a disassembled washing machine that stood near some open packing cases, strolling past a heavy steel pillar that held up the ceiling—not unlike the one Panzram had been chained to in the Washington Jail—and stood surveying the washing machine. Then he turned, and realized that Carl Panzram had been standing behind the steel pillar, and that he was holding a crowbar that had been used to open the packing cases. Warnke had no time to notice anything else as the crowbar was brought down on his head, shattering the bone. Panzram screamed with rage and satisfaction as he went on pounding the skull of the fallen man's head to a pulp. Then, when he was sure Warnke was dead, he turned on the other prisoners and guards; they fled in all directions as he flourished the bloodstained crowbar.

Like some great limping ape, Panzram shambled down the street outside, and into the office of the Deputy Warden. Fortunately for Zerbst, he was late that morning. Panzram opened the door of the mailroom and limped in, swinging the bar; yelling clerks scattered in all directions. A convict who came in with a message was chased down the street. Then Panzram made his way back to the locked gate of the isolation unit. "Let me in."

"Not with that in your hand," said the startled guard.

Panzram threw away the crowbar, and the guard unlocked the steel door. Now Panzram's rage was all dissipated, he looked relaxed and almost serene as he walked into the nearest cell.

When Warden Peak heard the news in Washington, he lost no time in summoning the press and saying "I told you so." Lesser was shocked and depressed—as much by the death of a fellow prison employee as by Panzram's predicament.

Panzram himself was startled when no one tried to beat him to death, or even drag him off to the Hole. Instead, he was placed in a large, airy cell, next door to a prisoner named Robert Stroud (who would become known as the "the Bird Man of Alcatraz"), and although he was kept locked in without exercise, he was allowed to read all day long. He told Lesser: "If, in the beginning I had been treated as I am now, then there wouldn't have been quite so many people in this world that have been robbed, raped and killed . . ."

In reply, Lesser suggested that he himself should try and raise support from influential people—like Mencken—to get Panzram a reprieve. Panzram replied: "Wake up, kid . . . The real truth of the matter is that I haven't the least desire to reform . . . It took me 36 years to be like I am now; then how do you figure that I could, if I wanted to, change from black to white in the twinkling of an eye?"

Lesser declined to take no for an answer, and persuaded a famous psychiatrist, Karl Menninger, to go and see Panzram. Forty years later, Menninger recalled how he had interviewed Panzram—under guard—in the anteroom of a federal court. When he told Panzram that he did not believe he would harm someone who had never done him any harm, Panzram's reply was to hurl himself at Menninger as far as his chains would allow him, and to shout: "Take these off me and I'll kill you before their eyes." Then Panzram went on to describe with gruesome satisfaction all his murders and rapes.

In spite of the fact that a Sanity Commission decided that Panzram was insane, on April 15, 1930 the jury in a federal courtroom in Topeka, Kansas, found him guilty, and the judge sentenced him to death. Panzram was pleased with the verdict, and interrupted his defense attorney to say that he had no wish to appeal.

One problem for the state was that executions in Kansas were illegal. Panzram's sentence caused indignation in anti-capital-punishment groups. One such group was permitted to appear outside his cell to ask him to sign a petition for clemency. They were startled to be met with shrieks of rage and obscenity. Subsequently Panzram wrote a long and brilliantly lucid letter to a penal reform group explaining precisely why he had no desire to escape the death sentence. He even wrote to President Herbert Hoover telling him not to interfere and reprieve him. He managed to make an unsuccessful attempt at suicide, eating a plate of beans that he had concealed until they had gone black and poisonous, and somehow slashing a six-inch wound in his leg. His magnificent constitution saw him through.

Shortly before six on the morning of September 5, 1930, Panzram was led from his cell, singing a pornographic song of his own composition. Seeing two men in clerical garb among the spectators in the corridor, he roared an obscenity about "Bible-backed cocksuckers," and told the warden to get them out. When this had been done, he said: "Let's get going. What are we hanging around for?"

On the scaffold, the hangman, who was from Ohio and therefore known as a "Hoosier," asked him if there was anything he wanted. "Yes, hurry it up, you Hoosier bastard! I could hang a dozen men while you're fooling around."

Moments later, the trap fell, breaking his neck.

Panzram remains one of the most fascinating cases in criminal history because he pursued hatred and revenge with a kind of ruthless logic. He possessed an extremely strong will—the kind of will that makes great statesmen and soldiers and reformers. It was a characteristic he shared with

Michelangelo, Luther, Beethoven and Lenin. But when Panzram met with opposition, and he was sure he was in the right, he charged like a mad bull. It made no difference if he ran into a brick wall; he almost enjoyed battering his head against brick walls. Attempts to beat him into submission only made him twice as determined—and twice as violent and dangerous.

Riding the freight trains at the age of 14, he had another lesson in inhumanity when he invited four burly tramps into the comfortable box car he had found. Ignoring his struggles, they held him down and raped him. The same thing happened again in a small town in the mid-west when he approached a crowd of loafers sitting around a fire and tried to beg food. They got him drunk on whiskey, and he only realized what had happened when he recovered consciousness. The lesson Panzram learned from this was simple: Might makes Right.

Panzram was a highly sexed youth, but even the cheapest whores were too expensive for a teenage tramp. Instead, he developed a taste for sodomy. On one occasion when a brakeman caught him hiding in a freight car, Panzram pulled out a revolver and sodomized him at gunpoint, then forced two other hoboes to do the same. It was his crude and simple method of taking revenge on the world.

Sexual frustration also turned Panzram into a rapist—but not of women. After catching gonorrhea from a prostitute, he decided that women were not for him. He picked up boys whenever he could, and when he robbed men, he often tied them to a tree to commit rape. If someone had accused Panzram of being homosexual, he would have been astonished. It was merely a sexual outlet—and an outlet for his aggression. By committing anal rape, he was somehow repaying what had been done to him; he called it the Law of Compensation.

Although he never actually says so, it is clear that he had acquired another curious perversion—pyromania, a tendency to experience sexual excitement from causing fires. He arrived in Houston, Texas, during the great fire of February 1912. "I . . . walked through the town, enjoying the sights of all the burning buildings, and listening to the tales of woe, the moans and sighs of those whose homes and property were burning. I enjoyed it all . . ."

His hatred of society—and of respectable people—dominated his life. Like the Marquis de Sade, he was convinced that society is built on corruption, and on the strong exploiting the weak. It gave him immense satisfaction to record the sins of those in authority—for example, of the warden of Deer Lodge Prison, Montana, who was also the mayor. "He wound up his career by blowing out his own brains because he was due for a bit of his own cells for charges of stealing the state funds and a host of other crimes."

What baffles the reader of Panzram's autobiography is why he never used his intelligence to avoid punishment. It is understandable why he tried to burn down the San Francisco jail when the authorities broke their word and sentenced him to seven years. But it is impossible to understand why the first thing he did at the Oregon jail was to throw a full chamberpot in a guard's face, earning himself thirty days of torment.

The answer has to be that Panzram never acquired any kind of self-discipline. And it may have been this recognition that led to the virtually suicidal activities of his final years. This becomes very clear in a story told by Lesser. He had been told to test the bars of Panzram's cell with a steel rod. As he left the cell, Panzram said in a strangled voice: "Don't ever do that again. Turning your back on me like that."

Lesser protested: "I knew you wouldn't harm me."

"Yes, you're the one man in the world I don't want to kill. But I'm so erratic I'm liable to do anything."

It was as if Panzram had trained a part of himself—a kind of savage dog—to leap at people's throats. But the dog was now out of control . . .

Perhaps the cruellest thing that ever happened to Panzram was Warden Murphy's offer to allow him to walk out of the jail if he promised to return. It was a proof that the murderous logic on which he had based his life was founded on a fallacy. To hate "Society" is to hate an abstraction. Society is a mass of individuals. And when he finally betrayed Murphy's trust, Panzram suddenly began to hate himself as well as other people. The subsequent murders were an attempt to kill something inside himself. But when Lesser sent him the dollar, and Panzram's eyes filled with tears, he knew that it was still alive. Suddenly, he experienced an overpowering need to cleanse himself through confession . . .

In the 1930s, America again had a series of murders as mysterious as those of the New Orleans Axeman; the killer was known as "the Mad Butcher of Kingsbury Run" or "the Cleveland Torso Killer," and the crimes are still unsolved.

On a warm September afternoon in 1935, two boys on their way home from school walked along a dusty, sooty gully called Kingsbury Run, in the heart of Cleveland, Ohio. On a weed-covered slope known as Jackass Hill, one challenged the other to a race, and they hurtled sixty feet down the slope to the bottom. Sixteen-year-old James Wagner was the winner, and as he halted, panting, he noticed something white in the bushes a few yards away. A closer look revealed that it was a naked body, and that it was headless.

The police who arrived soon after found the body of a young white male clad only in black socks; the genitals had also been removed. It lay on its back, with the legs stretched out and the arms placed neatly by the sides, as if laid out for a funeral. Thirty feet away, the policemen found another body, lying in the same position; it was of an older man, and had also been decapitated and emasculated.

Hair sticking out of the ground revealed one of the heads a few yards away, and the second was found nearby. The genitals were also found lying nearby, as if thrown away by the killer.

One curious feature of the case was that there was no blood on the ground or on the bodies, which were quite clean. It looked as if they had been killed and beheaded elsewhere, then carefully washed when they had ceased to bleed.

Medical examination made the case more baffling than ever. The older corpse was badly decomposed, and the skin discolored; the pathologists discovered that this was due to some chemical substance, as if the killer had tried to preserve the body. The older victim had been dead about two weeks; the younger man had only been dead three days. His fingerprints enabled the police to identify him as 28-year-old Edward Andrassy, who had a minor police record for carrying concealed weapons. He lived near Kingsbury Run and had a reputation as a drunken brawler.

But the most chilling discovery was that Andrassy had been killed by decapitation. Rope marks on his wrists revealed that he had been tied and had struggled violently. The killer had apparently cut off his head with a knife. The skill with which the operation had been performed suggested a butcher—or possibly a surgeon.

It proved impossible to identify the older man. But the identification of Andrassy led the police to hope that it should not be too difficult to trace his killer. He had spent his nights gambling and drinking in a slum part of town and was known as a pimp. But further investigation also revealed that he had male lovers. Lead after lead looked marvelously promising. The husband of a married woman with whom he had had an affair had sworn to kill him. But the man was able to prove his innocence. So were various shady characters who might have borne a grudge. Lengthy police investigation led to a dead end—as it did in another ten cases of the killer who became known as "the Mad Butcher of Kingsbury Run."

Four months later, on a raw January Sunday, the howling of a dog finally led a black woman resident of East Twentieth Street—not far from Kingsbury Run—to go and investigate. She found the chained animal trying to get at a basket near a factory wall. Minutes later, she told a neighbor that the basket contained "hams." But the neighbor soon recognized the "hams" as parts of a human arm. A burlap bag proved to contain the lower half of a female torso. The head was missing, as were the left arm and lower parts of both legs. But fingerprints again enabled the police to trace the victim, who had a record for soliciting. She proved to be a 41-year-old prostitute named Florence Polillo, a squat, double-chinned woman who was well known in the bars of the neighborhood.

Again, there were plenty of leads, and again, all of them petered out. Two weeks later, the left arm and lower legs were found in a vacant lot. The head was never recovered.

The murder of Flo Polillo raised an unwelcome question. The first two murders had convinced the police that they were looking for a homosexual sadist; this latest crime made it look as if this killer was quite simply a sadist—like Peter Kurten, the Düsseldorf killer, executed in 1931; he had killed men, women and children indifferently, and he was not remotely homosexual. And now the pathologist recalled that, a year before that first double murder, the torso of an unknown woman had been found on the edge of Lake Erie. It began to look as if the Mad Butcher was quite simply a sadist.

At least the Cleveland public felt they had one thing in their favor. Since the double killing, the famous Elliot Ness had been appointed Cleveland's Director of Public Safety. Ness and his "Untouchables" had cleared up Chicago's Prohibition rackets, then, in 1934, Ness had moved to Cleveland to fight its gangsters. With Ness in charge, the Head Hunter of Kingsbury Run—another press soubriquet—would find himself becoming the hunted.

But it was soon clear to Ness that hunting a sadistic pervert is nothing like hunting professional gangsters. The killer struck at random, and unless he was careless enough to leave behind a clue—like a fingerprint—then the only hope of catching him was in the act. And Ness soon became convinced that the Mad Butcher took great pleasure in feeling that he was several steps ahead of the police.

The Head Hunter waited until the summer before killing again, then lived up to his name by leaving the head of a young man, wrapped in a pair of trousers, under a bridge in Kingsbury Run; again, two boys found it on June 22, 1936. The body was found a quarter of mile away and it was obvious from the blood that he had died where he lay. And medical evidence showed that he had died from decapitation. It was not clear how the killer had prevented him from struggling while he did it. The victim was about 25, and heavily tattooed. His fingerprints were not in police files. Three weeks later, a young female hiker discovered another decapitated body in a gully; the head lay nearby. The decomposition made it clear that this man had been killed before the previously discovered victim.

The last "butchery" of 1936 was of another man of about 30, found in Kingsbury Run; the body had been cut in two, and emasculated. A hat found nearby led to a partial identification: a housewife recalled giving it to a young tramp. Not far away there was a "hobo camp" where down-and-outs slept; this was obviously where the Butcher had found his latest victim.

The fact that Cleveland had been the scene of a Republican Convention, and was now the site of a "Great Expo," led to even more frantic police activity and much press criticism. The murders were reported all over the world, and in Nazi Germany and Fascist Italy were cited as proof of the decadence of the New World.

As month after month went by with no further grisly discoveries, Clevelanders hoped they had heard the last of the Mad Butcher. But in February 1937, that hope was dashed when the killer left the body of a young woman in a chopped-up pile on the shores of Lake Erie. She was never identified. The eighth victim, a young negress, *was* identified from her teeth as Mrs. Rose Wallace, 40; only the skeleton remained, and it looked as if she might have been killed in the previous year.

Victim no. 9 was male and had been dismembered; when he was fished out of the river, the head was missing, and was never found. This time the killer had gone even further in his mutilations—like Jack the Ripper. It was impossible to identify the victim. Two men seen in a boat were thought to be the Butcher with an accomplice, but this suggestion that there might be two Butchers led nowhere.

The Butcher now seems to have taken a rest until nine moths later. Then the lower part of a leg was pulled out of the river. Three weeks later, two burlap bags in the river proved to contain more body fragments, which enabled the pathologist to announce that the victim was female, a brunette of about 25. She was never identified.

The killer was to strike twice more. More than a year after the last discovery, in August 1938, the dismembered torso of a woman was found on a dump on the lakefront, and a search of the area revealed the bones of a second victim, a male. A quilt in which the remains of this twelfth victim were wrapped was identified as having been given to a junk man. Neither body could be identified.

One thing was now obvious: the Butcher was selecting his victims from vagrants and down-and-outs. Ness decided to take the only kind of action that seemed left to him: two days after the last find, police raided the "shantytown" near Kingsbury Run, arrested hundreds of vagrants, and burned it down. Whether or not by coincidence, the murders now ceased.

The suspects? Two of the most efficient of the man hunters, Detectives Merylo and Zalewski, had spent a great deal of time searching for the killer's "laboratory." At one point they thought they had found it—but, like all leads, this one faded away.

Next, the investigators discovered that Flo Polillo and Rose Wallace—victim no. 8—had frequented the same saloon, and that Andrassy—no. 2—had been a "regular" there too. They also learned of a middle-aged man called Frank who carried knives and threatened people with them when drunk. When they learned that this man—Frank Dolezal— had also been living with Flo Polillo, they felt they had finally identified the killer. Dolezal was arrested, and police discovered a brown substance like dried blood in the cracks of his bathroom floor. Knives with dried bloodstains on them provided further incriminating evidence. Under intensive questioning, Dolezal—a bleary-eyed, unkempt man—confessed to the murder of Flo Polillo. Newspapers announced the capture of the Butcher. Then things began to go wrong. The "dried blood" in the bathroom proved not to be blood after all. Dolezal's "confession" proved to be full of errors about the corpse and method of disposal. And when, in August 1939, Dolezal hanged himself in jail, the autopsy revealed that he had two cracked ribs, and suggested that his confession had been obtained by force.

Yet Ness himself claimed that he knew the solution to the murders. He reasoned that the killer was a man who had a house of his own in which to dismember the bodies, and a car in which to transport them. So he was not a down-and-out. The skill of the mutilations suggested medical training. The fact that some of the victims had been strong men suggested that the Butcher had to be big and powerful—a conclusion supported by a size 12 footprint near one of the bodies.

Ness set three of his top agents, Virginia Allen, Barney Davis and Jim Manski, to make enquiries among the upper levels of Cleveland society. Virginia was a sophisticated girl with contacts among Cleveland socialites. And it was she who learned about a man who sounded like the ideal suspect. Ness was to call him "Gaylord Sundheim"—a big man from a well-to-do family, who had a history of psychiatric problems. He had also studied medicine. When the three "Untouchables" called on him, he leered sarcastically at Virginia and closed the door in their faces. Ness invited him—pressingly—to lunch, and he came under protest. When Ness finally told him he suspected him of being the Butcher—hoping that shock tactics might trigger a confession—Sundheim sneered: "Prove it."

Soon after this, Sundheim had himself committed to a mental institution. Ness knew *he* was now "untouchable," for even if Ness could prove his guilt, he could plead insanity.

During the next two years Ness received a series of jeering postcards, some signed "Your paranoid nemesis." They ceased abruptly when "Sundheim" died in the mental institution.

Was "Sundheim" the Butcher? Probably. But not certainly. In Pittsburgh in 1940, three decapitated bodies were found in old boxcars (i.e., railway coaches). Members of Ness's team went to investigate, but no clue to the triple murder was ever discovered. But then, the Mad Butcher was also blamed for the horrific Black Dahlia killing in Hollywood in 1947, in which model Elizabeth Short was tortured before the killer cut her body in half at the waist, although no serial killer has ever been known to leave an eight-year gap between murders. The Torso case remains unsolved.

6

THE 1940s

THE DECADE OF THE 1940S HAS MANY SEX MURDERS—MORE than the previous decade—yet almost no mass murders like those of the 1920s and 1930s. Perhaps the mass slaughter of the Second World War kept potential serial killers otherwise occupied. One of the few exceptions is the German Paul Ogorzov—the "S-Bahn rapist"—who, in fact, began his career of violence shortly before the war.

His first victim, a gym teacher named Frieda Lausche, was traveling on the S-Bahn (short for Schnell-Bahn, or fast railway) on the evening of September 20, 1940, when the man sitting opposite her in the dimly lit carriage suddenly flung open the door and hurled her out. Because she was supple and in good training, she succeeded in falling safely, and hurried to the police. They were frankly incredulous. Why should a man simply fling a woman from a moving train, with no attempt at either assault or robbery? And why was she not scratched and bruised? They agreed to look into the case, then quietly forgot about it.

Three weeks later they had to revise their opinion. On October 11, 1940, a secretary named Ingeborg Goetz was traveling on the elevated railway between Rummelsberg and Karlshorst around midnight when a man in the carriage struck her on the head with some sort of club, then slashed her stomach with a knife. After this he opened the door and threw her out. She recovered in the hospital, but was unable to describe her attacker, except to say he wore a peaked cap and some kind of uniform with brass buttons.

Now the police were inclined to wonder if the attacker might have been responsible for a murder that had happened a week before the attack on Ingeborg Goetz: a war widow named Gerda Dietrich had been found stabbed to death in her cottage near the S-Bahn, in the suburb of Sommerland. It had been assumed she was the victim of a burglar, but wounds in the stomach—similar to those of Frau Goetz—suggested the madman who hurled women from trains.

Three weeks later, on December 3, the corpse of a girl was found near the S-Bahn station at Rummelsberg; she was identified as 22-year-old Matilda Hollesch, and she had been clubbed to death with a blow on the back of the head, and then raped. A few hours after this attack, another woman was found by the S-Bahn track nearby; she had been struck violently on the head and hurled from the train. This victim, 20-year old postal clerk Irmgard Frank, had not been raped.

The following day, a passenger found the murder weapon down the back of a seat: a two-foot piece of lead-covered cable, stained with blood and human hairs. Forensic tests established that it had been used to kill both women.

Nearly three weeks later, at 7 o'clock in the morning on December 22, the killer bludgeoned and hurled from the train a housewife named Maria Bahr, again killing her.

Now Detective Wilhelm Ludtke, one of Berlin's leading investigators, decided to try placing decoys on the trains—armed policewomen or volunteers. He also decided that "official guides" would escort young women who had to travel home late at night. But only two weeks later, on January 3, 1941, a man who had claimed to be an official guide pushed a cinema usher out of the train; fortunately, she was only scratched and bruised. But forty-eight hours later, a 23-year-old telephone operator named Sonia Marke died when she was hurled from a train.

The skill shown by the S-Bahn rapist in avoiding traps suggested either a policeman or a railway employee: the description of survivors suggested the latter. But soon after the last murder one of the women "decoys" almost succeeded in arresting the killer. Alone in a carriage with an S-Bahn employee, she became suspicious of his sudden movements and his evident desire to make her nervous, and announced that she was a policewoman and that he was under arrest. The man leapt from the train as it pulled into a platform and disappeared.

On February 11, another woman, Martha Zernowski, was killed as she was clubbed and hurled from a train. On February 20, Lisa Novak, a 30-year-old factory worker, was raped, clubbed and hurled to her death from the train.

This time an arrest was made—a known sex offender named Richard Bauer, whose footprint was found in the girl's blood. He insisted that he had merely stumbled over her in the dark, but was kept in custody as a suspect.

Another possible suspect—among many—was a 28-year-old railway worker named Paul Ogorzov, a married man with two children. The Rummelsberg stationmaster admitted that he was friendly with Ogorzov, and often told him what measures the police were planning. But Ogorzov was at work at the time of many of the murders, and workmates vouched for him; he was dropped as a suspect.

The attacks now ceased until July 3, 1941, when a woman named Olga Opell was found dead beside the tracks. Since

Bauer was in prison, he was automatically exonerated and re-leased.

But investigators now learned that Paul Ogorzov had slipped away from his job as a telegraph operator at about the time of the murder of Olga Opell—he had been seen climbing over a fence. Under interrogation, Ogorzov admitted this, and explained that he had a girlfriend who lived nearby. This proved to be true; moreover, the girl declared that Ogorzov had been with her at the time Olga Opell was attacked. But when traces of blood were found on Ogorzov's tunic, the questioning was renewed. He explained that one of his children had cut his finger. But Ludtke now took a long look at the map showing where attacks had taken place, and observed that most of them were along the route between the Rummelsberg station and Ogorzov's home. This seemed too much of a coincidence, so he began pressing Ogorzov about reports from women that a man had shone his torch in their eyes. Ogorzov finally admitted that he had done this on two occasions. Pressed to name precisely where this had happened, Ogorzov became confused, then mentioned a location where, in fact, a rape had occurred.

The victims who had escaped were brought in to confront Ogorzov; one positively identified him, and mentioned that he had worn a coat with a very wide collar; when police found such a coat in Ogorzov's home, he admitted to attempted assault on four women. Asked to pinpoint the places, he mentioned Sommerland, where Gerda Dietrich had been stabbed to death in her cottage. His state of confusion was now so great that he admitted that Gerda Dietrich had been one of the women he had beaten with his fists. This left Ludtke in no doubt that there had been so many victims that he was mixing them up.

Finally, shock tactics worked where long questioning had

failed; when Ludtke showed him the smashed skulls of several victims, the harassed Ogorzov suddenly broke down, and admitted that he was the S-Bahn killer. He also admitted that he had been guilty of a number of sexual attacks on women since 1939, mostly in the course of attempts to pick them up.

The incident that had turned him into a killer had occurred a few weeks before he threw the first victim—the gym teacher—from the moving train. He had accosted a woman near the Rummelsberg station, and she had screamed, bringing her menfolk from a nearby house. They beat up Ogorzov so badly that he had to spend a week in bed. He emerged vengeful and ruthless. Women would pay for this affront to his dignity . . .

And so the first two victims were hurled from the train, an act that he confessed gave him sadistic pleasure—his voice became hoarse as he described the sensation of opening the door and throwing them out into the darkness. But he quickly progressed to rape and murder, killing most victims with a tremendous blow from the lead-covered cable.

Perhaps because Ogorzov was a member of the Nazi Party, and the authorities wished to avoid embarrassment, his trial (on July 21, 1941) was rushed through in one day, and he was beheaded the following day.

The same embarrassment seems to have led the Nazis to hush up the crimes of another serial killer, Bruno Lüdke.

Lüdke was born in 1909; he was definitely mentally defective, in the same way as Earle Nelson. He began his murders at the age of eighteen. During the war he found it easy to kill. He was arrested for a sexual assault and sterilized by order of Himmler's SS. He was a petty thief (like Kürten) and a sadist who enjoyed torturing animals and (on one occasion) running down a woman with his horse-drawn van. (He worked as a laundry roundsman.)

On January 29, 1943, a 51-year-old woman, Frieda Rösner, was found strangled on the outskirts of a wood near Berlin where she had been collecting fuel. Kriminal Kommissar Franz, in charge of the case, examined all the known criminals in Köpenick, the nearby village. These included Lüdke, who lived at 32 Grüne Trift. When he was asked if he had known the murdered woman, Lüdke admitted that he had, and that he had last seen her in the woods. Asked if he had killed her, he sprang at his interrogator and had to be overpowered; he then admitted he was the murderer, and added that under Paragraph 51 (concerning mental defectives) he could not be indicted for the crime. Lüdke went on to confess to killing eighty-five women throughout Germany since 1928. His normal method was strangulation or stabbing with a knife, and although he stole their belongings, rape was the chief motive. Franz investigated the murders and after a year, reported that it seemed to be true that Lüdke was responsible for all the crimes he confessed to. But it is also true that local police chiefs blamed all their unsolved murders on Lüdke, the ideal scapegoat.

Lüdke believed that he could never be indicted because he was insane. In fact, the embarrassment of various police forces who had arrested innocent men for Lüdke's crimes led to the case being hushed up and treated as a State secret. Lüdke was sent to a hospital in Vienna where he was a guinea-pig for various experiments, and one of the injections killed him on April 8, 1944.

In London during the days of the blitz, another sadistic killer was responsible for a brief reign of terror that was comparable to that of Jack the Ripper.

In the early hours of February 9, 1942, a 40-year-old

schoolmistress, Miss Evelyn Hamilton, was found strangled in an air-raid shelter in Montagu Place, Marylebone. Her handbag was missing; she had not been sexually assaulted. On February 10, Mrs. Evelyn Oatley, known as Nita Ward, a 35-year-old ex-revue actress, was found dead in her Wardour Street flat. She was found naked on the bed; her throat had been cut and the lower part of her body mutilated with a can-opener. Fingerprints were found on the can-opener and a mirror.

On February 11, a Tuesday, another woman was murdered, although the police did not find out about it until three days later. She was Mrs. Margaret Lowe, aged 43; she lived alone in a flat in Gosfield Street in the West End. She had been strangled with a silk stocking, and mutilated with a razor blade in the same way as Mrs. Oatley. She was discovered on Friday by her 14-year-old evacuee daughter who came to pay a visit.

Some hours after Mrs. Lowe's body was found, the fourth victim was also discovered. She was Mrs. Doris Jouannet, whose husband was the night manager of a Paddington hotel. When he returned home on Friday evening he noticed that the milk had not been taken in. Mrs. Jouannet had been strangled with a stocking and mutilated with a razor blade. It soon transpired that Mrs. Jouannet had been in the habit of picking up soldiers in Leicester Square pubs while her husband was on night duty; he had last seen her alive at ten o'clock on the previous evening.

Shortly after Mrs. Jouannet's body was discovered, a young airman tried to accost a Mrs. Heywood in a pub near Piccadilly. She refused, and he followed her out into the blacked-out street, saying "You must at least kiss me good night." He dragged her into a doorway and throttled her into unconsciousness. A passer-by heard the scuffle, and investigated; the man ran away, leaving behind his gas-mask. This had his service number stenciled on it.

The young airman immediately picked up another woman and drove with her in a taxi to her flat in Southwark Street, Paddington. She was Mrs. Mulcahy, known as Kathleen King. In her room, the light failed, and the airman seized her by the throat. Her terror of the "ripper" who had already killed four women made her fight violently and scream. The airmen fled, leaving behind his belt.

From the gas-mask case, the attacker was identified as Gordon Frederick Cummins, a 28-year-old RAF cadet, married and living in North London. He was arrested within twelve hours of the attack on Kathleen King, on returning to his billet in St. John's Wood.

Cummins had a curious record. Although he came from a good family and was well educated, he had been dismissed from a series of jobs as unreliable and dishonest. He had married in 1936 the private secretary of a theatrical producer. One of his companions declared he was a "phoney," that he spoke with a fake Oxford accent and claimed he had a right to use "honorable" before his name because he was the il-legi-timate son of a member of the House of Lords. He was known as "the Duke" to his companions.

His fingerprints corresponded with those on the mirror and can-opener; also, like the killer, he was left-handed. It appeared later that another prostitute had had a narrow escape from death; Cummins had accompanied her home on the night he killed Mrs. Oatley, but she had mentioned that she had no money, and Cummins, who killed for cash, left her alone.

He was sentenced to death at the Old Bailey, and executed on June 25, 1942 during an air raid. Sir Bernard Spilsbury, who had performed the post-mortem on Mrs. Oatley, also performed one on Cummins.

Like Cummins, Neville Heath would have undoubtedly gone on to commit more murders if he had not been caught—or, in fact, virtually given himself up. Born in 1917, Heath was one of those men who seem to be born to be petty crooks. By the age of 20 he had been dismissed from the RAF for bouncing checks and stealing a car. After that, posing as "Lord Dudley," he bounced more checks and received probation; still under 21 he was sent to Borstal for three years for stealing jewelry from a family he was staying with—he was engaged to the daughter. (Heath was immensely attractive to women—one brother officer called him the male equivalent of the *femme fatale*.) At the outbreak of the war he was allowed to join the army, but was soon in trouble in Cairo for somehow getting the paymaster to give him two salaries, and was again cashiered. On his was back to England on a troopship, he seduced a mother and her 17-year-old daughter, and terrified the daughter by hitting her as he made love, inflicting some unpleasant bruises. He decided to remain in South Africa, and swindled a bank in Durban by producing an apparently genuine letter on Air Ministry notepaper authorizing a bank to pay him money. When Durban began to see through him he moved to Johannesburg and swindled hotels with plausible stories about money that was on its way from England. Then, incredibly, he was admitted into the South African Air Force, and even when they learned that he was a con-man, they allowed him to remain. By this time he had married a girl from a wealthy family, and for a year at least, the marriage was happy. Then, in 1944, he was seconded to the RAF again, and at Finmere, Oxfordshire, succeeded in getting engaged to nine girls at the same time. (The reason, almost certainly, is that "respectable" girls would only go to bed with a man when he had promised marriage.) When the body of a WAAF was found not far from the station, with bruises and injuries to her genitals,

Heath was suspected, but never charged. Back in South Africa, he was involved in a car accident that left a young nurse burned to death—Heath claimed he had been thrown out of the car by the crash. His wife divorced him. Arrested again for dud checks and posing as a lieutenant-colonel, he was cashiered from the South African Air Force and deported to England.

In February 1946 the police were called to the Strand Palace Hotel in London, where Heath had been caught—naked—whipping a nearly unconscious girl. Because she refused to lodge a complaint he was released. Soon after this he was fined ten pounds for posing as an Air Force officer. Not long after, he was again caught flogging a naked girl, who was tied to a bed in a hotel bedroom; again the woman refused to charge him.

Finally, on June 21, 1946, Heath was carried away as he flogged a 32-year-old artist named Margery Gardner, and this time no one interrupted them—perhaps because he made sure that her face was rammed into the pillow. She suffocated to death—but not before Heath had flogged her with a riding whip, bitten her nipples until they were almost detached, and rammed a poker into her vagina. The body was discovered the next morning by a chambermaid. By that time Heath was already on his way to the Ocean Hotel at Worthing, from which he telephoned the girl who had spent the previous Saturday night with him in the same hotel where he had killed Margery Gardner—the Pembridge Court in Notting Hill. On a visit to the girl's parents, he learned that the police wanted to question him about the murder, whereupon he wrote them a letter claiming that he had lent his room key to Margery Gardner and a male friend, and found her body when he visited the room early the next morning.

A week later, on July 3, he was staying in the Tollard Royal Hotel in Bournemouth, posing as Group Captain Rupert Brooke. There he met a pretty ex-Wren named Doreen Marshall. He persuaded her to have dinner with him, and to allow him to walk her back to her own hotel, the Norfolk. Witnesses who saw them together could see that she was nervous and tense. Five days later, Doreen Marshall's body was found in a wooded dell called Branksome Dene Chine, beaten, mutilated and stabbed to death. The major injury was a Jack-the-Ripper-type slash from the inside of the thigh to the breast, By then, Heath had already volunteered his help to the local police, and they had recognized him as the man wanted by Scotland Yard. A cloakroom ticket in Heath's pocket led them to a briefcase that contained the riding whip with which Margery Gardner had been lashed.

Heath was tried for the murder of Margery Gardner—an odd decision, since her death was probably accidental—and executed at Pentonville on October 16, 1946. If, as seems likely, he was also guilty of the two earlier murders, then he certainly qualifies for a place in this book as a serial killer.

Even Germany—with its astonishing record of serial murder, from Grossman to Ogorzov—became relatively quiescent in the 1940s. Apart from Lüdke, there is only Rudolf Pleil, a sex murderer who committed suicide in his cell in 1958. Pleil was a habitual criminal, a burglar among other things, who began by attacking women in order to rob them. (He always robbed his female victims as well as raping them.) Since 1945 he reckoned to have killed fifty women. He was a small, fat man with a friendly face (although he had a receding forehead which produced an ape-like effect).

Pleil, like Kürten, enjoyed murder, and referred to himself boastfully as "der beste Totmacher" (the best death-maker). Full details of his crimes are unfortunately not available at the time of writing. Like Kürten, he used many weapons for his murders—stones, knives, hatchets and hammers to kill and mutilate his victims. When in prison he often wrote to the authorities, offering to reveal the whereabouts of another murder; in this way he would get an "airing" to the town where he had buried one of his victims. On one occasion, he wrote to the mayor of a town offering his services as hangman, and telling him that if he wanted to study his qualifications, he should look in the well at the end of the town; a strangled body was discovered in this well. Pleil was a vain man who took pleasure in the horror he aroused and described himself as "quite a lad." He is quoted as saying: "Every man has his passion. Some prefer whist. I prefer killing people."

America has no cases of mass murder that date from the war years. But in June 1946, an 18-year-old Chicago student named William Heirens was caught as he tried to burgle an apartment building, and was grilled by the police until he confessed to three murders: those of Josephine Ross, a widow who was stabbed in the throat on June 3, 1945; Frances Brown, who was shot and then stabbed in her apartment; and Suzanne Degnan, a 6-year-old girl who was removed from her bed on January 7, 1946 and dismembered. Heirens claimed that the murders were actually committed by an alter ego called George, and explained that he had started burgling apartments to steal women's panties. He was sentenced to life imprisonment. In recent years, Heirens' defenders—like Dolores Kennedy (author of *William Heirens: His Day in Court*)—have argued that the confession was forced out of him by threats of the electric chair; Heirens himself continues to insist that he is totally innocent of everything but burglary. He also claims that the famous inscription written in lipstick about he body of Frances Brown—"For heaven's sake catch me before I kill more I cannot control myself"—was written by a reporter. In an anthology called *Murder in the 1940s*, I have printed Heirens' own account of the case, which makes some telling points in favor of his innocence. *If* he is innocent, of course, this would be one of the most disturbing miscarriages of justice in legal history. But even if not, it could be argued that a man who has served more than forty-five years in jail has more than paid for crimes committed as a teenager, and deserves to be paroled. (In fact, Heirens has had his application for parole rejected several times.)

The crimes of Marcel Petiot, a French doctor who, under the pretense of helping Jews to escape from occupied France, murdered them in a gas chamber and stole their possessions, belong to the realm of mass murder for profit rather than serial killing. So do the murders committed by Raymond Fernandez and Martha Beck, the "Lonely Hearts" killers. Fernandez answered "lonely hearts" advertisements, seduced the women, then absconded with their savings. A woman he married in 1947 died on their honeymoon in Spain under mysterious circumstances, almost certainly poisoned by her husband. When Fernandez met Martha Beck, he was hoping to swindle her; in fact, she fell frantically in love with him, and all his efforts to escape were a failure. Together—with Martha posing as his sister—they plotted the death of Fernandez's latest bride, Myrtle Young, who died of a brain hemorrhage after a massive dose of barbiturates. The next bride, Janet Fay, was murdered by Martha with a hammer after a quarrel, and was buried in a cellar in Queens, New York. Fernandez then married a widow with a 2-year-old daughter, Delphine Dowling. Delphine was despatched with her former husband's service revolver, and her daughter Rainelle was drowned in a washtub. Suspicious neighbors alerted the police, who soon uncovered the two bodies in the basement. The two killers, labeled "America's most hated murderers," were electrocuted in March 1951.

The main interest of the case in this context is that Fernandez had been a normal, law-abiding citizen until he received a heavy blow on the head from a falling hatch on board a ship, and that it was after this that he turned into a "sex maniac," an insatiable seducer of lonely women who kept many affairs going at the same time—in one case he even seduced a seriously deformed woman. When we recollect that Earle Nelson and Albert Fish had suffered similar accidents (and that the same is true of the 1970s serial killer Henry Lee Lucas), it raises the interesting question of whether such a blow could stimulate sex hormones to a degree that would turn such a person into a "sex maniac?" (Ken McElroy, the town bully of Skidmore, Missouri, who was murdered by angry fellow citizens in 1981, also received a severe head injury when he was 18, and turned into a thief and rapist.) It is a question that is worth bearing in mind in the investigation of serial killers.

Another American murderer who deserves a brief mention in this survey is Howard Unruh, as the first of the "crazy gunmen"—men who go berserk and kill at random. Unruh was an ex-GI who returned to his home in Camden, New Jersey, after the war. He enrolled at the university, and spent all his spare time studying the Bible. Over the years he became increasingly paranoid, developing a particular hatred of various neighbors who had treated him with what he considered to be a lack of respect. He began to collect high-powered weapons. When, on September 5, 1949, some prankster removed a gate he had installed in his garden fence, his control snapped, and he left the house with two loaded pistols. In the next twelve minutes he shot to death thirteen people—Unruh was a crack shot—then barricaded himself in his bedroom until the police persuaded him to surrender. He was found to be insane and committed to an asylum.

Unruh was not a serial killer—in the perfectly obvious sense that all his murders were committed at the same time;

he was what FBI agent Robert Ressler calls a "spree killer." But the resentment, the smoldering hatred of "society," is typical of the serial killer, and during the next four decades, the "crazy gunman" syndrome would become almost as familiar as the closely related problems of the political terrorist and the serial killer.

7

THE 1950s

WHEN I BEGAN TO ASSEMBLE AN ANTHOLOGY OF FAMOUS murder cases of the 1950s, I noticed that I had approximately twice as many to choose from as in the earlier volumes on the 1930s and 1940s. One reason, I knew, was partly that the murder rate began to climb steadily after the war, as it does after most wars. But a glance down the list revealed something more disturbing: that an increasing number of people began to experience the *compulsion* to kill—from Christie, who turned his house into a kind of private morgue, and Werner Boost, who liked to murder courting couples, to Heinrich Pommerencke, who admitted that he became a wild animal when he killed. All these were, of course, sex crimes, and in retrospect they can be seen as a prelude to the epidemic of "serial murder" that becomes apparent in the 1970s.

Another interesting change can be seen if we compare killers like Christie and Glatman with killers like Manuel, Boost and Rees. Christie and Glatman seem to belong to an "older" type of killer, the conventional little man with a violent sexual appetite that drives him to rape in much the same furtive spirit as a poacher stealing game. In Manuel, Boost and Rees we encounter a type of criminal who will become increasingly familiar in the following decades: the rebel against society who seems to feel that he has a *right* to kill. It is significant that the "Moors murderer" Ian Brady cited Nietzsche, Sade and Dostoevsky among his intellectual mentors. Christie had no intellectual mentors—although a number of witnesses described his desire to be known as a doctor and a man of learning. It is also possible to infer from the trial evidence that he possessed at least one characteristic of the successful doctor—a soothing bedside manner that lulled his victims into a state of trust.

The climax of what has been called "the greatest murder mystery of all time" developed on the afternoon of March 24, 1953 at a tiny, shabby house in London's Notting Hill area. A Jamaican tenant named Beresford Brown was preparing to redecorate the ground-floor kitchen, and was looking for a place where he could put up a shelf. When he tapped the wall in the corner it sounded hollow, and he realized that he was looking at a cupboard that had been covered over with wallpaper. He peeled back a strip of wallpaper from the corner and discovered a hole in the door; he switched on a torch and peeped through. And what he saw was unmistakably the back of a naked woman, who seemed to be bending forward with her head between her knees, as if being sick. It explained the offensive smell in the kitchen, not unlike that of a dead rat.

The police were there within minutes; so was the pathologist Dr. Francis Camps. The cupboard door was opened, and the seated body was seen to be supported by a piece of blanket which was knotted to her brassiere. The other end of the blanket was part of the covering of a tall object leaning against the wall. A closer look revealed this was another body. And beyond it, against the back of the cupboard—which had obviously been a coal cellar—there was yet another object that looked ominously like an upright body.

The first corpse proved to be that of a rather pretty young woman, with a mark around her throat indicating that she had been strangled to death; a "stalactite" of mold was growing out of her nose. Medical examination showed she had been dead about a month. Bubbling from her vagina was a large quantity of sperm—about five cc—suggesting that her killer had either had a tremendous orgasm, or had raped her more than once. The second body also proved to be of a young woman, wearing only a cardigan and vest; she too had been raped and strangled. The body had been placed in the cupboard upside down. Medical examination showed that she had been in the cupboard about two months. Body three was again of a young woman, upside down and wrapped in a blanket. And, as in the case of body two, a piece of cloth had been placed between the legs in the form of a diaper. She was wearing only a pink silk slip and bra, with two vests. She was six months pregnant, and had been in the cupboard from two to three months.

These were not the only remains found at No. 10 Rillington Place. Beneath the floor boards in the front room there was another naked body wrapped in a blanket. This proved to be a middle-aged woman, who had been dead for between three and four months. Between her legs there was also a piece of silk in the position of a diaper. A search of the garden revealed that a bone propping up a fence was a human femur. Digging revealed bones belong to two more female bodies.

There was no problem about identifying the killer. He was John Reginald Halliday Christie, who had lived in the ground floor flat for the past fifteen years, and had had the exclusive use of the garden. Christie was described as a tall, thin, bespectacled man with a bald head. The corpse under the floorboards was that of his 54-year-old wife Ethel. Christie had left the flat four days earlier, sub-letting it to a couple named Reilly (from whom he took rent of £8). That same evening the Jamaican landlord, Charles Brown, had arrived and found the Reillys in occupation; he had ordered them to leave the following morning—since Christie had no right to sub-let the flat.

Now the hunt was on for Christie; police naturally feared he might commit more sex murders. One week later, on March 31, 1953, a police constable near Putney Bridge thought he recognized a man staring gloomily into the water and asked him if he was Christie; the man admitted it quietly, and accompanied PC Ledger to the station. He seemed relieved it was over.

The finding of the bodies brought to mind another tragedy that had occurred in the same house five years earlier. On December 2, 1949, the police had found the bodies of 20-year-old Beryl Evans and her one-year-old daughter Geraldine in the wash-house outside the back door. The husband, an illiterate laborer named Timothy Evans, had been charged with both murders and hanged. Now everyone was asking the question: was Christie the killer of Beryl and Geraldine Evans? Christie himself answered part of this question a few weeks later when he confessed to strangling Beryl Evans with a stocking; he claimed she had asked him to help her commit suicide. But Christie strongly denied murdering the baby Geraldine.

Reg Christie (as he was known) was born in Yorkshire in April 1898, the son of a carpet designer who bullied and ill-treated his family. He was a weak child who was regarded as a "sissy" by his schoolfellows. He was often ill, and frequently in trouble with the police for minor offences—he was the unlucky type who always seemed to get caught. At the age of fifteen he became a clerk to the Halifax police, but was sacked for pilfering. And when he lost a job in his father's carpet factory for petty theft, his father threw him out of the house. He served in the First World War and, according to his own statement, was gassed. In 1920 he got a job as clerk in a wool mill, and began courting a neighbor, Ethel Waddington, a plain, homely girl of a passive disposition; they married in 1920.

But Christie continued to be a petty criminal. In 1921 he was a postman, and people complained that letters and postal-orders failed to arrive. Investigation revealed that Christie had been stealing them, and he was sentenced to three months in jail. In 1923 he was put on probation for obtaining money by false pretenses. In 1924 he was sentenced to nine months for theft. This was too much for Ethel, and she left him. He moved to London and settled down with another woman whom he met on a coach going to Margate. But Christie's dislike of work led to quarrels, and after one of these he hit her with a cricket bat, almost shattering her skull. For this he was sentenced to six months for malicious wounding. And in 1933 he received another three months for stealing the car of a priest who had befriended him. He wrote to Ethel in Sheffield, asking her to come and visit him in prison. When he came out, they again moved in together. Their new home was the small, shabby house at the end of a cul-de-sac called Rillington Place. The rent was twelve shillings and nine pence a week.

In September 1939 Christie became a war reserve policeman, and he became unpopular in the area for his bullying and officious behavior—he loved to run in people for minor blackout infringements. During this period, Ethel often went to visit her family in Sheffield, and in 1943 Christie began to have an affair with a young woman from the Harrow Road police station. Her husband, a soldier, heard about it and went and caught them together at Rillington Place. He beat Christie up, and later divorced his wife, citing Christie as co-respondent.

It may have been this humiliation that led to Christie's first murder. Some time soon after the divorce scandal, Christie picked up a young Austrian prostitute named Ruth Fuerst—she had been stranded in England by the war—and took her back to Rillington Place. Ethel was in Sheffield. As they had sex, he strangled her with a piece of rope. The fact that he used rope suggests that the murder was premeditated; he probably decided to kill her while she undressed. But why? The answer was supplied to me by Dr. Francis Camps, the pathologist on the case, when I met him in 1959. Camps told me that one of the odd things about the case that never came out in court was that he found dried sperm in the seams of Christie's shoes. For Camps, this showed clearly that Christie had masturbated as he stood over a corpse. And this, in turn, indicates that Christie had to *see* the corpse to achieve maximum stimulation. In short, he was a necrophile. In fact, he admitted later that the most overwhelming emotional experience of his life was to see the corpse of his grandfather when he was 8 years old.

Christie was almost certainly lying when he said he had normal intercourse with Ruth Fuerst. In his teens, Christie was the laughing stock of the local youths because he was reputed to be impotent; after a humiliating experience with a local girl, he became known as "Reggie No-Dick" and "Can't do-it Christie." With shy, passive women (like Ethel) he could achieve intercourse, although he claims that they had been married for two years before they had sex. The same is probably true of the soldier's wife with whom he had an affair. But with most women he was impotent unless they were unconscious or dead. So when Ruth Fuerst came back to his flat, he probably prepared a piece of "strangling rope" (with a knot at either end) and placed it under the pillow, intending to kill her and make sexual use of the corpse until Ethel came back. In fact, he was interrupted. A telegram arrived shortly after the murder, announcing her return. He had to conceal the body hastily under the floor boards, and bury it in the garden at the first opportunity. Now he had killed a woman, the aching sense of inferiority—brought to a head by the beating from the angry soldier—was assuaged.

In December 1943 temptation came his way again. Now no longer a policeman, he worked for a firm called Ultra Radio, and met a plump, attractive little woman called Muriel Eady. She told him she suffered from catarrh, and Christie had an idea. He told her had a cure for catarrh, and invited her back to Rillington Place while Ethel was away. The cure, he said, was to lean over a bowl of steaming Friar's Balsam, with a cloth over the head to keep in the steam. Christie ran a rubber pipe from the gas tap, and inserted it under the cloth. Muriel Eady passed out peacefully. Trembling with excitement, Christie moved her on to the bed, removed her clothes, and raped her. Looking at the body, he later described how he experienced a sense of exquisite peace. "I had no regrets." Muriel Eady also found her way into the garden.

Six years passed before he killed again, and it is possible the murder was unpremeditated. Timothy and Beryl Evans had moved into the upstairs flat, but they quarreled a great deal; one of the quarrels was about a blonde girl who had moved in with them; the girl had to leave. In one of his confessions, Christie claimed that he strangled Mrs. Evans at her own request, because she wanted to die. There may be an element of truth in this. But what Christie failed to mention is that Beryl Evans had again discovered herself to be pregnant, and wanted an abortion. Christie, who loved to swagger, had told Timothy Evans that he had once studied to be a doctor. And Evans asked Christie if he could perform an abortion.

What happened next is a matter for conjecture; but the view of Ludovic Kennedy, in his book *Ten Rillington Place*, is well argued. Christie went into the room, where Beryl Evans was waiting for him; she removed her knickers and lay down with her legs apart. Christie inserted a finger, or perhaps a spoon, then was overcome with sexual desire, and tried to climb on her. Christie strangled her, and then raped her. When Timothy Evans came home, Christie told him that his wife had died as a result of the abortion, and that he, Evans, would almost certainly be blamed.

Evans, a man of subnormal intelligence, panicked. He allowed Christie to do his thinking for him. And what Christie apparently advised was that the baby should be looked after by some people in Acton, and Evans should vanish. Evans *did* vanish—to Merthyr Vale, in Wales, and spent ten days with an aunt and uncle; then he decided to go back to London, to give himself up to the police. They came and found the bodies in the wash-house, and Evans was charged with murder.

And here we encounter the first mystery of the case. Evans then made a full confession to murdering his wife and baby by strangulation. This was, admittedly, his second confession—in the first he had stated that Beryl had died as a result of an abortion performed by Christie. But he repeated his confession to murdering his wife and child the following day. So although he withdrew this second confession a fortnight later, the police had no reason to believe his assertion that the real killer was Christie. At the trial, Christie appeared as a witness for the prosecution, and Evans was hanged on March 9, 1950.

Ethel Christie had a strong suspicion, amounting to a certainty, that her husband was somehow involved in the murders—she had noticed his extreme nervousness at the time. She confided her belief to a neighbor, and when Christie came in and caught them discussing the case, he flew into a rage. This could explain why, on December 14, 1952, he strangled her in bed. It could also have been that he experienced a compulsion to commit more sex crimes, and Ethel stood in the way. Christie told her family in Sheffield that she was unable to write because she had rheumatism in her fingers.

In mid-January 1953 Christie picked up a prostitute called Kathleen Maloney in a pub in Paddington, and invited her back to his flat. As she sat in a deck-chair in the kitchen, he placed the gas pipe under the chair; she was too drunk to notice. When she was unconscious, he raped her and put her in the cupboard.

The next victim, Rita Nelson, was six months pregnant; Christie may have lured her back with the offer of an abortion. She also ended in the cupboard—the second body.

About a month later, Christie met a girl called Hectorina Maclennan, who told him she was looking for a flat. She and her boyfriend actually spent three nights in Christie's flat, now devoid of furniture (Christie had sold it). On March 5th Hectorina made the mistake of going back to the flat alone. She grew nervous when she saw Christie toying with a gas-pipe and tried to leave; Christie killed her and raped her. When her boyfriend came to inquire about her, she was in the cupboard, and Christie claimed not to have seen her. As Christie gave him tea, the boyfriend noticed "a very nasty smell," but had no suspicion he was sitting within feet of Hectorina's corpse.

This was Christie's last murder. Two weeks later, he left Rillington Place, and wandered around aimlessly, sleeping in cheap lodgings and spending the days in cafés until he was arrested. He confessed to all the murders of women, usually insisting that it was *they* who made the advances. He was executed July 15, 1953.

The major mystery remains—was Timothy Evans innocent? Long after his death, he was officially absolved of all responsibility and guilt; yet that leaves some major questions unanswered. For example, why did he confess to the murders?

Ludovic Kennedy, in *Ten Rillington Place,* takes the view that Evans was innocent of both murders. He confessed, says Kennedy, out of misery and confusion. But this is almost impossible. Evans had had ten days in Wales to think things over. There is no earthly reason why he should have confessed to strangling Beryl (after a quarrel) and then Geraldine. (Kennedy argues that he was too fond of both.)

In *The Two Stranglers of Rillington Place*, Rupert Furneaux takes the opposite view. He points out that Beryl and Timothy Evans often quarreled violently, and that nothing was more likely than that Evans would kill Beryl in a rage. He argues closely and convincingly, and is, on the whole, more plausible than Kennedy. And he believes that it was Christie who murdered the baby.

But this still leaves a major mystery: why, in that case, did Evans also confess to murdering Geraldine?

The answer is surely supplied by a curious piece of evidence from another murderer, Donald Hume, who was in prison at the same time as Evans, on a charge of murdering a man named Stanley Setty and throwing pieces of his body out of an airplane. Evans asked Hume's advice, and when Hume asked, "Did you kill your wife?" Evans replied: "No, Christie murdered her." Here he could well have been lying, for by now his defense was that Christie had killed her in the course of an abortion. But when Hume asked if he killed the baby, Evans made the surprising statement that Christie had strangled Geraldine while he, Evans, watched. He said that the baby's crying had got on his nerves.

This rings true. Evans was in a frantic state, and he could well have stood by while Christie killed Geraldine. In doing so, he had become, in effect, her killer, so his confession to murdering her was not far short of the truth. Guilt probably increased his sense of being her murderer. And this, I would argue, is almost certainly the answer to the riddle. There *were* two stranglers of Rillington Place. And baby Geraldine was, in a sense, killed by both of them.

The question of whether Peter Manuel should be classed as a serial killer is a difficult one. John Bingham's book *The Hunting Down of Peter Manuel* (1973) begins: "Peter Thomas Anthony Manuel was found guilty of murdering seven people. He certainly killed nine. In addition to the murders, he raped one woman, assaulted others, and was a housebreaker of some renown, being in all a versatile criminal." And a few pages later: "Manuel did kill for pleasure. He liked killing. The act of killing thrilled him." This certainly sounds like a precise definition of a serial killer.

Manuel seems to have been one of those habitual crooks who find it impossible to stay out of trouble. Unfortunately, little is known of his childhood, and the circumstances that turned him into a criminal. Born in Manhattan in 1927, he returned to England with his British parents at the age of 5. His parents were good Catholics. The family lived in Motherwell, Scotland, then moved to Coventry. There, at the age of 12, Manuel made his first appearance in court for burgling the shop of a cycle dealer, and received twelve months' probation. When he appeared before the same court five weeks later for housebreaking he was sent to an approved school. He escaped eleven times, and was usually returned after being caught housebreaking with a hammer. In 1942 he robbed and indecently assaulted the wife of a school employee, and was eventually caught hiding in the school chapel. This time he was sent to Borstal. After being released two years later, he rejoined his family, who had returned to Scotland. His father worked as a foreman in the local gas-

works, and was on the District Council. Soon afterwards
Manuel was acquitted on yet another charge of housebreaking.

Manuel's problem was that, as a criminal, he was not particularly competent. Worse still, he was unlucky. Soon after
midnight on February 16, 1946, he broke into a bungalow in
Sandyhills, near Glasgow. A local constable called Muncie
was called to the scene, and spent most of the night searching the house, in case the burglar was still concealed there.
He was not, so Muncie went home for breakfast. Soon, he
was called back to an empty bungalow very close to the one
he had already investigated—a neighbor had reported seeing
an intruder. In fact, Peter Manuel was hiding in the loft, but
Muncie failed to find him, and left after a search. Later that
morning, Muncie remembered that he had left behind a
teacup with fingerprints on it, and drove back to the bungalow with a colleague. While the colleague was collecting the
keys from a neighbor, a well-dressed youth—Manuel was
19—walked towards Muncie's car from the direction of the
bungalow; Muncie stopped him and asked his identity. The
youth said he was Peter Manuel, then admitted that he had
come from the garden of the bungalow, where he had been
"watching." At the police station, he was found to have in his
possession a gold watch that Muncie had last seen in the
bungalow. Manuel was placed under arrest and charged with
burglary.

Unfortunately, he was allowed out on bail. And within two
weeks, he had committed three sexual attacks. The first two
were unsuccessful; a woman with a 3-year-old child fought
and screamed so hard that he ran away, and a nurse was
saved by the appearance of a motorcyclist. Muncie had already recognized the description of the attacker as that of the
burglar, but Manuel was nowhere to be found. The third victim, a married woman, was attacked from behind on a lonely

road after dark. She had only just been released from the hospital, and was in no condition to resist. Manuel dragged her to a railway embankment, beat her into submission, then raped her.

The next day Muncie caught up with him. In an identity parade, the first two victims immediately identified Manuel as the attacker. The third victim had not seen his face; but fragments of red sandstone—from the railway embankment—in Manuel's clothes left no doubt that he was the rapist. He received an eight-year sentence.

Back in Glasgow in 1953, he worked for the Gas Board and British Rail, and even became engaged for eleven months to a bus conductress. There was a curious episode during the engagement that throws light on Manuel's complex psychology. The girl received a letter alleging that Manuel's real father had been electrocuted in America, and that Manuel himself had been in the Secret Service. Manuel shrugged it off as a calumny; in fact, he had written it himself. It was typical of his desire to "be" someone, to appear as more interesting and exciting than he actually was. In fact, the girl canceled the marriage because Manuel refused to go to confession. (Both were Catholics.)

During this period, Manuel tried hard to make trouble for Muncie by alleging perjury in the rape case; he also offered information about two murders, claiming to know the identity of the killer. The police dismissed the claims. In December 1954, Manuel also tried to gain American citizenship, and tried to support the claim by offering information about various crimes he claimed to know about, and information about national security. The Americans decided he was a liar and fantasizer, and sent him away. Muncie, who interviewed him again about these claims, decided that he had an overpowering craving for attention.

On July 30, 1955—the day he was supposed to have been

married—Manuel made another bungled attempt at rape. The girl, Mary McLaughlin, was forced into a field at knife point, but her screams were heard, and people began searching nearby fields with torches. Manuel forced her to the ground and placed a knife at her throat, threatening to kill her and cut off her head. He also put his hand inside her underwear. When the searchers had gone away, the girl tried talking him out of rape, asking if he was in trouble, and Manuel told her that he had been due to get married that day, but that the girl, a bus conductress, had broken it off the previous evening. Then, after smoking cigarettes and talking for more than an hour, they made their way back across the fields. Manuel had thrown away the knife with which he threatened her. When he asked her if she meant to report him to the police, she told him that she intended to forget the whole thing.

In fact, after telling her mother and sister what had happened, she went to the police. Muncie recognized the description as being similar to Manuel, and soon Manuel was under arrest. At first he alleged an alibi, which was quickly disproved. But in court, he elected to defend himself, and soon revealed that he was a highly articulate young man. He told the jury that he and Mary McLaughlin had been courting, but had quarreled. They had met by accident on the day of the alleged assault, and she had gone with him voluntarily . . .

He told the story so plausibly that the jury—who knew nothing of his criminal record—decided that he deserved the benefit of the doubt, and brought in a Scottish verdict of "not proven." Subsequently, Manuel's father saw Mary McLaughlin at a bus stop and spat at her.

Manuel's next attack on a woman proved fatal. Ten weeks later, on January 4, 1956, a man taking a walk in a copse near the East Kilbride golf course saw a girl lying face down, her head battered in. She proved to be 19-year-old Anne

Knielands, who had set out the previous evening to meet a boyfriend. But her young man was celebrating Hogmanay, and had forgotten about their date.

She had been attacked from behind, and had run away across a field, losing both shoes and scrambling over barbed wire that had lacerated her. Finally, she had been overtaken, and struck on the back of the head with a piece of angle iron so violently that the skull was shattered into fifteen pieces. Yet although her panties—and one stocking—were missing, she had not been raped.

Not far from the site of the murder, men from the Gas Board were working at a building site, and among the workers was Peter Manuel. The man who had found the girl's body learned that Manuel had a criminal record that included sex attacks, and informed the police. Manuel was questioned, and explained that the scratches on his face had been acquired in a brawl. He had been at home on the evening when Anne Knielands had been killed. His father supported his alibi, although he knew some of his son's statements were false. The police had to accept his word.

In March, police received a tip that Manuel and another man intended to rob a colliery at Blantyre, near Manuel's home. They pounced as the men were breaking in; one was arrested, but the other—Manuel—ran away. However, he left behind a fragment of clothing on a barbed wire fence, and was finally charged with the attempted break-in. His trial date was set for October 2, seven months away. Meanwhile, he was released on bail.

Six months later, in September 1956, there were three burglaries in Lanarkshire. The first, on September 12, was in an empty house in Bothwell. The burglar had scattered soup on the floor, walked on the bed cover in dirty boots, and slashed the mattress and quilt. He had drunk the juice from a can of pears and left the pears on the carpet. A stopwatch, an electric razor and some tools were missing, but other valuable items were untouched.

The second burglary took place in High Burnside, not far from East Kilbride, on September 15. Again, soup was scattered on the carpet, as well as spaghetti; there were dirty footmarks on the bed. But all that had been stolen were four pairs of nylon stockings and two gold rings.

Two days later, the daily help arrived at 5 Fennsbank Avenue, High Burnside, the home of baker William Watt, and found a glass panel broken in the front door. In the house, three women lay dead, shot in the head at close range: Mrs. Marion Watt, her sister, Margaret Brown and her 16-year-old daughter Vivienne. All were wearing nightclothes, although Margaret Brown's pajama bottoms had been torn, and Vivienne's had been removed. A brassiere, apparently torn from her body, lay on the floor of Vivienne's bedroom. The girl had a bruise on her chin where she had obviously been struck but there was no sign of rape or sexual assault. A cigarette had been stubbed out on the carpet.

William Watt had been away on a fishing trip when the women were murdered, but ten days later he was arrested and charged with the murders—the policeman who had arrested him had felt that he did not behave like a man whose family has just been slaughtered, and a check of his alibi convinced the police that he *could* have returned home during the night and committed the crimes.

Yet the police also had reason to suspect Manuel. Further along Fennsbank Avenue, at number 18, another burglary was discovered. The burglar had again poured tomato soup on the carpet and stubbed out a cigarette. A pair of nylon stockings was found on a chair in the lounge.

They had another reason. An informant told the police that Manuel had boasted that he intended to "do a Jew's house" on the evening of the murders, and to use a revolver. He told the informant that he had tested the revolver by shooting a cow up the nostril.

By chance, Muncie—now a chief inspector—had noticed a dead cow in a field, and learned from the vet that it had blood in its nostril. Unfortunately, it already lay in a vat at the knacker's yard. In an attempt to find the bullet, Muncie and a squad of policemen spent four days searching through piles of stinking offal; unfortunately, they were unable to find anything.

Manuel was questioned—his father blustered that he was going to complain about police harassment to his local MP— and Manuel simply refused to account for his movements on the evening of the murders. Soon after, he was sentenced to eighteen months for the colliery burglary. He was placed in Barlinnie Jail, alongside William Watt . . .

Now Manuel behaved in the strangely irrational manner that seems typical of a certain type of serial killer—unless, that is, he was suddenly struck by remorse, or a flash of human decency. He sent for Watt's lawyer and told him that he, Manuel, knew that Watt was innocent, and that he knew the name of the man who had actually committed the murders. To prove this, he described the position of certain articles of furniture in the Watts' house, claiming that the murderer had told him—and that he had also asked him to dispose of the gun. The lawyer checked the furniture and found that Manuel's statement was accurate. But there was still no proof that Manuel was the murderer. Finally, after sixty-seven days in jail, Watt was released.

Almost a year later, in November 1957, Manuel was also released. His first action was to arrange a meeting with William Watt, and tell him that the murders had been committed by a man called Tallis. His description of the inside of the house was so accurate that Watt accused him of having been inside it. Manuel denied this. There was nothing Watt could do about his suspicion that he had spoken to the killer of his wife, daughter and sister-in-law.

On December 8, a few days after this talk with William Watt, Manuel went to Newcastle upon Tyne, and hired the taxi of a driver named Sidney Dunn. Near Edmundbyers, he shot Dunn in the back of the head, then cut his throat; then he smashed the windows and headlamps of the taxi, and dragged the body onto the moorland grass. He left the driver's wallet untouched. The precise motive—apart from the pleasure of killing—remains a mystery.

Twenty days after the Newcastle murder, Manuel killed another girl. On the evening of December 28, 1957, Isabelle Cooke set out from her home in Mount Vernon to go to a dance. She failed to reach the dance or return home. A woman who lived nearby heard a woman cry out.

The police were still searching for the body on New Year's Eve when Manuel massacred another family. Peter Smart, a successful civil engineer of 45, lived with his wife and 10-year-old son in a house he had built himself at Sheepburn Road, Uddingston. His relatives had been expecting him to drop in for Hogmanay celebrations, but when he failed to arrive, simply assumed that he had found something else to do. When he failed to arrive at work on January 6, and the police reported finding his car abandoned in a Gorbals street, two of his colleagues went to the house in Sheepburn Road; when there was no reply to their knocks, they called the police. The three Smarts were found dead in their bed; all had been shot at close range in the head.

Two local residents named McMunn shivered when they heard the news. On January 4, a burglar had peered round their bedroom door, but had fled when Mr. McMunn asked his wife: "Where's the gun?" and she replied "Here it is." The burglar had gained admittance by breaking a window.

Peter Manuel was an immediate and obvious suspect. And

suspicion of his involvement increased when Joe Brannan, a friend of Manuel's who was now in the police force, reported that Manuel had been broke on New Year's Eve and spending freely on New Year's Day. And now, at last, the police had the break they had been hoping for. Peter Smart had been to the local bank on New Year's Day and had drawn out £35. The money, as it happened, was in new notes, in consecutive numerical order. The customer who had drawn out cash immediately after Peter Smart was interviewed, and still had some of his notes, also numbered consecutively. From this, the police could deduce the numbers of the notes drawn out by Peter Smart. They then went around hotels and pubs where Manuel had spent money on New Year's Day, and were able to trace notes he had spent; they were from the lot drawn out by Peter Smart.

Early on January 13, 1958, the police swooped on the house of Manuel's father. He was as aggressive and unhelpful as ever, threatening again to complain to his MP. Peter Manuel was roused from sleep, and became angry. "You haven't found anything yet—you can't take me." The word "yet" convinced the police that they were on the right track.

In the house they found a camera and a pair of gloves lined with lambswool. On Christmas Day, there had been a burglary at the home of the Reverend Alexander Houston, in Mount Vernon, in which a camera and gloves lined with lambswool had been stolen. When the minister identified them as his property, the police at last had something with which they could charge Peter Manuel. For good measure, his father was also charged.

Peter Manuel's reaction was as unexpected and irrational as ever. He asked to see the police superintendent, and told him that the money had been given him by a man called Samuel McKay, in payment for showing McKay around the

Sheepburn Road area, with a view to spying out suitable houses for burglary.

When told of this accusation, McKay—who was not normally the kind of man who would help the police—became indignant, and offered them a useful piece of information: that just before Christmas, Manuel had been in possession of a Beretta pistol.

And now, two days after his arrest, the totally unexpected happened, and Manuel decided to confess. He asked to see the inspector in charge of the murder team, and told him that he could help him clear up some unsolved crimes. Then, in front of members of the team, he wrote a statement declaring that he would give information about the murders of Anne Knielands, Isabelle Cooke, the Watt family and the Smarts, if they would release his father. Then he confessed—verbally—to breaking into the Smarts' house and killing all three. His parents were sent for, and Manuel repeated his confession to them. After that, Manuel took the police to the spot where he had buried Isabelle Cooke. In the grave—in a field not far from where she had last been seen—the girl's almost naked body was uncovered.

Later, Manuel was able to lead the police to the place beside the River Clyde where he had thrown the Beretta; this was recovered by a diver. The pistol was wrapped in a pair of Mrs. Smart's gloves.

The trial, which opened on May 12, 1958, should have been an anticlimax, since Manuel had confessed, and the police had overwhelming evidence against him. But Manuel still had a few surprises. He dismissed his defense counsel and undertook his own defense—no doubt recalling the previous occasion when this tactic had succeeded in producing a verdict of "not proven." His basic assertion was that his "confessions" had been forced from him, in that his father was also in custody, charged with burglary. He also charged that William Watt had murdered his own family, and had confessed this to him. But when he examined his own mother, she admitted that when she and her husband had been called to the police station, her son had said "I don't know what makes me do these things." Manuel tried hard to get her to retract this, without success. The jury, understandably, felt that if Manuel's own mother was willing to acknowledge that he had confessed, then there could be little doubt of it.

They took two hours and twenty-one minutes to find Manuel guilty on all counts except the Anne Knielands murder, on which the judge had instructed them that the evidence was insufficient. Manuel was sentenced to death.

In Barlinnie Jail, Manuel had to be kept apart from other prisoners—rapists and child killers are always unpopular. Precautions were even taken to make sure he could not be poisoned. When his appeal was rejected, Manuel suddenly stopped speaking, and gave up smoking; for three weeks he was silent. Two days before his execution, when he heard that the Home Secretary had rejected an appeal for clemency, he suddenly became his old self again, talking in the odd, compulsive way that had already caused him so many problems. On July 11, 1958, he made his confession to a priest, ate breakfast with a large tot of whiskey, then went quietly to meet the hangman.

From the point of view of this book, the main interest of the Manuel case lies in the fact that Manuel was one of the earliest "self-esteem killers." Fellow prisoners knew him as a braggart who wanted to be respected as a master criminal. His most urgent desire was to be "known," to be famous or notorious. Yet unlike other boastful killers—for example, Richard Speck, the murderer of the eight Chicago nurses—he was a man of considerable intelligence, and psychiatrists noted that he could be articulate and well-mannered. But he continued to refuse to acknowledge the murders, claiming that the police had "framed" him. He explained his burglaries by saying with disarming candor that he was a dishonest person who happened to have been born that way.

But how do we explain the fact that, except in one case, his female victims were never raped? John Bingham has suggested that the reason is that Manuel would reach orgasm before he arrived at this point. After the Mary McLaughlan assault, semen stains were found in his trousers, and this could explain why, after groping around inside her underwear, he suddenly calmed down and smoked a cigarette. Vincent Verzeni and Peter Kürten often achieved orgasm in the act of throttling victims; when this was over, they became harmless.

Manuel may also have been an underwear fetishist. Anne Knieland's knickers, and her missing stocking, were never found. In one of his burglaries, Manuel left a pair of nylon stockings on a chair; he may have used them to cover his hands and prevent fingerprints, but also because they sexually excited him. The torn pajama trousers in the case of Margaret Brown, the removal of Vivienne Watts's pajama trousers, and the fact that most of Isabelle Cooke's clothes had been removed, point unmistakably to a sexual motive. Yet the bus conductress to whom Manuel was engaged said that he never made sexual advances. This seems to suggest that Manuel was interested in sex only when it was associated with the "forbidden." What excited him was tearing off a girl's underwear or pajamas; while doing this the excitement may have been so great that he achieved a climax.

Another curious detail is that neighbors of the Smarts noticed that the curtains were sometimes drawn and sometimes undrawn in the days following New Year's Day. This suggests that Manuel returned to the house day after day. John Bingham's theory is that his murders sprang out of an association of violence with sexuality, and even that this may have had something to do with the phases of the moon. Whether or not this is true, it seems clear that Manuel was one of those for whom criminality itself is somehow sexual. But he lacked insight into his own condition; he was undoubtedly speaking the truth when he told his parents: "I don't know what makes me do these things."

One thing seems very clear—and explains the amount of space devoted to this curiously untypical case. In spite of his intelligence, Manuel was driven by a totally irrational resentment. Like Panzram, he wanted to "get his own back" on society. This could well have been the result of his period in Borstals—we have already seen that this was one of the major factors that led "Brides in the Bath" Smith to become a criminal. Manuel followed the search for Isabelle Cooke with gloating satisfaction, and even dropped hints to his policeman friend Joe Brannan that he knew something about it. It didn't worry him that he knew Brannan was a policeman, and that he had probably been told to report on him. It made the game more interesting. As he and Brannan sat on top of a bus, looking at police searching a high railway viaduct, Manuel said: "Wouldn't it be a fine sight to see one of those bastards hanging by the neck from the viaduct? Preferably one with stripes on his arm . . . " He was obviously *glad* to have a policeman there as an audience; at last he was being allowed to give them "a piece of his mind," just as if he was standing on stage under a spotlight with an audience of coppers . . . A comment like this enables us to understand Manuel's mentality in a single flash. He was saying: "If I can't be a part of society—with the pre-eminence I deserve—then I'm going to do my best to screw things up, until the bastards feel sorry they *didn't* pay me more attention . . . "

This is an attitude we shall see again and again in later serial killers. Lacenaire was perhaps the first notable criminal to embody this irrational resentment, and he would have regarded Manuel as a worthy—if somewhat unimaginative—successor, lacking the foresight and cunning that make a truly great criminal.

Lacenaire might well have entertained a higher opinion of the criminal who might be regarded as the German counterpart of Peter Manuel: Werner Boost, who was arguably Germany's most dangerous serial killer since Peter Kürten. And, unlike Manuel, he certainly could not be accused of lack of planning: he spent hours in libraries reading the lives of notorious criminals, studying their methods and making notes on how to avoid their mistakes.

For the Düsseldof police, the story began on the cold, snowy night of January 7, 1953. Shortly before midnight, a fair-haired young man who was bleeding from a head wound staggered into the police station and said that his friend had just been murdered. The "friend," it seemed, was a distinguished lawyer named Dr. Lothar Servé. The officer on duty immediately telephoned Kriminal Hauptcommissar Mattias Eynck, chief of the North Rhineland murder squad, who hurried down to the station. The young man had identified himself as Adolf Hullecremer, a 19-year-old student, and explained that he and Dr. Servé had been sitting in the car "discussing business," and looking at the lights on the river, when both doors of the car had been jerked open by two men in handkerchief masks. One of the men began to swear, then shot Servé in the head. As Hullecremer begged for his life, the second man whispered that if he wished to stay alive, he should "sham dead." He then hit Hullecremer on the head with a pistol. As he lost consciousness, Hullecremer heard him say: "He won't wake again." When the men had gone. he made off as fast as he could . . .

After Hullecremer's head had been bandaged, he said he

felt well enough to take the police and the doctor back to the car. It was parked in a grove of trees on the edge of the river, its engine still running. Across the rear seat lay the body of a man of about 50, bleeding from a wound in the temple. The doctor pronounced him dead.

The motive was clearly robbery—the dead man's wallet was missing. Eynck concluded that the robbers were "stick-up men" who had chosen this spot because it was known as a "lovers' lane." The fact that the two had been in the rear seat when attacked suggested a homosexual relationship.

Forensic examination revealed no fingerprints on the car, and falling snow had obliterated any footprints or other tire tracks. The murder inquiry had reached an impasse when, a few weeks later, a tramp found a .32 caliber pistol—of Belgian make—in the woods, and forensic tests showed it to be the murder weapon. Photographs of its bullets were sent to all police stations, and the Magdeburg police—in East Germany—contacted Eynck to say that the same gun had been used in a murder a few years earlier in a small town called Hadersleben. Two East Germans attempting to flee to the West had been shot with the same weapon. This seemed to suggest that the murderer was himself an East German refugee who had moved to Düsseldorf. But there the trail went cold—thousands of East Germans had fled the communist regime to the large cities of West Germany since the war.

Almost three years later, in October 1955, Eynck found himself wondering whether the double killers had struck again. A young couple had vanished after an evening date. The man was 26-year-old Friedhelm Behre, a baker, and his fiancée was 23-year-old Thea Kurmann. They had spent the evening of October 31, in a "bohemian" restaurant called the Cafe Czikos, in the old quarter of Düsseldorf, and had driven off soon after midnight in Behre's blue Ford. The next day, worried relatives reported them missing. But there was no sign of the couple or of the blue car. Four weeks later, a contractor standing by a half-dredged gravel pit near Düsseldorf was throwing stones at a metal object when he realized that it was the top of a blue car. He called some of his men, and they heaved it ashore. In the back seat lay two decomposing corpses. They proved to be those of the missing couple, the girl dressed in her red satin evening dress, which had been torn and pulled up.

The medical report revealed that Friedhelm Behre had been shot through the head at close range. The girl had been garrotted, possibly by a man's tie, after being raped. It looked as if the killer had wrenched open the rear door as the couple were petting, shot the man, then dragged the girl out. After rape, her body was thrown into the back seat, and the car driven to the gravel pit, where it was pushed into the water.

To Eynck, this sounded ominously like the Servé murder. Again, there were no fingerprints—suggesting that the killer had worn gloves. The bullet had disappeared. It had gone right through the victim's skull, but it should have been somewhere in the car. Its absence suggested that the murderer had removed it to prevent the identification of the gun.

The murder caused panic among Düsseldorf's young lovers, and over the Christmas period the usual lay-bys were deserted. Meanwhile, Chief Inspector Botte, in charge of the investigation, quickly found that he had run out of clues.

Three months later, on the morning of February 8, 1956, a businessman named Julius Dreyfuss reported that his Mercedes car was missing—together with its chauffeur, a young man named Peter Falkenberg. The chauffeur had failed to arrive to pick up his employer. It seemed possible that Falkenberg had driven away to sell the expensive car. But an hour or so later, a woman reported that a black car was parked in front of her house with its headlights on. It proved to be the missing Mercedes. And there was a great deal of blood inside—in both the front and the rear seats.

At about the same time, a woman had reported that her daughter, 23-year-old Hildegard Wassing, had failed to return home after a date. A few days before, Hildegard and a friend had met a young man named Peter at a dance; he had told them he was a chauffeur. Hildegard had agreed to go out with him the following Tuesday, February 7, and her brother had noticed that he was driving a black Mercedes. To Eynck, it sounded as if Peter Falkenberg and Hildegard Wassing had fallen victim to the "car murderer."

The next morning, a gardener was cycling to work near the small village of Lank-Ilvereich, near Düsseldorf, when he saw the remains of a burning haystack some distance from the path. He strolled over to look—then rushed for the nearest telephone as he saw the remains of two corpses among the burnt hay.

Eynck arrived soon after, and noticed the smell of petrol. Both bodies were badly charred, but rain had prevented the fire from totally incinerating them. Forensic examination revealed that the man—identified from dental charts as Peter Falkenberg—had been shot through the head. Hildegard Wassing had been raped and then strangled—the rope was still sunk in the burnt flesh.

Thousands of Düsseldorf residents were questioned, but once again, there were no obvious leads. The car killer was evidently a man who took great care to leave no clues. Then a detective named Bohm came upon a possible suspect. In the small town of Buderich, not far from the burnt haystack, he was told of a young man named Erich von der Leyen, who had once attacked some children with a manure fork, and was regarded as a "loner" by his neighbors. He was originally from East Germany, and now lived in lodgings in a place called Veert. Von der Leyen worked as a traveling salesman for agricultural machinery, so his log-book should have shown precisely where he was when the couple were murdered. But the entry for February 7, had been made later, and the traveling times for drives seemed implausible. Moreover, there were red spots on the front seat-covers. These were sent for forensic examination, and were reported to be human bloodstains. Erich von der Leyen was placed under arrest. Stains on his trousers also proved to be blood.

Von der Leyen insisted that he had no idea where the stains came from—the only way he could account for them was to recall that his girlfriend's dachshund had been in his car when it was in heat. That sounded unlikely. The police asked another forensic expert to examine the bloodstains on the trousers, and see if he could determine their age. Under the microscope, he saw epithelial cells—evidence that it *was* menstrual blood. The stains on the car seat were re-tested, and the laboratory admitted with embarrassment that these were also of menstrual blood—and, moreover, from a dog. The police had to release von der Leyen, and to apologize for the intense interrogations he had endured.

Soon after this, on the evening of June 6, 1956, a forest ranger named Erich Spath was walking through woods near Meererbusch, not far from the burnt haystack site, when he saw a man lurking in the undergrowth, and peering from behind a tree at a car in which a courting couple were petting. The man was so absorbed that he did not hear the ranger. Then Spath saw him draw a revolver from his pocket, and creep towards the car.

Spath placed his rifle to his shoulder and crept up behind the young man. "Drop it!" The man turned round, then threw away his gun and ran. Spath chased him and soon caught up with him, crouching in a hollow.

Half an hour later, the car with the courting couple—and

also containing the ranger and his captive—pulled up in front of Düsseldorf's main police station. The suspect—who was dark and good-looking—had accompanied them without protest and without apparent concern, as if his conscience was clear. And when they stood in the office of Kriminal Hauptkommissar Mattias Eynck, Spath understood why. The young man—who gave his name as Werner Boost—explained that he had merely been doing a little target practice in the woods, and had thought *he* was being attacked. He obviously felt that no one could disprove his story and that therefore the police would be unable to hold him.

"Is your gun licensed?" asked Eynck.

"Well . . . no. It's a war trophy . . .

"In that case, I am charging you with possessing an illegal weapon."

The gun was found in the undergrowth where Boost had thrown it. Nearby was a motorcycle, which proved to have been stolen. Boost was also charged with its theft. A magistrate promptly sentenced him to six months in jail, which gave Eynck the time he needed to investigate the suspect.

At first the trail seemed to be leading nowhere. The pistol had not been used in any known crime; Boost was, as he said, an electrical engineer who worked in a factory, and who was regarded as a highly intelligent and efficient worker; he had been married for six years, had two children, and was a good husband and provider. His wife, Hanna, told Eynck that he spent most of his evenings at home, working in his own laboratory or reading—he was an obsessive reader. Occasionally, she admitted, he became restless and went out until the early hours of the morning.

She led Eynck down to the basement laboratory. There he discovered various ingredients for explosives, as well as some deadly poisons. He also found a quantity of morphine.

Back in the flat, Eynck noticed a letter postmarked

Hadersleben. He recalled that the Belgian pistol, which had been found within a few hundred yards of Boost's flat, had been used in a double murder in Hadersleben, near Magdeburg. "Do you know someone in Hadersleben?" he asked. Hanna Boost told him that it was her home town, and that she had married her husband there.

"How did you both escape from East Germany?"

"Werner knew a safe route through the woods."

But she insisted that, as far as she knew, her husband had never owned a gun.

Now, at last, the case was beginning to look more promising. Back in his office, Eynck looked through the latest batch of information about Boost. This had come from a town called Helmstedt, which had been taken over by the Russians in 1945. And at about this period, there had been a great many murders—about fifty in all—of people trying to escape from the Russian to the British zone. Werner Boost had been in Helmstedt at the time. Then he had moved to Hadersleben, and the murders had ceased. But the two would-be émigrés had been shot in Hadersleben while trying to escape . . .

There was another interesting item—a notebook which had been found in the saddle of Boost's stolen motorcycle. And it contained an entry: "Sunday, June 3. Lorbach in need of another shot. Must attend to it."

Eynck sent for Boost and questioned him about the item. Boost said smoothly:

"Franz Lorbach is a friend of mine, and we go shooting together. On that day, he just couldn't hit the bull's eye, so I made a note to give him another shot."

Eynck did not believe a word of it. He asked Boost about his days in Helmstedt, and whether he had ever helped refugees to escape. Boost admitted that he had, and said he was proud of it. "And did you ever shoot them?" Boost looked horrified. "Of course not!"

Eynck now sent out one of his detectives to try to locate Franz Lorbach. This was not difficult. Lorbach proved to be a man of 23 with dark curly hair, whose good-looking face lacked the strength of Werner Boost's. He was a locksmith, and insisted that he only had the most casual acquaintance with Boost. Eynck knew that he was lying. He also noticed Lorbach's dilated pupils, and surmised that he was a drug addict, and that Boost was his supplier. He was certain that, when his craving became strong enough, Lorbach would talk. He held him in custody for questioning.

Meanwhile, Boost and Lorbach were placed in a police lineup, wearing handkerchief masks over the lower half of their faces. Adolf Hullecremer, the student who had been with Dr. Servé when he was shot, was able to identify Boost as Servé's assailant. He said he recognized the eyes. But he failed to identify Lorbach.

After a day or two in custody, Lorbach began to show symptoms of withdrawal from drugs. And one day, as Eynck was questioning Boost again—and getting nowhere—he received a phone call saying that Lorbach wanted to talk to him.

Lorbach was pale, his eyes were watery, and his nose twitched like a rabbit's.

"I want to tell you the truth. Werner Boost is a monster. It *was* he who killed Dr. Servé, and I was his accomplice . . .

Lorbach admitted that it was a love of poaching that had drawn the two of them together in 1952. They often went shooting in the woods. But Boost seemed to have a maniacal hatred of courting couples. "These sex horrors are the curse of Germany." So they would often creep up on couples who were making love in cars and rob them. Then, he said, Boost had an idea for rendering them unconscious. He had con-

cocted some mixture which he forced them to drink. Then he
and Lorbach would rape the unconscious girls. "Some of
them were very lovely. I feel ashamed—my wife is going to
have a baby. But it was Boost who made me do it. I had to
do it. He kept me supplied with morphine, which he obtained
from the chemist who sold him chemicals."

He insisted that he had taken part only in the attack on
Servé and Hullecremer. Boost had been indignant to see two
men in a car together, and had ordered him to kill the young
man. But Lorbach had not the stomach for it. Instead, he had
whispered to him to pretend to be dead. Lorbach's failure to
shoot Hullecremer enraged Boost—he made Lorbach kneel
in the snow, and said: "I ought to kill you too . . . "

Lorbach led the police to a place at the edge of the forest,
where Boost kept his loot concealed. In a buried chest, they
found watches, rings and jewelry. There were also bottles of
poison, some knives and a roll of cord which proved to be
identical to that which had been used to strangle Hildegard
Wassing.

Lorbach also disclosed that Boost had ordered Lorbach to
kill his wife, Hanna Boost, if he was arrested. There was a
vial of cyanide hidden behind a pipe in his flat, and Lorbach
was to slip it into her drink, so that she could not incriminate
her husband. Eynck found the vial exactly where Lorbach
had said it was.

Lorbach also confirmed that he and Boost had been involved in an earlier attempt at crime, a year before the murder of Dr. Servé. The two men had placed a heavy plank
studded with long nails across the road, to force motorists to
stop. But the first car to come along had contained four
men—too many for them to tackle—and it had driven on to
the verge and around the plank. Two more cars also contained too many passengers. Then a security van came, and a
man with a gun removed the plank. After that, police ar-

rived—evidently alerted by one of the cars—and Boost and Lorbach had to flee. In fact, as long ago as 1953, Eynck had suspected that Dr. Servé's murderer was responsible for this earlier attempt.

Lorbach also detailed Boost's plans to rob a post office by knocking everyone unconscious with poison gas, and to kidnap and murder a child of a rich industrialist for ransom.

Werner Boost had been born on May 6, 1928 in an industrial area of Hadersleben, the son of an unmarried mother who was only 17; he never knew the identity of his father. He had been placed in a government-run home, and been in trouble with the law from an early age. Leaving school in 1942, at the age of 14, he had worked in a series of menial jobs. He was released from a juvenile institution just before the war ended, and conscripted into the army. Taken prisoner by the British, he was set free within two months.

Unable to find work as an electrician, he had engaged in black marketeering and any other illegal activity that would pay. This is the period when, it is believed, he began smuggling would-be escapees across the border into West Germany, murdering them en route and stealing all they had. Since they would be carrying all their wealth with them, it would have been a profitable occupation.

Back in Hadersleben, in 1950, Boost married, and seems to have been an affectionate husband and father (the couple had two daughters). But there is evidence that he murdered the pair who were shot with the Belgian pistol, perhaps to finance an escape to West Germany. There he chose Lorbach as a partner in crime, and embarked on a career of robbery and murder.

On December 11, 1956, Boost was charged with the murders of Dr. Servé, Friedhelm Behre, Thea Kurmann, Peter Falkenberg and Hildegard Wassing. But when Lorbach, the main prosecution witness, suffered a nervous breakdown due to drug problems, the trial had to be postponed. Meanwhile, Boost was extradited to Magdeburg for questioning about the murder of the couple at Hadersleben. But he stonewalled his questioners as he had tried to stonewall the Düsseldorf police, and was finally returned to Eynck's jurisdiction with no additional charges against him.

Boost's trial began in the courthouse at Düsseldorf on November 3, 1961, before Judge Hans Naecke, two associate magistrates, Dr. Warda and Dr. Schmidt, and a six-man jury. Boost maintained his total innocence, and his layer, Dr. Koehler, lost no time in pointing out that the testimony of a drug addict like Franz Lorbach was hardly reliable. Lorbach himself was a poor witness, who mumbled and became confused. But he was able to tell one story that strengthened the case against Boost. Lorbach confessed that Boost had blackmailed him—by threatening withdrawal of his drug supply—into taking part in another attack on a couple. They had held up two lovers in the woods. Boost had tried to kill the man, but the gun had misfired. The girl had run away screaming, and Boost had ordered Lorbach to catch her. Lorbach had done so—but then whispered to her to lie low for a while. When he returned, Boost had knocked the man unconscious—but Lorbach had warned him there was a car coming, and they had roared away on Boost's motorbike.

Eynck told the court that he had traced this couple, and that they had confirmed the story in every detail. They were not married—at least not to one another—which is why they had failed to report the incident. But Eynck was able to offer their deposition in evidence.

Boost's lawyer counter-attacked by pointing out that there had recently been a murder of a couple in a car near Cologne, and that Boost was obviously not guilty of this crime.

After a month of listening to this and similar evidence, the six jurors decided that the evidence that Boost had murdered the two couples was insufficient. But they found him guilty of murdering Dr. Servé. He was sentenced to life imprisonment, and Lorbach to three years as his accomplice—much of which he had already served. Boost's sentence was exactly the same as if he had been found guilty on all charges.

The psychiatric examination had uncovered some of the causes of his criminality. Fatherless, brought up under harsh and loveless conditions, Boost—like Panzram and Manuel—reacted by making a conscious decision to become an "enemy of society." An account of Boost by George Vedder Jones contains the lines: "He developed an almost fanatical jealousy towards men who had been rich and successful through opportunities that had been denied him in his youth," and "His bitter hatred of mankind—originating in his warped childhood and manifested by his fantastic plans for mayhem and violence—seemed to supply motivation for the five Lovers' Lane murders."

But it must also be recognized that Boost was primarily a *sex* criminal—a man of immense sex drive whose "hatred of society" simply provided a rationalization for rape-murder. In this sense, there was an element of self-deception, of unconscious dishonesty, in Boost's hypocritical attitude about lovers petting in cars—"These sex horrors are the curse of Germany"—when he himself then went on to rape the women.

It should finally be noted that in spite of his ruthlessness, Boost was a victim of self-pity, convinced he had never been given a chance. Like so many criminals, it would never have entered his head to consider placing some of the blame on himself. Here again we have a basic key to the mind of most serial killers.

Boost's contemporary Heinrich Pommerencke was an altogether more straightforward killer—an uncomplicated example of a man driven by such an urgent craving for sex that it overrode all other considerations. This emerged clearly in an exchange that took place when the prosecutor Franz Schorp asked Pommerencke if he felt no remorse after his murders. Pommerencke shook his head. "All I felt was the physical desire to possess these women." "Do you know what people call a man who can commit such crimes and feel no remorse?" Pommerencke answered softly: "A monster."

On the morning of June 5, 1959 a pretty blonde girl was found dead by the railway line south of Freiburg. It was immediately obvious to police commissioner Gut, of the Freiburg murder squad, that this was a sex crime; her red dress was torn down the front, and she lay in the typical rape position, her underwear in the bushes beside her. Her body was covered with scratches and bruises, and there were cinders embedded in her flesh.

As it happened, Gut already knew her identity, because he had been involved in the search for her. She was 21-year-old Dagmar Klimek, a trainee teacher from Heidelberg. Three days earlier, she had boarded the Riviera Express with a group of twenty-nine other young women, en route for a package holiday in the Italian lakes. At about 11:30 at night, she had said goodnight to her friends and made her way to the toilet in the next coach—she had paused to ask the tour director where it was. Then she had vanished. A few minutes later, someone had pulled the communication cord and jumped from the train.

Commissioner Gut could have no doubt what had happened. A man had been waiting on the small open platform at the end of coach 405—this was established by the fact that someone had removed the light bulbs from this particular platform—and had hurled her from the train as she passed him. Then he had pulled the communication cord and run back to find her. The girl had still been alive, but probably unconscious, as the man dragged her into the bushes, and raped her. Then he had stabbed her in the chest, killing her instantly. The body was so well concealed that it was not found until three days later.

Only two witnesses had seen the killer. One was a salesman who had boarded the train at Freiburg, climbing on at the platform of coach 405. He had noticed the tall, slim young man with blond hair because he looked somehow furtive. The man had been wearing a shabby grey suit.

The other witness had been dozing in the same carriage when the train braked to a halt. He had seen a man jump from the train and run out of sight behind bushes; he described him as tall and gaunt, and wearing a loose-fitting grey suit that made him look like a scarecrow.

A check into Dagmar Klimek's background indicated that she had no male admirer who might have killed her. The killer was clearly a sex maniac who had chosen her at random because she walked past him on her way back from the toilet.

On the supposition that the killer must have been bloodstained, the police checked cleaning establishments from Frankfurt to Freiburg, looking for the grey suit; they met with no success. Careful interrogation of dozens of known sex offenders also produced no result. Every railway ticket clerk south of Frankfurt was asked if he recalled a tall skinny man in the grey suit; no one did.

Could this killer have struck before? When Gut looked through the record of unsolved sex crimes in Baden-Württemberg, he found three that sounded as if they might have been committed by the same man. Towards the end of February 1959, a Karlsruhe waitress named Elke Braun had been walking home when a man had seized her from behind and thrown her on the ground. He was brandishing a knife and ripping at her clothes when a passing taxi driver heard her screams. The man—who was tall and blond—ran off as the taxi driver approached. The girl said her attacker had "the face of a baby," with soft skin. But his expression as he attacked her left her in no doubt that he intended to kill her.

The following morning, the body of a 34-year-old cleaning woman named Hilde Konther was found in bushes near her home. She had been beaten and raped, then strangled. It looked as if the waitress's attacker had been lying in wait for her as she returned home from work in the early hours of the morning.

The other crime that sounded as if it had been committed by the same man had taken place a month later, on March 26, 1959. In the nearby town of Hornberg a beautician named Karin Walde had also failed to return home from work. The next morning, her parents found her naked body in bushes close to her home. She had been battered to death with a heavy stone and raped.

One more sex crime had an ominously similar ring. On May 30, an 18-year-old girl had been attacked in her bedroom in Zingen, another small town on the Karlsruhe railway line. Someone had climbed in through the window while she was asleep, beaten her insensible before she could resist, then raped her. It had been a moonlit night, and she had seen him clearly—a tall man with piercing eyes and a "baby face." He had escaped by the way he came in.

Three days after the body of Dagmar Klimek was found, another girl disappeared. Rita Walterspacher was an 18-year-old office worker who traveled by train from her home in Rastatt, south of Karlsruhe, to her job in Baden Baden, a mere ten kilometers to the south. On June 8, 1959, she telephoned her parents to say she would be a little late arriving home; she expected to be back by seven. When she had failed to return by the next morning, her parents inquired at the local railway station—to be told by the stationmaster that he had seen their daughter alight from the 6:06 train.

Rita's way home lay south along a wooded road. The police organized a search party, and there was an appeal on local radio for anyone who might have seen her. Soon after this, a woman from a neighboring town drove to the Rastatt police station. She had been on a slightly later train the evening before, she explained, and at about 6:15, just before they reached Rastatt, she saw a girl running along the road beside the track, pursued by a man. She was screaming, but the woman thought they were simply two lovers having fun. The man—who was tall, with blond hair—grabbed the girl and dragged her into the woods. The woman thought no more about it until she heard the appeal on the radio.

When she added that the man was wearing a grey suit, the detective realized that this was almost certainly the rapist of the Riviera Express. A larger search party was organized, and spread out through the woods near the spot where the woman had seen the incident. The girl's body was found a few hours later by a farmer's dog, hidden under a pile of fir branches, not far from the railway line. From her position, it was clear that she had been raped there, then covered over. The cause of death was strangulation.

When Commissioner Gut saw the body he had no doubt that this was the man he was looking for. This was clearly a sex maniac in the most precise meaning of the term. When he was trying to rape a girl, he went into a frenzy, beating her violently and tearing at her clothes until they were in tatters. The fact that he might have been seen from the passing train did not deter him. Until the rape was accomplished, he became a wild animal incapable of any other thought.

Two rape-murders within a week suggested that the killer was reaching a peak in a cycle of violence that is typical of sex criminals, and that he had to be caught quickly. But the area over which he had committed his crimes was enormous, ranging from Karlsruhe in the north to Hornberg, a hundred kilometers south.

On the off-chance that the killer lived in the Rastatt area, the police instituted door-to-door inquiries, looking for anyone who might resemble the Riviera rapist—who had by now acquired himself a press nickname: the Monster of the Black Forest. Many suspects who matched the description were brought in for questioning, but all were able to prove their innocence. Again there was an extensive search for a bloodstained suit at local cleaners, but it was as unsuccessful as before. As the days went by, Gut experienced an increasing frustration, realizing that all he could do was to wait for the next attack to occur, and hope that this time the "Monster" left some clue.

Fortunately, the Riviera rapist was caught before he could kill again.

On the morning of June 19, a tailor named Johann Kohler opened his shop at eight o'clock. Soon after this, his first customer arrived—a young man named Heinrich Pommerencke, who had worked as a waiter in Hornsberg's Hotel Baren. Kohler was glad to see him, for the youth had ordered some clothes two months earlier—a sports jacket and trousers—and had paid a deposit. But he had failed to collect them.

Pommerencke had a soft, almost girlish face, with pink, smooth skin. Although tall, he looked much younger than his twenty-two years. He was wearing a baggy grey suit.

Pommerencke apologized for the delay in collecting the clothes, explaining that he now worked in a hotel in Frankfurt, and had been unable to get to Hornberg. He asked the tailor how much he owed, and paid from a wad of notes.

"Would you mind if I changed my clothes here? I can't stand this old suit a moment longer."

Kohler indicated the changing cubicle, and Pommerencke vanished inside, leaving a bulging briefcase on a chair in the shop. He emerged a few minutes later, and surveyed himself with satisfaction in the mirror.

"Now all I need is a haircut. Could I leave you to wrap up my old suit while I go?"

When Kohler had packed the suit, he moved the heavy briefcase on to the floor. As he did so, the defective catch burst open, and Kohler was startled to find himself looking at a rifle whose barrel and butt had both been shortened with a hacksaw.

At that moment, his wife came into the shop. The tailor showed her the weapon.

"I can't understand what such a quiet young man is doing with a gun like this. He doesn't look as if he'd say boo to a goose."

Frau Kohler shook her head. "A weapon like that could have only one purpose—robbery. You ought to report it to the police."

Within minutes, an inspector named Posedowski had arrived from the local station on his bicycle. He viewed the sawn-off rifle with distaste, then looked through the briefcase. It contained some soiled clothing, money, pornographic books, a bottle of pink liquid labeled "love cocktail," a box of bullets and a ticket stub from Karlsruhe to Zingen.

The suit itself was unpacked, and Posedowski saw why its owner was anxious to change it. There were many spots where cleaning fluid had been used to remove some dark stain, and these showed as unsightly blotches.

Like every other policeman in Baden-Württemberg, Posedowski knew about the Monster of the Black Forest and his grey suit. And although this pink-cheeked young man hardly sounded like a multiple killer, his reasons for carrying a sawn-off rifle obviously demanded investigation.

Heinrich Pommerencke looked mildly surprised to find a policeman waiting for him, but raised no objection when asked to accompany him to the local police station. He seemed so unconcerned that Posedowski relaxed his vigilance, and was taken by surprise when the young man took to his heels. Posedowski blew his whistle and pursued him on his bicycle. Fortunately, they had almost arrived at the station, and another policeman soon joined the chase. They eventually cornered Pommerencke in the grounds of a carnival on the edge of town. Posedowski snapped handcuffs on him, and the two policemen marched him back to the station.

When Commissioner Heinrich Koch saw the sawn-off rifle, he reacted with satisfaction.

"I've just been notified of a burglary at Durlach station last night. A track worker walked in on the robber, who threatened him with a sawn-off rifle, then ran away." The thief had stolen some money from a cashbox.

The rest of the contents of the briefcase also intrigued the commissioner. The "love cocktail"—presumably a mild aphrodisiac—and the pornography certainly suggested a man with sex on his mind. The stub of the rail ticket from Karlsruhe to Zingen reminded Koch of the rape of the 18-year-old girl in her bedroom by a man with a "baby face."

The grey suit was sent to Freiburg for forensic analysis; the blood serum test would reveal whether spots that still showed under the cleaning fluid were human blood.

Koch then interviewed the youthful suspect, and accused him without further ado of being the Durlach burglar. He noticed that, far from looking worried, Pommerencke seemed relieved. He admitted that he had purchased the rifle in a pawnshop, and had used it in the burglary the night before. He also admitted to three other recent burglaries—of a textile mill, an ammunition factory and a cafeteria in Rastatt. These admissions gave Koch the grounds he needed to charge his suspect, and Pommerencke was taken to the cells.

The investigation into Pommerencke's background was continued by the police in Frankfurt. In his room in the hotel they found papers that established that he had lived in various West German cities, including Karlsruhe, and that he had served a prison sentence for burglary. He had apparently worked as a house painter and handyman, as well as a waiter. Those who worked with him in Hornberg and Frankfurt said that he was a "loner" who spent much of his time at the cinema or in his room. He was known as a good worker who neither smoke nor drank.

Four days after his arrest, Pommerencke was taken to Freiburg, where the two commissioners who had been in charge of the case—Gut and Zismann—were waiting to interview him. They had also prepared a surprise for him. He was given a grey suit, and placed in an identity parade. The girl who had been raped in her bedroom in Zingen instantly identified him as her attacker.

Pommerencke indignantly denied it. "I may be a burglar but I've never attacked a girl."

But there were still four witnesses to view the police lineup. They were the two men who had seen the rapist on the Riviera Express, the woman who had seen Rita Walterspacher being attacked near Rastatt, and the waitress who had been saved by the taxi driver in Karlsruhe. All of them picked out Pommerencke.

Zismann told his suspect that they now had powerful circumstantial evidence to link him with Karlsruhe—where Hilde Konther had died—with Hornberg, where Karin Walde had died, and with Rastatt and the Riviera Express. Faced with this evidence, Pommerencke sullenly admitted that he had been the man who had attacked the girl in Zwingen and the waitress in Karlsruhe. But he strongly denied the rape-murders.

When the results of the test on the grey suit came from the forensic lab, Zismann was also able to tell Pommerencke that they now had evidence to link him to Hilde Konther, Dagmar Klimek and Karin Walde—the blood on the suit corresponded to their blood groups. And hairs on the suit had been identified as being from the head of Rita Walterspacher.

It was fortunate that Pommerencke was ignorant of forensic science, or he would have known that—at that time—neither blood nor hairs could be identified as coming from a particular person. Blood could only be "grouped"—and in fact, the stains had been too faint for grouping. The lab had only been able to establish that they were of human origin. Moreover, there had been no hairs on the suit.

But Pommerencke was taken in by the bluff. His defiance suddenly collapsed. With averted eyes, he asked for a pencil to write his confession.

What this document made clear was that Pommerencke had been attacking and raping women for years—he had no idea of how many rapes he had committed. He had also committed scores of burglaries.

Heinrich Pommerencke had been born in Bentwisch, near Rostock in East Germany, in 1937. He was the child of a broken marriage, and described himself as an extremely lonely little boy. But he seems to have inherited an extremely powerful sexual urge, which troubled him from an early age. "When I was a boy I never had a friend in the world. After a while I got the urge to assault females. I had a girlfriend once but we split up, and I went back to my old ways. Other men always had girlfriends with them. I wanted girlfriends too, but I never succeeded."

Pommerencke claimed—almost certainly untruthfully—that he had seduced his first girl at the age of 10. At the age of 15 he began to hang around the local dance hall in Bentwisch and made a few clumsy attempts to attack girls. Because of one of these attempts at rape, he fled from Bentwisch in 1953, when he was 16 and went to Switzerland. There he served a prison sentence for burglary, and was deported. He drifted around West Germany, living in Hamburg, Heidelberg, Düsseldorf, Karlsruhe, Hornberg and Frankfurt.

Living alone in rented rooms, reading pornography and indulging in sexual daydreams, Pommerencke's fantasies had reached an intensity that sooner or later had to be translated into action. He was not of high intelligence, and tended to be inarticulate—which meant that he completely lacked the arts of a seducer. "Whatever I did (when with girls) was always wrong. I was never a good dancer, and girls avoided me because of that. When I was alone with them, I didn't know what to say." This social inadequacy, combined with an overpoweringly strong sexual urge, meant that rape was virtually his only way of obtaining the sexual favors he craved. And it was finally in Hamburg, according to his confession, that he gave way to the compulsion and committed seven rapes between 1955 and 1957. It was after this that he was jailed for burglary.

But his first murder had been committed in Karlsruhe soon after he moved there in 1959. There he had been to see Cecil B. DeMille's film called *The Ten Commandments* with Charlton Heston. In the scene with the half-naked women dancing around the Golden Calf, he had suddenly decided that many women are evil, and deserve to die. When he left the cinema he bought a knife, then walked around until he saw the waitress Elke Braun. But as he was attacking her, the taxi driver had interrupted, and he had been forced to flee. But the compulsion was now overpowering, and he had attacked the cleaning woman a few hours later, battering her unconscious when she resisted, then strangling her. But Pommerencke admitted that it was after killing his second victim, beautician Karin Walde, in Hornberg, that this violent method of obtaining satisfaction became a fixed obsession that drove him to seek further victims.

Pommerencke's trial opened in Freiburg on October 3, 1960, before Judge Friedrich Kaufmann. The defense evidence consisted mainly of character testimony from many people who said that the prisoner was extremely shy, and blushed when he talked to women. His mother came from Switzerland to testify that her son certainly did not hate women; he adored them. Girls who had been out with him testified that he was too nervous even to attempt to kiss them.

His factual account of his various murders chilled the spectators. He described how, after throwing Dagmar Klimek from the train, he had had to walk back for half an hour along the tracks before he found her. He had dragged her into the bushes and torn off her clothes in a frenzy, then, after raping her, had stabbed her to death. Then he had walked to the nearest village, washed in the public fountain, and hitched a lift back to Frankfurt from a passing motorist.

He admitted that he had felt no remorse after the murders, because he had been so overwhelmed by a desire to possess women. But now, he conceded, he saw that "everything I did was cruel and bestial. From the bottom of my heart I would like to undo all this."

After a five-week trial, Heinrich Pommerencke was sentenced to eight terms of life imprisonment, plus a further 156 years, a sentence to be served with hard labor. It meant that he would spend the rest of his life in jail.

On the other side of the Atlantic, at the time when Heinrich Pommerencke was nerving himself to commit his first sex attack, another mild little man was collecting pornographic photographs and fantasizing about rape. But his tastes were less straightforward than Pommerencke's; being of a timid disposition, Harvey Glatman dreamed only of violating girls who were tied hand and foot.

On the evening of August 1, 1957, Robert Dull, a young pressman on the *Los Angeles Times*, called at a Hollywood apartment block to see his estranged wife, and was not surprised to hear that she was not at home. Judy was an exceptionally beautiful girl, greatly in demand as a photographic model, and it was this that had led to the break-up of their marriage—Robert Dull objected to her posing in the nude.

Judy's flatmate, Lynn Lykles, explained that she had gone off with a photographer called Johnny Glynn at about two that afternoon.

"Do you know where she went?"

"No, but he left a telephone number."

"Would you ask her to call me at work when she comes in?"

But two hours later, there was still no sign of Judy. By that time, two photographers had called in to complain that she had failed to keep appointments. At 9 p.m., a young contractor telephoned to say that Judy had failed to show up for a dinner date, at which she was supposed to meet a lawyer to discuss her marital problems. Lynn gave him Johnny Glynn's telephone number. A few minutes later, he called back.

"That number was a machine shop in Pico. They'd never heard of a photographer called Johnny Glynn."

Now they were both seriously worried. There had been a number of attacks on girls in Hollywood recently, and only two evenings before, Judy had complained that a strange man had followed her home.

The contractor hurried off to look in a number of Sunset Strip cafes that Judy frequented; meanwhile, Lynn rang Robert Dull, who hurried over immediately. They telephoned

Judy's parents, relatives and friends without success, then went to report her disappearance at the West Hollywood police station. And when a routine check of hospitals failed to locate her, the sheriff put out a call to radio cars cruising Sunset Strip, asking them to watch out for a pretty 19-year-old blonde. He asked:

"Who is this Johnny Glynn?"

Lynn described how, two evenings before, a little rabbit-like man with jug-handle ears had knocked on the door of their apartment, asking to see Lynn. It so happened that the only person at home was Betty Carver, a recent arrival from Florida; like Lynn and Judy, she was a photographic model. And, since Betty had a friend with her, she allowed the little man into the apartment. He identified himself as Johnny Glynn, a magazine photographer, and said he had obtained Lynn's name from an agency. Would it, he asked, be possible to see her portfolio? But when Betty returned with it, he pointed to the photograph of Judy on the wall. "Now she's the type I'm really looking for. Could I see her portfolio as well?" As he leafed slowly through it, Betty could see that he was fascinated. When he had finished, he asked for Judy's personal telephone number.

Two mornings later, the three girls were eating breakfast when Johnny Glynn telephoned. He had a rush assignment, he explained, and wanted Judy to pose for him that afternoon. Judy was reluctant; she had a busy schedule, and Betty's description of Johnny Glynn aroused her suspicions. But when he mentioned that his own studio was being used, and that he would have to use Judy's apartment, her doubts evaporated, and she agreed to see him at two that afternoon.

He arrived looking as scruffy and unprepossessing as on his previous visit; moreover, he was without his photographic equipment. This, he explained, was because a friend had agreed to lend him his own studio. When Judy mentioned her hourly fee, he agreed immediately. And a few minutes later, they left the apartment, with the photographer carrying Judy's case. Lynn Lykles had felt uneasy as she watched them leave.

At mid-morning the following day, a bulletin was issued listing Judy Van Horn Dull as a missing person, possibly kidnaped; she was described as 19 years old, five feet four inches tall, with golden hair and a suntanned complexion. Johnny Glynn was described as about 29 years old, of slim build, five feet nine inches tall, with horn-rimmed glasses, and dressed in a rumpled blue suit.

Sergeant David Ostroff, who was handed the assignment, checked on all the Hollywood photographers and modeling agencies he could find; none of them had heard of Johnny Glynn, or knew anyone who answered his description.

The disappearance of the beautiful model made newspaper headlines, and Ostroff was kept busy for weeks following up tips. It soon became clear that the modeling business was not Hollywood's safest occupation. Several young models came forward to describe how they had been rash enough to accept jobs from unknown "photographers" who had then forced their attentions on them, sometimes at knife- or gunpoint. A number of men were questioned, but none of them had the distinctive appearance of Johnny Glynn. Ostroff recalled the disappearance of a beautiful young actress named Jean Spangler eight years before, in October 1949, but although they studied her file, it failed to throw any light on Judy's disappearance.

Even Judy's husband Robert seemed a possible suspect; he and Judy had not been on the best of terms since he had seized their fourteen-month-old daughter Suzanne while Judy was at work. But a little investigation cleared him of suspicion; he was known to be still in love with his wife, and hoping for a reconciliation. None of Judy's friends could offer any clue to the mystery. After following up dozens of futile leads, Sergeant Ostroff concluded that Johnny Glynn was a false name, and that the rabbit-like man was probably some kind of sex pervert. It seemed likely that Judy Dull was dead.

Or was it possible that Judy had gone into hiding before the court case that would decide the custody of her daughter? At the hearing—on August 9, 1957—there was an unusual number of reporters and photographers. Judy was known to be deeply attached to her daughter—so attached that she was even considering giving up modeling to devote more time to her. When there was no sign of her in court, her husband told the press that he was certain she had been murdered.

Five months after her disappearance, on December 29, 1957, a ranch worker walking in the desert near US Highway 60, between Indio and Thousand Palms—130 miles east of Los Angeles—wondered what was causing his dog to bark. It was standing above a human skull that lay in a cotton field. He summoned the police, and they discovered a half-buried skeleton not far from the skull. The moldering brown dress and underwear revealed that it was a woman. Remains of hair sticking to the skull indicated that she was a blonde. It was impossible to determine the cause of death.

Could this be Judy Dull? She had been last seen wearing a brown dress. And the skeleton was the same height as Judy—five feet four. But a forensic expert concluded that the dead woman was in her mid-thirties, and when Judy's husband failed to identify the pearl ring found on the finger, Ostroff concluded that this was not the woman he was looking for.

As it happened, he was mistaken . . .

On Sunday, March 9, 1958, the Los Angeles police heard about another disappearance. The woman's name was Shirley Ann Loy Bridgeford, a 24-year-old divorcee with two children. The night before she had gone out with a stranger on a blind date, and had not been seen since.

From Shirley's mother, the San Fernando Valley police learned that Shirley had been lonely and bored. And since a man she had been hoping to marry had suddenly lost interest in her, she had also been depressed, convinced that she was now "on the shelf." A friend had suggested that Shirley should join a Lonely Hearts Club, and she had seized on the idea with the enthusiasm of the desperate. For a fee of $10, she had become a member of a dating club in Los Angeles. Her first date had arrived early on Saturday evening—an unprepossessing, bespectacled man with jug-handle ears and an appearance that suggested he had no interest in clothes. He had introduced himself as George Williams; a plumber who lived in Pasadena. Shirley had introduced him to the family—her mother, grandmother, brother and sister, and he had looked awkward and embarrassed. A few minutes later they had left—he said he was taking her to a square dance. No one had bothered to look to see what kind of car he was driving.

The obvious lead was the Lonely Hearts Club. Its organizer was able to provide the police with George Williams's address, but it turned out—as they expected—to be false. Another girl—a Hollywood secretary—who had actually spent an evening with "George Williams" told them that he had been a "perfect gentleman," and that they had spent the evening quietly in her apartment. She was unable to offer any leads.

To Sergeant Ostroff, it sounded as if George Williams and Johnny Glynn might be the same person. But this was no help to the investigation, since it was impossible to find any trace of either. The only thing that was clear was that "George Williams" had almost certainly joined the club with the intention of abducting a girl. The Hollywood secretary had described him as clean shaven, yet Shirley's family said he wore a moustache. Since he had dated Shirley only two days after the secretary, that meant it had to be a false one. Since only a man with some misdemeanor in mind would go out on a blind date with a false moustache, the likeliest conclusion was that Shirley Bridgeford was now dead. Another was that unless the abductor was caught, he would strike again.

When another model vanished in late July, Lieutenant Marvin Jones of the Los Angeles police suspected that this is exactly what had happened. The landlord of a small apartment block on West Pico Boulevard, in the Wilshire district of Los Angeles, reported that one of his tenants was missing. She was 24-year-old Ruth Rita Mercado, who—using the alias Angela Rojas—worked as a stripper and a nude model. Her landlord had passed her door on the evening of July 23, and heard her inside talking to her collie dog. There was a "Do Not Disturb" sign on the door. When, four days later, he observed the mail piling up in her mailbox, he used his pass key to enter the apartment. It was empty, with no sign of a struggle; but the collie pup was in the bathroom, exhausted from lack of food. Her parakeets were in a similar condition—fortunately they had been found in time. It seemed obvious that Ruth had not left them voluntarily. She had cared for her pets as though they were babies.

Oddly enough, the landlord wrote to Ruth's mother in Plattsburg, New York, instead of going to the Los Angeles police and Lieutenant Jones learned of the model's disappearance from the New York police. He sent Sergeant Paul A. Light to investigate. Light felt he had found a promising lead when he learned that Ruth had left her previous apartment on South Kenmore Avenue because she had been receiving obscene phone calls, and had one evening found an obscene note pushed under her door. And when, with some help from the local police, he tracked down the author of the note, he felt that he might have found his man. His hopes collapsed into disappointment. The man had been harassing the girl because he objected to having a model as a neighbor, and he was able to prove that he had nothing to do with her disappearance.

When Lieutenant Jones checked the files of other disappearances, he observed the similarity to the case of Judy Dull. And it was clear that Ruth Mercardo's way of life involved even more risk than Judy's. As well as being a stripper, she advertised her services as a nude model in newspapers, and even provided photographic equipment for amateurs. And since she lived alone, she had less protection than Judy in her shared apartment. Her boyfriend—a piano player—was at present in Bermuda, so could be eliminated as a suspect. And so, eventually, were several other photographers who had worked with both Judy Dull and Ruth Mercado. And this time there was not even a description of the abductor. As he surveyed the total absence of clues, Lieutenant Jones surmised that he would turn out to have jughandle ears and a disheveled appearance.

Three months after Ruth Mercado's disappearance, late on the evening of Monday, October 27, 1958, Officer Thomas F. Mulligan of the California Highway Patrol turned his motorcycle into a dark avenue near the small town of Tustin, 35 miles southeast of Los Angeles, and was startled when his headlight illuminated a couple who were struggling at the side of the road. At that moment, the couple separated, and as he braked to a halt and shouted to ask what was happening, he saw that the woman was holding a gun, which she was pointing at a man. The woman was small and plump, and her clothing was in a state of disarray. The Highway Patrolman raised his revolver and ordered them to stand still and hold up their hands. Both did so immediately. The woman, who was almost hysterical, shouted: "He's a killer. He was going to rape me." The man made no attempt to deny this, or to escape as Mulligan radioed Tustin for assistance. A few minutes later, the Tustin police arrived.

Meanwhile, the girl—who identified herself as Lorraine Vigil—told Mulligan what had happened. A model named Diane, who also ran a modeling agency, had telephoned her two hours ago to ask if she wanted to do a modeling job. Lorraine was a secretary who was determined to break into the modeling business, and she accepted immediately. But before the client arrived, Diane rang her back to tell her to be on her guard. Although she knew the man—Frank Johnson—and had done some modeling for him before, she felt uneasy about him. That was why she herself had refused to accept the job unless she was allowed to take a chaperone along. And Johnson had refused . . .

Frank Johnson arrived at her Wilshire apartment soon afterwards, and Lorraine saw why Diane was uneasy. He was a shifty little man with jug-handle ears and an untidy appearance—he looked as if he slept in his clothes. He didn't even come to her door, but blew his horn outside. When she went out, she asked for money in advance, and he handed her $15. Then they drove off in the direction of downtown Los Angeles. But instead of heading for Diane's agency in Sunset Strip, he turned south-east. When Lorraine objected, he explained that he was going to take her to his own studio in Anaheim.

In fact, he drove straight through Anaheim. And in the dark road near Tustin, he pulled up and told her he had a flat tire. Then he pulled out a small automatic, ordered her to keep quiet, and produced a length of rope. Lorraine pleaded not to be tied up, offering to do whatever he wanted. But as a car came past, she tried to open the door. He grabbed her and pulled her back, then threatened her again, and tried to tie her up. She began to struggle and he became increasingly angry and abusive. As he pointed the gun at her, she grabbed it and tried to pull it away. It went off, and she felt the bullet burn her thigh. But the man seemed as shocked as she was by the sound of the shot. As he stared at the smoking gun in bewilderment, she leapt across him, forced open his door, and fell out on to the road with the man underneath her. Clinging tightly to his gun, she tried to pull it out of his hand; when he tried to point it at her, she bit him as hard as she could. He gave a cry of pain, and released the gun. Lorraine pointed it at him and tried to pull the trigger. It was at that moment that they were illuminated by the patrolman's headlight.

Taken to the Santa Ana police station, the man gave his name as Harvey Murray Glatman, aged 30, a TV repairman. He proved to have nearly a thousand dollars on him, which led the police to suspect him of being a holdup man. He made no attempt to deny his attempt to assault Lorraine Vigil, but said it had been a sudden impulse, and he was sorry. He also admitted that he had a police record and had been in prison. He had come to Los Angeles, he said, in the previous year. But when the police asked him what he had been doing since then, he was evasive, and they felt he was concealing something.

A bulletin describing the arrest was sent to police throughout the area, asking if the suspect could be linked to any other crimes. When it landed on the desk of Lieutenant Marvin Jones, he immediately noted that the suspect, as well as his intended victim, lived in his area. Moreover, Glatman lived a few blocks from Ruth Mercado on San Pico Boulevard.

When the police called at the white shingle bungalow at 1011 South Norton Avenue, they noted its run-down appearance, the tar-paper on the roof and the bars on the windows. Inside, they found the walls covered with nude pinups, in some of which the girls were bound and gagged. There were also a number of lengths of rope. It seemed that Harvey Glatman was interested in bondage.

The following day, Glatman was asked if he would take a lie detector test, and he agreed. Two sergeants from Wilshire went to Santa Ana to watch. They walked in while Glatman was being questioned—wired up to the lie detector—and when they were introduced as two detectives investigating the disappearance of two girls, the polygraph recorded no sudden alarm. But when he was asked about "Angela"— Ruth Mercado—the stylus gave a nervous leap. A few minutes later, Glatman was confessing to killing Ruth. "I killed a couple of other girls too."

And now, at last, the police heard the full story of the disappearance of three women.

Harvey Murray Glatman was born in Denver, Colorado, in 1928; he was a "mother's boy" who was also an excellent student (A later test showed that his IQ was 130.) When he was 12 years old, his parents came home one day to observe that he had red marks around his neck. Under pressure, Harvey admitted that he had been in the attic, tied a rope round his neck, and tightened the noose until he experienced sexual satisfaction. (Many masochists accidentally hang themselves when obtaining release in this way.) The family doctor was consulted, but advised them not to worry—Harvey would outgrow it. Meanwhile, the best way to avoid more self-strangulation was exercise . . .

Girls at school found the scrawny, jug-eared boy unattractive; he made his bid for attention by snatching their purses, running away, then flinging them back at them. Mrs. Glatman is quoted as saying tolerantly: "It was just his approach."

When he was 17, Glatman tired of frustration and sexual fantasy; one night in Boulder, Colorado, he pointed a toy gun at a teenage girl and ordered her to undress. She screamed and he lost his nerve and ran. Picked up by the police, he was released on bail—and broke bond to make his way to New York. There he satisfied his aggressive urges against women, robbing them at gunpoint; he became known as the "Phantom Bandit." He also graduated to burglary, but was soon caught, and sentenced to five years in Sing Sing. Once inside, he proved a docile prisoner, seemed to respond to psychiatric treatment, and was released in 1951. He moved back to Colorado, and worked at TV repairs. In 1957, he moved to Los Angeles, where his doting mother, who took a lenient view of his "mistakes," found the money to set him up in a TV repair business.

Glatman's problem was simple: a powerfully inferiority complex made him incapable of the normal courtship procedures. In order to maintain a state of sexual excitement, he had to have the girl completely at his mercy—preferably bound and gagged. The result was that at 28 he was still a virgin, whose sex life was confined to lurid daydreams of bondage.

He may have thought of the idea of becoming a photographer after seeing pictures of bound girls on the covers of true detective magazines. He soon learned that even an amateur photographer could pay to photograph unclothed girls in public studios. But his glimpses of female nudity only made his celibacy more agonizing. Which is why, on July 29, 1957, he called at the apartment of Lynn Lykles to try and persuade her to pose for him. But when he saw the photograph of Judy Dull on the wall, he realized that she was the girl he had always wanted. Two days later, his dream was fulfilled; Judy was in his old black Dodge, being driven to his "studio"—no doubt he had removed the pinups and bondage photos from the wall for the occasion.

Judy was wearing a dress; Glatman told her to remove it

and put on a pleated skirt and cardigan. When he produced a length of rope, Judy reacted with alarm. He soothed her by explaining that he was taking photographs for the cover of a true detective magazine, and she had to be bound and gagged. And when she was seated in an armchair, her knees tied together, her hands behind her, a gag in her mouth, Glatman pushed up her skirt to reveal the white underskirt. Then, having taken some pictures, he unbuttoned the cardigan, pulled down her bra, and unzipped the skirt at the waist. Then, unable to contain himself any longer, he lifted her on to the floor—she was only five feet four inches tall, and very light—and removed everything but her panties. When he began to fondle her, Judy struggled and tried to scream; Glatman felt his excitement evaporating. He rushed out of the room and returned with an automatic pistol. He placed this against her head and told her that if she resisted, she would be killed—he was an ex-convict, and would not hesitate to shoot. When she nodded her acquiescence, he removed the gag.

He found the sight of a bound girl so satisfying that he decided to prolong the pleasure; he left her tied on the floor while he had something to eat. Now anxious to pacify him, Judy promised to do whatever he wanted, and not to report him to the police. She explained that she was due to appear in court in ten days' time, hoping to obtain the custody of her daughter, and that if she went to the police, it would only confirm her husband's contention that she was unfit to be a mother.

Glatman responded with apparent concern. When Judy's nose began to bleed, he stanched the blood with a pillowcase. Then he made her sit on the settee for more bondage photographs. Finally, he did what he had been waiting to do; he removed his own clothes and raped her twice.

After that, he switched on the television, and the two of

them sat naked and watched it, while she allowed him to fondle her. Now it was all over, he was not sure what to do next. Could he believe her when she said she would not report him to the police? If he did, and she broke her word, he would be in jail for the rest of his life . . .

Finally, he explained what he had decided to do. He would take her to some remote spot, then release her. After that, he would leave town. Judy tried to persuade him to let her take a taxi back home, but he refused. She apparently believed his threat to shoot her, for she made no attempt to escape when he forced her to climb into his car. They drove out on the San Bernardino freeway, then into the desert. There he made her pose for more "cheesecake" photographs on a blanket, which he took with a flash. Finally, he made her lie on her stomach, and looped the rope around her neck; then he bent her legs back and tied it around her ankles. At this point, Judy must have realized she was going to die, and began to struggle. It was too late; Glatman pulled on the rope until she lay still.

Glatman was not a violent man; now she was dead he felt sorry. He apologized to her body before dragging it farther into the desert, and burying it in a shallow grave,. A fetishist to the end, he took her shoes for souvenirs.

For weeks, Glatman lived in fear of being caught. Would Judy's flatmates provide the police with enough clues to track him down? Would they visit some of the agencies and studios he had used. But as the weeks went by, he began to feel calmer. After Christmas, the craving for another woman became too strong to resist. This time he joined the Lonely Hearts club, and arranged a date. The first girl he visited was the Hollywood secretary. But she was simply not his type—a talker. She offered him tea and biscuits and they conversed. It was impossible for Glatman to feel master of the situation.

So he took his leave, and rang the club for another date. They gave him the name of Shirley Ann Bridgeford.

As soon as he saw Shirley Ann, he knew she found him a disappointment; for a moment he was afraid she would find some excuse not to go out. But once they were in the car she seemed to reconcile herself to the evening ahead; she even raised no objection when he explained that he was not fond of square dancing, and suggested they go for a drive instead. This time they drove past Long Beach and down south towards San Diego. But when he stopped the car on a side road in the Anza desert, and put his arm around her, she balked. Wasn't it about time to go home? Glatman's anger surged, but he controlled it; they were still too close to a main road to risk force. He pretended to agree, and said they would find a drive-in for a meal.

As he drove with one hand on the wheel, he tried to fondle her, and his resentment was fueled by her resistance. Finally, on a dark mountain road inland, he stopped the car and produced his automatic. Then he ordered her into the back seat, and told her to undress. When she resisted, he tore off her clothes, then raped her. After that, he drove on into the desert, and stopped where a track came to an end. He removed his photographic gear, spread out the blanket on which he had killed Judy Dull, and ordered Shirley—now once again wearing her dress—to sit on it while he took some photographs. And when he had enough souvenirs, he made her lie on her stomach, looped the rope around her neck, and garrotted her. This time he was too lazy to dig a grave; he covered her body over with brushwood; before leaving, he removed her red panties as a keepsake.

He had allowed almost seven months to elapse between his first and second murders. Now, as with most sex criminals, the urge became more insistent. And when he saw a newspaper advertisement in which the model offered to be photographed nude, it seemed too good an opportunity to miss. He called on Angela Rojas on the evening of July 22, 1958, and was not particularly surprised when she shook her head and explained that she felt ill. He was used to rejection. The following evening he went back, and found the apartment in darkness. He whiled away an hour in a bar, then returned; this time, the light was on. When she showed no sign of being willing to admit him, he pulled out the gun and ordered her inside. Like Judy Dull, Ruth Mercado was small, and he liked this. He ordered her into the bedroom, made her undress, then tied her up and raped her. After that he took souvenir photographs. Before they left the apartment he had raped her several times more.

When she mentioned that she was expecting her boyfriend soon—a lie—he told her he wanted to take her for a picnic. He seemed so convincing that she believed him, and even offered to provide two bottles of brandy. They drove off down towards San Diego, beyond Escondido, and in the early hours of the morning they were thirty or so miles from the spot where he had killed Shirley Ann Bridgeford.

This time Glatman had decided to take his time. In this lonely spot they were unlikely to be interrupted. He and Ruth Mercado spent the whole of the following day out in the desert; they slept, ate, drank, took photographs and made love. Ruth had decided that she had nothing to lose by trying to please him, and Glatman found himself increasingly unwilling to kill her. She was the kind of girl he would enjoy living with. Yet he again had to recognize the impossibility of allowing her to stay alive. More than twenty-four hours after kidnaping her, as she lay face downward in nothing but her panties, Glatman garrotted her in the same manner as the other two. He again took the panties as a memento, as well as all her identification. Like Shirley Ann Bridgeford, she was left unburied.

That was the conclusion of Harvey Glatman's two-hour confession. By the light of the full moon, the detectives drove down to the Anza desert, and with Glatman's help, located the bones of Shirley Ann Bridgeford and Ruth Mercado. Back in prison, Glatman was questioned about more unsolved sex killings in Los Angeles, but his openness convinced police that he knew nothing about them. Meanwhile, police searching his apartment again found a locked toolbox that contained the bound photographs of his victims, two pairs of panties and one pair of shoes.

In court in San Diego in November, 1958, Harvey Glatman pleaded guilty to the murders of Shirley Ann Bridgeford and Ruth Mercado. His lawyer had proposed a plea of guilty but insane, but Glatman opposed it, saying he would prefer to die rather than spend a life behind bars. Superior Court Judge John A. Hewicker duly obliged, and on September 18, 1959, Harvey Glatman died in the gas chamber at San Quentin.

One of the most sensational cases of the late 1950s was that of the necrophile Ed Gein. Strictly speaking, Gein does not qualify as a serial killer; yet it is impossible to doubt that, in the psychological sense, he belongs in the same gallery as Pommerencke and Glatman.

On the freezing afternoon of December 8, 1954, a customer who dropped into Mary Hogan's tavern in Plainfield, Wisconsin, found the place deserted, and a large bloodstain on the floor. A spent .32 cartridge lay near it. Bloodstains ran out of the back door and into the parking lot, where they halted beside tire tracks that looked like those of a pickup truck. It looked as if Mary Hogan had been shot and then taken away.

Police were unable to find any clues to the disappearance. But a few weeks later, when a sawmill owner named Elmo

Ueeck spoke of the disappearance to a little handyman called Ed Gein, Gein replied with a simplicity reminiscent of Stan Laurel: "She isn't missing. She's at the farm right now." And Ueeck who, like most of the residents of Plainfield, regarded Gein as little brighter than Stan Laurel, could not even work up the interest to ask him what he meant.

Three years passed. On the evening of November 16, 1957, Frank Worden returned from a day's hunting to find his mother's hardware store locked up, although the lights were on. A local garage attendant told him that he had seen Mrs. Worden's delivery truck driving away at about 9:30 that morning. With sudden foreboding, Frank Worden rushed home and collected the spare key to the store. Inside, as he expected, there was no sign of his mother. But the cash register was missing, and there was a patch of blood on the floor.

"He's done something to her," said Worden.

"Who?" asked sheriff Art Schley.

"Ed Gein. My mother said he'd been hanging around and behaving oddly recently . . ."

The sheriff lost no time in driving to Gein's farm, six miles west of Plainfield. It was deserted. But he knew that one of Gein's few friends was his cousin Bob Hill. As Schley arrived at Hill's house, he saw Gein's pickup truck about to drive away; Gein was at the wheel, with Bob Hill and his sister Darlene. The sheriff halted them, and asked Gein to get in the squad car for questioning. Gein's replies sounded typically inconsequential and inconsistent, but when he remarked that someone was trying to frame him for Mrs. Worden's death, Sheriff Schley decided to take him into custody. No one had mentioned Mrs. Worden.

The doors of Ed Gein's farmhouse were locked, but the door of a woodshed—or "summer kitchen"—at the rear opened when Schley pushed it with his foot. Since the farm had no electricity, the sheriff had to use a torch. What it showed him was the naked corpse of a woman hanging up-side down from a crossbeam, the legs spread wide apart, and a long slit running from the genitals almost to the throat. But the throat, like the head, was missing. The genitals and the anus were also missing. Bernice Worden had been disem-boweled like a deer.

When a portable electric generator had been installed, the investigators were able to explore the farmhouse. It looked as if it had not been tidied or cleaned for years, and there were piles of rubbish everywhere, as well as dozens of horror comics and magazines. More ominously, there were also human skulls, two of which adorned Gein's bedposts. The seat of a chair proved to be made of human skin. So did a lampshade, a wastepaper basket and even a drum. They also found a shirt made of human skin, and a number of shrunken heads, one of which proved to be Mary Hogan's. The head of Bernice Worden was in a sack, while her entrails and heart were neatly wrapped nearby.

Who were the other corpses (ten of them)—or rather, whose body parts? Gein cleared this up after confessing to the shooting of Mrs. Worden; he had dug them up in the local graveyard. Asked if he had had sexual relations with them, Gein shook his head vigorously. "No, they smelt too bad."

Slowly, his story emerged. His mother, Augusta Gein, had been crankily religious. Every time it rained heavily, she would read him the story of Noah from the Bible and proph-esy the end of the world. She was convinced that the modern world was so full of sin that God would destroy it at any minute—women wearing lipstick and short skirts ... Ed Gein was the younger of two brothers, and he became a mother's boy. His father died in 1940, and his brother Henry two years later. Henry had also been a bachelor—their moth-er's upbringing had made both men very nervous of women—and he died in 1944, the same year in which Augusta Gein also suffered a stroke. Her son nursed her until she died in the following year. Ed was then 38, a small, thin man with a pleasant smile, well liked by everyone. Admittedly, there was an odd story about him. His nearest neighbors, the Bankses, had invited him to their house in 1942 when a female relative was in the house; she was wearing shorts, and Gein clearly found it hard to keep his eyes off her legs. That night, a man broke into the woman's house and seized her small son by the throat, asking him where his mother had gone. The man fled before he found out, but the boy thought he recognized Gein. Ever since then, the Bankses had had reservations about their quiet, pleasant neighbour.

What happened seems fairly clear. Gein was a sexually normal man—his mother's undivided attention had not turned him into a homosexual—but he was frightened of women, and not very attractive to them. He had a woman friend, with whom he went out for twenty years, but she finally decided against marrying him. She said his conversation was all about murder. Alone in the farmhouse, he thought endlessly about sex, until one day he saw a newspaper report of a woman who had been buried that day. In the middle of the night, he set off with his pick-up truck and a spade. He dug up the woman, unscrewed the coffin, and put her into the truck; then replaced the coffin and carefully remade the grave. Then he took the corpse home, feeling happier than ever before. At last he had a woman alone and all to himself. He was probably so enthusiastic that he didn't know how to start. But he had plenty of time ... He explained: "It gave me a lot of satisfaction."

Gein's graveyard excursions were not very frequent. Over ten years there were only nine. He suffered from remorse, and decided every time never to do it again. The craving was so strong that it went beyond the desire to perform normal acts of love. He ate parts of the bodies, and made waistcoats of the skin, which he wore next to his flesh. His grave digging expeditions—and murders—were always at the time of the full moon.

Gein understood himself well enough to realize that his mother was the root of all the trouble. Consciously, he loved her, unconsciously, hated her; hence his choice of elderly women as the only two victims he actually murdered.

At Christmas, 1957, it was decided that Gein was insane, and he was committed to Waupan State Hospital for life. No doubt some of the people of Plainfield for whom he acted as a baby-sitter think about their narrow escape; but there is no evidence that Gein was violently inclined towards young women or children. Gein died of cancer on July 26, 1984, at the age of seventy-eight.

Another case of the late 1950s deserves to be mentioned at this point, because although it cannot be classified as serial murder, it is among the best known cases of "spree killing" in American criminal history. "Spree killing" describes a murder rampage—a group of murders that occur over a short period of time, in which the killer seems to decide that he may as well be hanged for a sheep as for a lamb, and goes on killing until he is stopped—usually by arrest or a policeman's bullet.

Nineteen-year-old Charles Starkweather, of Lincoln, Nebraska, was an admirer of film star James Dean. His girlfriend, Caril Ann Fugate, was five years his junior. In January 1958, Starkweather had an argument with Caril's mother—who believed her daughter to be pregnant—and shot her dead. He went on to kill her stepfather and two-year-old sister. After two days alone in the house with Caril, he fled when police began to try to gain entrance.

In a brief murder rampage, Starkweather killed seven more people: a farmer named August Meyer, a young couple, Robert Jensen and Carol King (the latter was raped), a businessman, C. Lauer Ward, his wife Clara and their maid, and a shoe salesman, Merle Collison, who was murdered as he napped at the wheel of his car beside the road. Another motorist, ordered to release the handbrake on Collison's car, grappled with Starkweather, and Starkweather fled in the car, pursued by police who had come upon the struggle. He surrendered when they shot out his rear window. Starkweather was electrocuted in June 1959, declaring that his last wish was to have Caril (who had turned against him) sitting on his knee. Caril Fugate was sentenced to life imprisonment by a jury that declined to believe that she had merely been a terrified captive, but was paroled in 1981.

A film, *Badlands* (1974), represented Starkweather exactly as he wanted to be remembered—as a courageous "rebel without a cause." In fact, his random killings required no courage, and as he surrendered, Starkweather was close to panic, complaining loudly that he had been cut by flying glass.

The 1950s ended with a case of serial murder that could be regarded as a portent of the future. Melvin Rees was a self-esteem killer, a man who felt he had every right to defy society in the name of his own moral standards.

On June 26, 1957, an army sergeant was driving home for a weekend with a girlfriend, Margaret Harold. They had stopped in a lonely spot near Annapolis, Maryland, when a green Chrysler pulled in front of them. A tall, thin-faced man got out, and identified himself as the caretaker of the property. He asked for a cigarette, then for a lift. Suddenly he pulled out a gun and climbed into the back seat. He demanded money, and wound his fingers into Margaret

Harold's hair, pulling her head back. "Don't give it to him," she said angrily. There was a shot, and she slumped forward. The sergeant pushed open the door and ran as hard as he could. A mile along the road he found a farmhouse and asked to use the phone. When the police arrived some time later, Margaret Harold was still across the front seat, without her dress. The killer had violated the corpse.

The police searched the area, and found a cinder-block building nearby, with a broken basement window. Inside, the walls were covered with pornographic photographs, and police morgue shots of women who had been murdered. One photograph stood out from the others as normal—it had been clipped out of a college yearbook. The girl in it was finally identified as a 1955 graduate of Maryland University, Wanda Tipson; but she had no recollection of dating any male who corresponded to the sergeant's description of the murderer.

On January 11, 1959, Carrol Jackson was out driving with his wife, Mildred; and their two daughters, Susan, aged 5 and Janet, eighteen months. Carrol Jackson was a non-smoker and teetotaler who had met his wife at a Baptist church; she was president of the women's missionary society. As he drove along a road near Apple Grove, Eastern Virginia, an old blue Chevrolet began to overtake, flashing his lights. When Jackson pulled over, the Chevrolet pulled in front and stopped. Jackson screeched to a halt, and was about to lose his temper when a man jumped out of the other car and waved a gun in his face. The tall, thin-faced man with long, ape-like arms and a beetling brow forced the Jackson family to get out of their car and into the boot of his Chevrolet. Then he drove off. Later that afternoon, Mildred Jackson's aunt drove along the same road and recognized her niece's husband's car, abandoned.

The search for the Jacksons revealed nothing. Then another couple came forward to say that they had been forced off the road earlier that afternoon by an old blue Chevrolet. A man had walked back towards their car, but they had quickly reversed and driven away.

Two months later, on March 4, two men whose car had bogged down on a muddy back road near Fredericksburg picked up armfuls of brush to gain traction, and found themselves looking at the body of a man. It proved to be Carrol Jackson, his hands bound in front of him with a necktie. He had been shot in the skull. Underneath him was the body of his eighteen-month-old daughter, who had simply been tossed into the ditch, and died of suffocation under her father's body. There was no sign of Mildred or Susan Jackson.

On March 21, boys hunting squirrels close to the spot where Margaret Harold had been murdered noticed freshly dug earth; they brushed some of it aside and saw the blonde hair of a little girl. Police uncovered the bodies of Mildred and Susan Jackson. Mildred had a stocking tied around her neck, but it was loose. Susan had been beaten to death with a blunt instrument. There was evidence that both had been raped. Police theorized that the stocking around Mildred Jackson's neck had been used as a tourniquet to force her to commit some sexual act that disgusted her.

The grave was within a few hundred yards of the cinder-block structure in which the obscene photographs had been found two years earlier. And a quarter of a mile away, the police found a broken-down shack with relatively fresh tire-marks nearby. Inside, police found a red button from Mildred Jackson's dress.

Again, the investigation came to a halt. But two months later, the police received an anonymous letter that accused a jazz musician called Melvin Davis Rees of the murders of Margaret Harold and of the Jackson family. The man, who said he was a salesman, said that he and Rees had been in a town not far from the spot where Margaret Harold had been murdered, and that Rees had been hopped up on Benzedrine. The writer said he had later asked Rees point-blank if he had killed the Jackson family; Rees had not denied it, but only evaded the question. Police searched for Rees—whose job as a jazz musician kept him traveling—without success. Then, early in 1960, the writer of the letter, who identified himself as Glenn L. Moser, went to the police, to say that he had received a letter from Rees, who was working as a piano salesman in a music shop in West Memphis, Arkansas. An FBI agent went into the store and told Rees he was under arrest. Later that day, the sergeant identified Rees in a line-up as the man who had murdered Margaret Harold.

Detectives hastened to the home of Rees' parents in Hyattsville, armed with a search warrant; in an attic they found a saxophone case containing a .38 revolver, and various notes describing sadistic acts—including the murder of the Jacksons.

"Caught on a lonely road ... Drove to a select area and killed husband and baby. Now the mother and daughter were all mine ... " He went on to describe a perverted sex act, probably forcing fellatio on her. "Now I was her master," he says with relish. He then described killing her slowly in a way that made it clear that his sexual hang-up was sadism.

Maryland police now discovered links between Rees and four other sex-murders of teenagers: two schoolgirls, Marie Shomette and Ann Ryan, had been intercepted in College Park, near the University of Maryland, and shot and raped; the bodies of Mary Fellers and Shelby Venable had been found in Maryland rivers.

Rees was tried in 1961, and executed for the murder of the Jackson family.

People who had worked with Rees (who played the piano, guitar, saxophone and clarinet) found it hard to believe that he was guilty of the crimes, and described him as mild-mannered and intelligent. The girl whose photograph had been found in the hut had, in fact, known him very well, and had given him up because he was married; it just never struck her that the killer of Margaret Harold could be the jazz musician.

Peter Hurkos, the psychic, was called into the case after the disappearance of the Jackson family, and his description of the killer was remarkably accurate—over six feet tall, left-handed, tattooed on the arm, with a walk like a duck and ape-like arms. At the scene of Margaret Harold's murder, Hurkos walked to a bush and plucked off the dead woman's torn skirt which had been there unnoticed since the murder. Hurkos added that the man had committed nine murders. This concurred with the figure the police themselves finally arrived at.

Rees had told Glenn Moser: "You can't say it's wrong to kill—only individual standards make it right or wrong"—the argument that Sade had advanced but never attempted to put into practice. We may also note Moser's comment: "I asked him point blank if he had killed these people. He evaded the question. He didn't deny it." H. H. Holmes would have cast his eyes up to heaven and said: "My dear fellow, what an appalling suggestion." Rees's self-esteem would not permit him to lie about it, even if—as happened—it cost him his life.

AFTERWORD

A WOMAN FRIEND ONCE TOLD ME THAT WHENEVER SHE WAS left alone in somebody else's house she felt an immediate compulsion to go through the drawers. What is interesting is that she was not a juvenile delinquent, but a middle-aged psychiatrist—admittedly, an extremely unconventional one. I recognized immediately that she had handed me a key to one of the fundamental problems of crime—in fact, of human nature itself. Human beings are purposive creatures; they need to be driven by a strong sense of motivation. When they lack motivation, they tend to become bored, then to look around for something they are not supposed to be doing.

Our basic human craving is for what might be called "the flow experience." We all recognize what this means on the crudest physical level—for example, the relief of going to the lavatory when the need has become urgent. Even scratching when you itch is an example of the flow experience. So is drinking when you are very thirsty and eating when you are ravenous. All these things release a flow of energy and relief. When our energies are blocked and our purposes frustrated, we experience a sense of stagnation, which can soon turn into a kind of mental constipation, in which our vital energies feel as if they had congealed into a leaden mass.

Human beings *need* the flow experience to change and evolve. Our energies could be compared to a river flowing over a plain. If the flow is too slow, the river begins to meander as it accumulates silt and mud. But a violent storm in the mountains can send down a roaring flood that sweeps away the silt and straightens out the bends, so that once again, the river flows straight and deep. This is why human beings crave the "flow experience."

This also offers us the key to sex crime. When Ted Bundy saw a girl undressing behind a lighted window, he experienced a flood of desire that turned him into a highly purposive creature. And since he was above average intelligence, and had a natural sense of his own superiority, this filled him with the conviction that he had discovered the key to his personal evolution. All he had to do was to use his charm to lure girls into a vulnerable position, then treat them as if they were a kind of tailor's dummy, an object designed for his pleasure. And after enough of these "flash floods," all his self-doubt and immaturity would be swept away; he would be as self-controlled and purposeful as Beethoven, Goethe, Napoleon—in fact, a kind of superman.

Our society is full of constraints, and the most obvious of these constraints is sexual. This remains as true today as in the time of Theodore Durrant, and will no doubt still be as true a century from now. So the highly sexed young man— and most young men *are* highly sexed—finds himself surrounded by desirable creatures whom he is forbidden to touch. If, like Bundy, the desire is strong enough and the constraints weak enough, he may decide to ignore the social taboos and use force to relieve his frustrations. Somewhere at the back of his mind there is the feeling that if he does it often enough, some inner blockage will be swept away and he will outgrow the need that causes him so much discomfort, and be an altogether more full and complete human being. Dostoevsky spent years planning a novel called *Life of a Great Sinner* in which the central character sins his way to salvation. The rapist has something like that in mind.

It is slightly alarming to realize that many perfectly respectable philosophers have been saying the same kind of thing for the past two centuries. William Blake remarked: "Rather murder an infant in its cradle than nurse unacted desire." Ibsen caused a scandal with *A Doll's House* when he made the heroine walk out on her husband and children, declaring that the need for self-development—Maslow's self-actualization—was more important than obeying the rules of conventional morality. Undershaft, the armaments manufacturer in Shaw's *Major Barbara*, justifies himself with the statement: "I moralized and starved until one day I swore I would be a full-fed free man at all costs; that nothing should stop me except a bullet, neither reason nor morals nor the lives of other men. I said 'Thou shalt starve ere I starve'; and with that word I became free and great. I was a dangerous man until I had my will: now I am a useful, beneficent, kindly person." He has, so to speak, sinned his way to salvation. Elsewhere in the play he explains that morality is relative: "For me there is only one true morality, but it might not fit you, as you do not manufacture aerial battleships . . . "

In *Civilization and Its Discontents*, Freud argues that man has created a civilization that has turned into a prison; it demands that he constantly repress desires that are natural to animals in the wild. Unlike Ibsen and Shaw, he is not arguing that we should cast off conventional morality; his purpose is simply to explain why our society is so riddled with neurosis. But Freud's argument could also be regarded as a justification for seeking the "flow experience" *at all costs*.

When Blake wrote *The Marriage of Heaven and Hell* there were no criminals capable of adopting his suggestions—he lived in the age of footpads and highwaymen. And when Ibsen wrote in his journal: "Liberation consists in securing for individuals the right to free themselves, each according to his particular need," there were no sex criminals to quote him as an excuse for rape. It was in the 1880s, when anarchists began to plant bombs on the grounds that all power is corrupt, that it gradually became clear that there is a negative side to individual self-development. Yet even *Major Barbara,* written in 1905, belongs to the "age of innocence" when criminals were more concerned with burglary and petty theft than heroic rebellion. It would be more than four decades before Melvin Rees would declare "You can't say it's wrong to kill—only individual standards make it right or wrong," and demonstrate that Undershaft's relativist morality could be used to justify rape and murder.

The struggle for what might be called "Criminal Liberation" has a long history. A decade before Blake wrote *The Marriage of Heaven and Hell,* Goethe's friend Schiller outraged his contemporaries with a drama called *The Robbers,* whose hero, Karl Moor, declares: "Law has never produced a man of true grandeur. It is freedom that incubates the colossal and the extreme." He explains that he is sick of his own age of professors and critics, and prefers the company of the men of action he finds in the pages of Plutarch. When he learns that his father has disinherited him (due to the machinations of his evil brother Franz), he curses the human race and declares that he will become a brigand. From their lair in the forest, his men put the philosophy of freedom into action as they storm cities, rob treasuries and violate nunneries. But even the highly romantic Schiller now found himself faced with an insoluble dilemma. It is true that Karl Moor acts out of noble motives—his hatred of oppression and tyranny—but how is it possible to justify murder and rape? Schiller declines to sidestep the problem by killing off his hero in battle, and ends the play with Karl's decision to hand himself over to the law.

It would be almost two centuries before Ian Brady, incensed at an unfair jail sentence, decided to emulate Karl Moor's example and carry out his own campaign of plunder and rape. But then, Brady had seen *The Third Man* several times when he was 11 and been impressed by Harry Lime's philosophy of moral relativism. Greene was not being serious when he made Lime describe human beings as insects, but when an idea is released into the atmosphere, it is no longer under its creator's control. I have also pointed out the significance of Brady's interest in the character of Stavrogin in Dostoevsky's *Possessed*. Stavrogin is a Byronic rebel who feels he has "done it all," and can now find nothing to do with his strength—in other words, no longer knows how to induce "the flow experience." So he commits all kinds of "gratuitous acts"—such as seducing a 10-year-old girl, then allowing her to kill herself—in an attempt to galvanize himself into positive feeling. He fails, and eventually hangs himself.

Now the point to note is that Schiller and Blake and Ibsen and Shaw were all concerned to "weigh up" the meaning of human life, to make what might be ponderously called a "philosophical-existential" judgement on it. And so, in a certain sense, were Melvin Rees, Ian Brady, Ted Bundy, Gerald Gallego and Leonard Lake. Gallego said he was searching for "the perfect sex slave." If he were persuaded to attend a philosophical seminar and explain what he meant, he would probably agree that "the perfect sexual experience" came closer to it. And why should he want the perfect sexual experience? Because all "positive" experience (i.e., pleasant as against unpleasant) helps to make us the masters of reality rather than its slaves. We have a clear sense, in certain moments, that life yields to a certain kind of effort, and that it is not "a tale told by an idiot." Schiller made his own attempt at stating this insight when he said: "It is freedom that incubates the colossal and the extreme." He puts it in a poem called "To a Moralist":

> Why check youth's ardour with thy dull advice,
> And teach that love is labor thrown away?
> Thou shiverest there amid the Winter's ice
> And speakst, contemptuous, of Golden May.[1]

Schiller is certain of one thing: he is a devotee of Golden May, and he hates the winter. Rebellion and revolution seem to be the solution, throwing off the trammels of "civilization and its discontents." But Schiller immediately betrays the weak point in his argument when he makes a clear distinction between Karl Moor and his merry men; *they* murder and rape while he reads Rousseau and gazes at the stars. The fact that Karl refuses to join in makes it clear that he recognizes this kind of "freedom" as morally wrong—that his dream of freedom and the Rights of Man involves actively depriving some people of their freedom and their lives. The same applies to Blake's "Rather murder an infant in its cradle . . . " (although he obviously intended it as a form of overstatement) and to Undershaft's admission that he decided to ignore reason and morals and the lives of other men in his determination to be a full-fed man. Even Nora's assertion of her right to "individual self-development" contains the seeds of criminality.

I am not trying to argue in favor of convention, good behavior and self-sacrifice: only to point out that what looks like an irrefutable argument in favor of human freedom leads us into a quicksand of moral ambiguity. For two centuries

[1] Translated by E. P. Arnold-Forster.

now philosophers have been engaged in a muddled argument about human freedom: now the chickens are coming home to roost.

Then what *is* the solution? Since I draw close to the end of this book, I may as well try to state my own view in a few sentences.

T. E. Lawrence once said: "Happiness is absorption." Every child has experienced that delicious sensation of curling up in bed and listening to the rain pattering on the windows. Every literate adult has experienced the sensation of becoming so absorbed in a book that he "doesn't want to put it down." We can *focus* the mind in the way that a magnifying glass can focus a beam of sunlight, until we experience a curious sense of inner warmth. It demands the total focus of *attention*. Most of us "leak" half the time, so never learn to focus our energies. Yet the sheer intensity of these moments of "focus" makes us aware that the human mind possesses powers that suggest that we are not "merely human." In some strange sense, we are gods in disguise.

Experiences we enjoy have the effect of focusing our emotions and energies, and producing a sense of being "more alive." But we fail to grasp the fact that the magnifying glass that focuses the energy is *the mind itself*. So we are inclined to go out looking for the experience instead of teaching ourselves to use the magnifying glass. And since the modern world has developed a whole "substitute experience" industry, from romantic novels to pornographic videos, we are in a far more fortunate position than our ancestors of a mere century ago, who expected life to be fairly dreary and repetitive. Most modern teenagers have had a wider range of experience—imaginative and actual—than most Victorian patriarchs. And when we take into account the loss of inhibition induced by alcohol and drugs, it suddenly becomes clear why an increasing number of young people are willing to risk breaking the law in pursuit of "experiences they enjoy" and of what they feel to be individual self-development.

In *Crime and Punishment*, Raskolnikov remarks that if he had to stand on a narrow ledge for ever and ever, he would prefer to do that rather than die at once. What would he *do* on the narrow ledge? In practice, probably jump off. Yet we can all *see* why he felt he would prefer *anything* rather than die at once. He has an intuition that *the mind itself* contains the answer, and that if he could learn the trick of "focusing" its energies, a narrow ledge would afford as much freedom as a ski slope in Switzerland or a beach on the Riviera.

Our everyday consciousness is concerned with "coping" with problems, and this is the basic source of criminality. If we compare consciousness to a spectrum, then modern man lives almost entirely at the "red end," preoccupied with purpose, activity, survival. When this need for activity vanishes—as when my psychiatrist friend was left alone in the house—we experience a kind of panic. The blue end of the spectrum seems to threaten us with stagnation. And crime—like alcoholism or drug abuse or any other form of overindulgence—is a protest against stagnation.

Yet when Raskolnikov says that he would prefer to be confined on a narrow ledge rather than die at once, he has suddenly recognized that he could live just as happily at the blue end of the spectrum—that far from representing stagnation, the "blue area" represents control, insight, exploration of one's own possibilities. Far from being a kind of blank that threatens us with boredom, exhaustion and nervous breakdown, it seethes with its own inner vitality, like some alchemical crucible that contains the elixir of life.

Regrettably, the human race remains trapped at the red end of the spectrum. It is only in moments of crisis that we glimpse the answer to our problems—the answer Dr. Johnson saw so clearly when he remarked that "the knowledge that he is to be hanged in a fortnight concentrates a man's mind wonderfully." In the meantime, we find ourselves in the highly dangerous position in which the "philosophy of freedom" has created one of the worst outbreaks of crime in the history of civilization.

The serial murderer is one of the most interesting—if frightening—symptoms of this melting-pot of moral attitudes. Whether they thought about it or not, Ted Bundy, Gerald Gallego, Leonard Lake believed that enough sex could concentrate the mind into a permanent state of intensity. Of course, it failed to work because what they were seeking— "the essence of sex"—is an illusion. Sex is a biological urge whose purpose is to persuade us to reproduce the species. To this end, it allures us in exactly the same way that the scent of a flower allures the bee. But if the bee were intelligent, it would realize that most flowers promise far more than they can fulfil; the scent is exquisite, but you cannot eat it or take it home with you. This explains why so many sex killers have ended with a curious sense of moral exhaustion and vacuity, a feeling of having been the victim of a confidence trick.

Jeffrey Dahmer expressed the essence of the problem when he said: "I couldn't find any meaning for my life when I was out there. I'm sure as hell not going to find it in here." And in saying this, he makes it clear why it is impossible to draw a clear and sharp dividing line between murderers and the rest of us. We *all* suffer to some extent, from the "Dahmer syndrome." Gurdjieff once explained that what is wrong with human beings is that the gods had implanted in us an organ called "kundabuffer," which makes us hopelessly confused about illusion and reality, and which prevents us from learning too much about our own stupidity. The only thing— says Gurdjieff—that could awaken us from this illusion of meaninglessness is another organ which would show us *the exact hour of our own death and the death of everyone we see. This* would shock us into a recognition of how we waste our lives.

But every time we study a murder case, with its moronic waste of life, we are momentarily traumatized out of our confusion and stupidity, our tendency to vegetate in a meaningless present. A few days ago I received a letter from a correspondent who remarked that reading Ann West's *For the Love of Lesley*, a book by the mother of Moors murder victim Lesley Ann Downey, had suddenly made him aware of the *reality* of murder, and of what it feels like to be the parent of a child who has disappeared. The book had made the same impact on me. And after re-living the experiences of Lesley's parents, I came back to my own life with a sigh of relief, like awakening from a nightmare. Suddenly I recognized that life without such a burden of misery is full of infinite possibility and potentiality and freedom. Yet we normally live it with a kind of bored casualness, as if fate were to blame for not making the world more interesting. The truth is that if we could use the imagination to grasp the reality of *any* murder, we would suddenly see life as a kind of unending holiday.

This is the ultimate justification of the study of murder: that there is something about its sheer nastiness that can galvanize us out of the "Dahmer syndrome" that causes human beings to waste their lives.